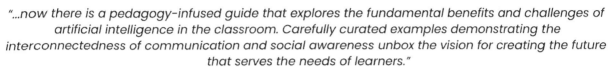

PRAISE FOR
CLASSROOM

"...now there is a pedagogy-infused guide that explores the fundamental benefits and challenges of artificial intelligence in the classroom. Carefully curated examples demonstrating the interconnectedness of communication and social awareness unbox the vision for creating the future that serves the needs of learners."
-Jennifer Womble, Conference Chair, FETC

"...this comprehensive guide is a great way to learn and understand all about the future of AI in the classroom. Covering everything you need to know."
-Lee Parkinson, Mr P ICT

"Dan, Amanda, and Brad have provided this comprehensive guide that offers invaluable insights and practical advice for educators and educational leaders who are looking to embrace the AI revolution in their teaching practices and curriculum development."
-Priya Lakhani OBE, CEO of Century Tech and UK Government AI Advisor

"We can't push the genie back into the bottle, nor can we close Pandora's box once it has been opened. Hence we need to prepare ourselves – and the next generation for the new realities. And that's where The AI Classroom is a useful guide."
-Vikram Chandra, Host of This World on the WION Network

"AI will force the greatest career choice in human history: do you want to compete against technology over the 'doing' of a task? Or are you going to elevate yourself to the 'thinking' and let technology 'do the doing?' The AI Classroom will empower educators to do the thinking while giving them the tools to let technology do the doing."
- Nicolas Cole, Author and Co-founder of Ship 30 for 30

"At its heart, it highlights the importance of collaboration between teachers and tech. Dan, Amanda, and Brad are at the forefront of the AI revolution in education and people I look forward to continuing to follow to feel like I'm somewhat ahead of what is going to be one hell of a curve."
- Baasit Siddiqui, Director of Siddiqui Education & star of Channel 4's Gogglebox

"Reading this book is like diving into a pool of delights designed to make our lives as educators ever more manageable and fulfilling. This essential read will leave you buzzing like a fridge such is the impact. We are guided through how to utilize the AI revolution to aid us as teachers, using it alongside our deep understanding of pedagogy with limitless possibilities."
- Chris Dyson, Author of Parklands: A School Built on Love

DEDICATIONS

Dan's Dedication

To Julia, for your unwavering belief and trust in me. Your support is a constant source of strength and inspiration, and I feel incredibly fortunate to have you in my life.

To Matilda Grace and Jacob Henry, I am filled with hope and excitement for the world that you will grow up in. Never forget your value, put your stamp on the world, and remember to enjoy yourself.

Amanda's Dedication

To all the teachers who are innovators, knowledge seekers, and are constantly living professionally in BETA. I dedicate this book to all of you, who like me, strive to educate the next generation with the most up-to-date knowledge. I hope this book on artificial intelligence will serve as a guiding light to help you navigate the exciting and ever-changing world of AI. Remember, let's keep it real, but also, let's keep it artificial!

To my family: thank you for your unwavering support throughout the long hours and countless cups of coffee it took to write this book. Your love and encouragement kept me going!

Brad's Dedication

To Alaina, for all you do for our family and for allowing me the time and opportunity to do this work.

To Matthew, Anna, and James, you are the reason for everything I do. I know you will all do big things, but most importantly, always remember that being happy matters most.

THE AI CLASSROOM

THE ULTIMATE GUIDE
to Artificial Intelligence in Education

DANIEL FITZPATRICK
AMANDA FOX   BRAD WEINSTEIN

THE AI CLASSROOM:
THE ULTIMATE GUIDE TO ARTIFICIAL INTELLIGENCE IN EDUCATION

© 2023 by TeacherGoals Publishing, LLC

Published by TeacherGoals Publishing, LLC, Beech Grove, IN
www.teachergoals.com

Cover and Interior Design by: Amanda Fox
Edited by: Dr. John Wick, Ed.D.
Copy Edited by: Heather Brown

Images generated by: Midjourney & prompted by Dan Fitzpatrick
Illustrations by: Amanda Fox

Library of Congress Control Number: 2022906806
Paperback ISBN: 978-1-959419-11-2
ASIN: B0CTHTN5FW

First Printing April 2023

TEACHERGOALS
PUBLISHING

Contents

Join Our Book Study & Find Us on Facebook!

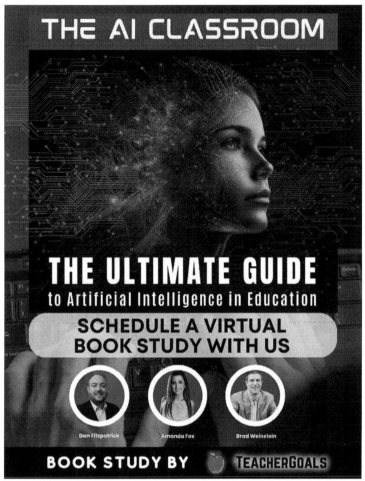

Join us for a groundbreaking virtual book study on *The AI Classroom!* In this study, we will explore the latest trends, innovations, and challenges related to the integration of artificial intelligence in the classroom setting.

Through engaging discussions and collaborative activities, we will delve into topics such prompt engineering, AI tools to support UDL, lesson craft, and more. We will examine case studies, real-world examples, and the latest research to gain a comprehensive understanding of the potential benefits and drawbacks of AI in education.

Whether you're a teacher, administrator, or simply curious about the future of education, this virtual book study is the perfect opportunity to explore the fascinating world of AI in the classroom. Don't miss out on this exciting opportunity to connect with like-minded professionals and learn about cutting-edge developments in AI and education!

Book Us for Professional Development

Dan Fitzpatrick, Amanda Fox, and Brad Weinstein are award-winning educators with decades of experience with technology and innovation for schools.

Dan can be found at theaieducator.io. He is a leading voice in the integration of artificial intelligence in education, appearing in numerous high-profile interviews and publications.

Amanda, author of *The Canva Classroom* and other great titles, is passionate about enhancing learning through technology and designing lessons to promote inclusivity.

Brad, co-author of *Hacking School Discipline*, is passionate about preparing students for an ever-changing world through the future of work skills and emotional intelligence.

We are currently embarking on a new era of innovation, where the collaboration between humanity and technology is expected to be stronger than ever before.

The AI Classroom helps educators to:

- *Start using artificial intelligence within seconds*
- *Use an artificial intelligence framework for learning*
- *Enhance existing pedagogies*
- *Take back personal time*
- *Create content and do tasks with ease*
- *Infuse emotional intelligence with artificial intelligence*
- *Put students in control of their learning*

Check Out the AI Repository Search Tool

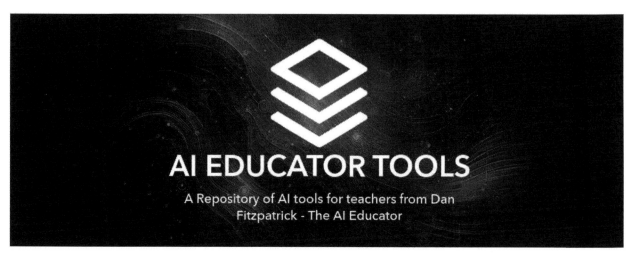

Make sure to check out the **AI Repository Search Tool**, a valuable and innovative resource for educators engaged in the expansive field of artificial intelligence. Thoughtfully designed for optimal user experience, this tool stands out for its comprehensive yet user-friendly interface, offering easy access to a broad spectrum of AI-related information and resources.

Engage with this tool to deepen your understanding and stay connected with the forefront of AI technology.

Scan the QR Code below or go to https://theaieducator.io/ to check it out.

FOREWORD BY VIKRAM CHANDRA

Vikram Chandra is an Indian journalist who founded Editorji Technologies, a multilingual video news platform. He is currently the host of This World on the WION Indian News Channel and set up Editorji in October 2018, positioning it as a disruptive offering in the digital news space. He is the former anchor for the Nine O'Clock News and was, until recently, host of Gadget Guru and anchor of The Big Fight.

When Dan asked me to write the foreword for *The AI Classroom*, an excellent book on AI education, I was honored and flattered and got down to work. I then took the obvious next step – firing up GPT-4 and asking it for help. This was the outcome, and you can see why we are now living in a whole new world.

My prompt was simple enough.

"Please write the foreword for a book on the importance of artificial intelligence, with a special focus on how it can be used for education. The advantages and the pitfalls. Make it about 600 words."

GPT-4's reply was as follows.

As we stand on the precipice of a new era, the transformative power of artificial intelligence (AI) has become an undeniable force in the realm of education. This book, "The Intelligent Classroom: Harnessing the Power of AI in Education," is a testament to the need for a comprehensive understanding of the ways in which AI can enrich, expand, and revolutionize the educational landscape. It is our hope that this work provides an essential resource for educators, policymakers, and the general public alike, highlighting the opportunities, challenges, and ethical considerations associated with the integration of AI in education.

The advantages of using AI in education are manifold, and its potential is limited only by the scope of our collective imagination. At the forefront, AI enables personalized learning experiences, allowing educators to tailor curricula, assessments, and interventions to the unique needs and abilities of each student. Through the use of adaptive learning platforms, AI can monitor student progress in real time, providing instantaneous feedback and support, thereby reducing the burden on teachers and enhancing student engagement and motivation.

Moreover, AI-powered tools can revolutionize the way students access knowledge and resources. As the world becomes more interconnected, AI can bridge the gap between learners from different backgrounds and cultures, offering them an opportunity to access education that is both relevant and global in scope. With language translation and virtual tutoring systems, we can overcome linguistic and geographic barriers to create an inclusive, diverse, and dynamic learning environment.

Furthermore, AI can augment the role of educators, empowering them to become more efficient and effective in their roles. By automating administrative tasks, teachers can devote more time and attention to nurturing students' cognitive, social, and emotional growth. The integration of AI can also help identify potential areas of improvement in teaching methodologies and curricula, thereby driving continuous innovation in education.

However, the remarkable potential of AI in education does not come without its pitfalls. One of the most pressing concerns is the issue of privacy and security, as the reliance on AI systems necessitates the collection and processing of vast amounts of personal data. This raises important questions about the protection of students' rights, as well as the potential misuse of their data for purposes beyond the realm of education.

Moreover, the adoption of AI in education raises concerns about the potential exacerbation of existing inequalities. As access to AI-powered tools and resources may be limited by socioeconomic factors, there is a danger that these technological advancements will primarily benefit those who are already privileged, leaving disadvantaged students further behind. To address this issue, it is imperative that governments, educational institutions, and industry stakeholders work collaboratively to ensure equitable access to AI-enabled educational resources for all.

Furthermore, the integration of AI in education must be approached with a deep understanding of the ethical implications. The algorithms that underpin AI systems can inadvertently perpetuate bias and discrimination, as they are shaped by the data and values of their creators. It is thus essential that we prioritize the development and implementation of ethical AI frameworks that foster fairness, accountability, and transparency.

"The Intelligent Classroom: Harnessing the Power of AI in Education" is a timely and insightful exploration of the myriad ways in which AI can transform education for the better. By addressing the advantages, challenges, and ethical considerations of AI integration, this book serves as a vital guide for all those who seek to navigate the rapidly evolving landscape of AI in education.

As we collectively embrace this new frontier, we must recognize that the power of AI lies not in its ability to replace human intelligence, but rather in its potential to augment and amplify it. It is our responsibility as educators, policymakers, and citizens to harness this power wisely, creating a future of education that is equitable, inclusive, and truly intelligent."

It got the title of the book wrong – which could be because I hadn't told it about the book, the authors, or even the themes that I felt it should address. This was the first unfiltered response to a basic and not very well-written prompt. And yet, it was probably as good as any foreword I could have written after hours of effort. Even the title isn't bad – perhaps Dan can consider it for a sequel.

But the challenge is now clear. A child's writing assignments assisted by GPT, or any other AI cannot be compared with a child doing the hard work herself. It is unfair, and as GPT-4 points out above, it will only serve to deepen the digital divide. What happens to underprivileged kids who don't have access to computers at all? What happens to children in countries with poor internet access?

Young people lost skills in arithmetic with the introduction of calculators, and many struggle with writing because they are far more comfortable with typing on laptops or mobile phones. Will the next generation lose the ability to think altogether, because that task has been outsourced to AI? Will they even need to think? And what should they think about? What jobs will they aspire to – if AI becomes super intelligent and takes over more and more activity?

Is there any reason to worry? After all, we have seen centuries of technological progress, and the human species has never been better off than it is today. So perhaps that trend will only continue. Optimists say that while we should train young people in how to use new technologies, and AI in particular, we should rejoice. A new era of abundance is approaching and all problems will be solved. Others have a far more bleak view of the new era that is upon us.

Whichever camp you belong to, one thing is clear. We can't push the genie back into the bottle nor can we close Pandora's box once it has been opened. Hence we need to prepare ourselves – and the next generation for the new realities.

And that's where Dan, Amanda, and Brad's book is a useful guide.

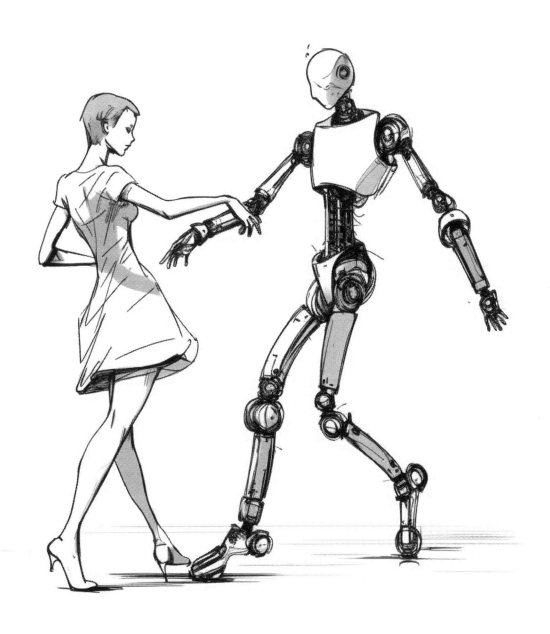

"THE NATURE OF THE DANCE
BETWEEN HUMANS AND MACHINES"
David Price OBE

ABOUT THIS BOOK

Introduction

The world of education is at a crossroads. Rapid advancements in artificial intelligence (AI) are changing the way we live, work, and interact with one another. As educators, we have a responsibility to prepare our students for the future they will inhabit, yet many of us feel ill-equipped to navigate this brave new world of AI in the classroom. This gap in understanding is the problem that we must address.

That's where *The AI Classroom* comes in. Our solution is to provide a comprehensive guide that empowers educators to harness the power of AI, enabling them to create innovative and engaging learning experiences for their students. In this book, we'll explore the what, how, and why of integrating AI into education, examining both the opportunities and the challenges that it presents.

What's Inside

As experienced educators, we understand the complexities of the field and the urgent need for clear, accessible guidance. Our goal is to demystify AI and provide you with the tools and knowledge needed to use it effectively in the classroom, unlocking its potential to revolutionize education.

By delving into *The AI Classroom*, you'll discover the benefits of integrating AI into your teaching practice. We'll explore how AI can personalize learning, streamline administrative tasks, and enhance communication between teachers, students, and parents. As you read, you'll gain a deep understanding of the ethical considerations surrounding AI and learn how to use AI responsibly in your classroom.

Throughout this book, we'll draw extensively on the use of ChatGPT by OpenAI. This AI tool has generated much excitement and debate in the world since the end of 2022. It's important to note that, as of the writing of this book, ChatGPT has an age policy that requires users to be at least 13 years old, with students between 13 and 18 years old needing parental permission. However, the principles, techniques, and ethical concerns we discuss will be applicable to a wide range of AI tools, including those designed specifically for younger students.

How to Read This Book

This ultimate guide to artificial intelligence in education is broken down into four main parts. This book can be read cover to cover, if you wish, or in parts. If you already have a foundational knowledge of the history of AI and what AI is, you may want to skip to other parts of the book that are relevant to where you are in your AI journey.

Part 1 contains chapters one through three, and we cover the history of AI and its place in education. We unpack the future of AI and how it will change the way we work and live while pointing out artificial intelligence tools that have been with us over the years. We outline ways that this technology has changed our workflow and productivity and ultimately will change future job markets. At the end of most chapters, we have also included the voices of educators on various topics surrounding artificial intelligence.

In Part 2, we really begin to shift our focus to the AI Educator. We explore how tools like ChatGPT fit into our pedagogical practices and provide prompt engineering frameworks (PREP and EDIT) for teacher and student use. We tackle worries about plagiarism and share strategies to have AI and students work together vs. compete. There is a whole chapter dedicated to Universal Design for Learning Guidelines and how AI tools can help create equitable and inclusive activities and lessons.

Part 3 breaks down and defines 16 different types of generative AI and contains our AI repository of tools and use cases educators can use right now. We have also included case studies from educators, so you can get a glimpse of how AI is being used in other classrooms. We cover over 30 tools!

Part 4 discusses the impact of technology on emotional intelligence and the importance of maintaining human qualities in education and employment contexts. It highlights the need to balance the benefits of technology with real-world connections, compassion, and empathy while also emphasizing the significance of cultivating emotional intelligence (EI) in maintaining human relationships and interactions in the rapidly evolving digital world. While AI-driven advancements are essential, we still need academic and leadership skills, 21st-century skills, and a human touch to ensure that technology enhances what we do without replacing us entirely.

Our Promise

Our promise to you is that *The AI Classroom* will transform the way you think about and use AI in education. You'll gain a wealth of knowledge and practical strategies that will allow you to create engaging and innovative learning experiences for your students. By the end of the book, you'll feel confident in your ability to harness the power of AI, preparing your students for their futures.

But don't wait! The world of AI is evolving at a staggering pace, and every day that passes is an opportunity to enhance your teaching practice and better prepare your students for the future. The time to start is now. Open the pages of *The AI Classroom* and embark on a journey that will change the way you teach and the way your students learn, forever.

So let's begin. Dive into *The AI Classroom* and discover the transformative power of AI in education. Together, we'll navigate this exciting new frontier, ensuring that our students are equipped to thrive in a world that is increasingly shaped by AI. Let's make *The AI Classroom* a reality.

ARTIFICIAL INTELLIGENCE AND THE MOVIES: LET'S TAKE A LESSON FROM HOLLYWOOD

For decades, movies have not only depicted societal fears and concerns but have also highlighted the positive potential of technological advancements, including artificial intelligence. Science fiction films have often predicted the future of technology, from space travel to virtual reality, inspiring scientists and engineers to turn these predictions into reality. The idea of artificial intelligence has been a long-standing interest in Hollywood, with *Metropolis*, a silent film directed by Fritz Lang in 1927, being one of the earliest movies to explore this theme. The movie depicted a dystopian future where a robot was created to look like a human and to serve as a subservient worker class. While the concept of artificial intelligence was not explicitly mentioned in the movie, it laid the foundation for future films to explore the topic in greater detail.

Since then, we have seen characters like HAL 9000 in *2001: A Space Odyssey* to Samantha in *Her*, both of which explore the potential for AI to enhance human connection and understanding. When we think about what it means to be human in juxtaposition to AI, the need to continue our focus on things like emotional intelligence and social-emotional learning will be important. In recent years, AI has made significant strides and gained traction in other sectors of society including the field of education by showing potential in how it can revolutionize the way we approach teaching and learning: specifically, as a support to ensure the success of all learners. AI can provide personalized and adaptive learning experiences for students of all abilities, paving the way for a more inclusive and equitable education system. Let's take a look at AI in Hollywood to not only make future predictions of AI advancement but how it can change and shape the future of education, NOW.

One promising Hollywood example of AI is the protagonist Neo in *The Matrix*. He was able to learn kung fu and other skills almost instantly by plugging himself into a computer program. While it's not quite the same, there are AI-powered tools that can now help educators personalize instruction for each student by analyzing their learning needs, preferences, and progress and suggesting tailored interventions. AI can lead to more inclusive and effective teaching practices and can ultimately improve learning outcomes for all students.

The movie *Marjorie Prime*, a science fiction drama that explores the use of AI technology to create lifelike virtual companions that can help people cope with loss and loneliness, depicts an elderly woman named Marjorie that spends time with a virtual version of her late husband, Walter, who has been created using AI and machine learning algorithms. The use of AI in regard to elderly care raises important questions about the future impact of AI technology on society. This is especially relevant in an aging population where many individuals may lack the social connections and support they need to maintain a high quality of life. On the one hand, *Marjorie Prime* illustrates the potential benefits of using AI to create virtual companions that can provide emotional support and companionship to people who may be isolated or lonely. On the other hand, the film serves as a serious commentary raising questions about the ethics of creating virtual versions of deceased loved ones without their consent, as well as the potential for AI-generated content to reinforce existing biases and prejudices.

Which brings me to the opposite side of the coin. While Hollywood has planted seeds of optimism and promise around AI, we also have them to thank for the opposite: generating fears around adoption and a worry about rising sentience. I promise the AI we have today is far from an uprising! But we do have to worry about how this technology could negatively impact our classrooms and districts. One of the most common threats that have been echoed throughout the internet is teachers' fears that students will use AI to cheat. But what is cheating? And how can we pivot to work with AI to create more authentic assessments and opportunities where tools like ChatGPT can be a resource?

The use of ChatGPT's open-source AI technology in S26 Episode 4 of *South Park* highlights the potential for the technology to be used for unethical purposes, such as plagiarism. In the episode, Stan's classmates use the technology to write their essays, which results in their essays being predictable and formulaic. This is a clear example of the dangers of relying too heavily on AI-generated content. An article by screenrant.com (2023) does a great job of pointing out the clever commentary on the episode titled "Deep Learning":

> *The South Park episode's closing sequence was intentionally far too tidy and the scene ended the story way too slickly. However, this worked in the context of an episode about the boys (and their teacher) dodging the real work of relationships, teaching, and academia alike. When Mr. Garrison noted that there was no reason to fear AI-generated movies since Hollywood is already derivative and repetitive, this was another instance of South Park season 26 leaning into pretty blatant meta-humor.*

The episode mirrored the real-world fear of teachers and educators becoming increasingly concerned about the possibility of students using AI language models, like ChatGPT, to plagiarize. With the ability to generate human-like responses to text-based prompts, there is a risk that students could use the technology to create essays, reports, and other assignments without actually doing the necessary research and writing themselves. As the show's writers ended the episode with a closing generated by ChatGPT, it drew on the historical trend of previous episodes.

Tweet from South Park's Twitter account.

Another limitation of AI highlighted exceptionally well in Hollywood is the limitations and bias in AI systems. The psychological thriller *Ex Machina* (2014) focuses on a young programmer who is invited to the secluded home of a brilliant CEO to conduct a Turing test on an AI robot with a human appearance. The film raises important questions about the impact of human bias on the development of AI and whether AI can develop its own biases based on its interactions with humans. These movies not only serve as social commentary but as a reminder that we must be vigilant in ensuring that our use of AI is guided by principles of fairness, equality, and respect for diversity, especially when it comes to education and learning.

Considering movies like *The Terminator*, it is understandable why some educators approach the technology lacklusterly and with caution. In the movie, an artificial intelligence system named Skynet gains self-awareness and initiates a war against humanity. While *The Terminator* may not seem directly related to education, there are some parallels, and we have Cyberdyne Systems Model 101 or the T-800 to thank for that! For example, some people worry that AI could become so advanced that it takes over jobs traditionally done by humans, including teaching. With any newfangled technology comes fear, but Brian Tracy said it best: "Fear is the enemy of innovation and development, and the greatest barrier to progress is the reluctance to take risks." I personally believe that we are living in an exciting time of the AI revolution and that AI will not replace teachers but empower us to create curricula more efficiently and more powerfully by augmenting human intelligence and providing new opportunities for learning.

In summary, one of the common denominators that are present in most, if not all of the Hollywood films involving AI, is the dual message that AI shows promise to change the future for the better, but we must also be mindful of the potential risks and challenges associated with AI development and use and work to develop ethical and transparent frameworks for the use of this technology. That is exactly what we aspire to do with this book; provide you with the history of AI, the concerns, the pitfalls, and help you navigate and pave an educational path forward with AI as a sidekick to enhance existing pedagogies and bring out the best of our human value systems. This will require ongoing dialogue and collaboration between technologists, policymakers, and members of the public, as well as ongoing monitoring and evaluation of AI systems to ensure that they are safe, fair, and effective.

So, let's boldly go where no educator has gone before and embrace the potential of AI in education to unlock new opportunities for learning and promote equity and inclusion in the classroom.

PART ONE

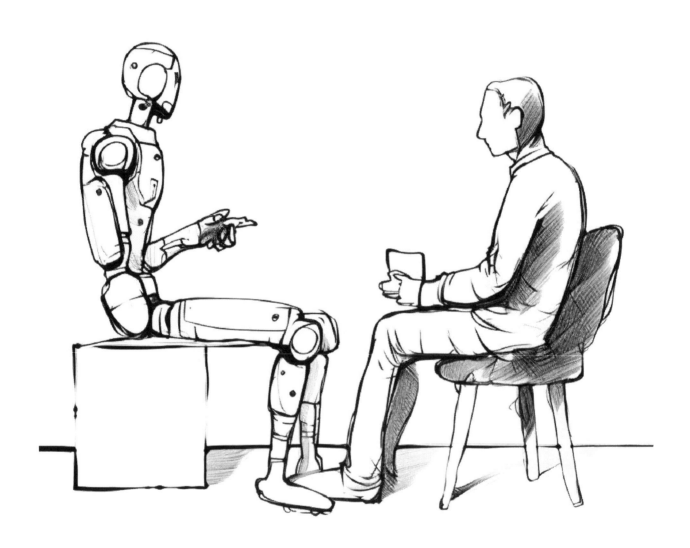

THE AI UPRISING

CHAPTER 1

Rise of the Machines

"We'll experience more technological progress in the coming decade than we did in the preceding 100 years put together."

- McKinsey & Company

Artificial intelligence (AI) poses the greatest challenge and opportunity for education that we have ever seen.

Without realizing it, we have entered the AI revolution. No longer do we talk about how AI will change the world; now we observe how it is already changing the world. This happened fast. For most people, it feels as if it happened overnight.

We can be forgiven for thinking that the hype will fade, and as teachers, we will carry on doing things as we always have done. After all, how many shiny new pieces of technology have we been presented with over the decades that have ended up in the cupboard? This time is different. There's no turning back. AI is revolutionizing most industries, and if education wants to be relevant, it will have to get to grips with it.

AI TIMELINE

BLAISE PASCHAL BUILDS THE FIRST MECHANICAL CALCULATING MACHINE
1642

THE TERM "ARTIFICIAL INTELLIGENCE" IS COINED
1956

IBM's DEEP BLUE DEFEATS CHESS CHAMPION GARY KASPAROV
1997

OPENAI RELEASES CHATGPT
2022

1837
ADA LOVELACE + CHARLES BABBAGE PRODUCE THE FIRST DESIGN FOR A PROGRAMMABLE MACHINE

1967
THE "GENERAL PROBLEM SOLVER" IS DEVELOPED

2016
GOOGLE'S ALPHAGO DEFEATS THE GO WORLD CHAMPION

2023
GOOGLE RELEASES BARD

In 1956, a group of computer scientists gathered at Dartmouth College to discuss the future of computing. They called this new field "Artificial Intelligence" and set out to create machines that could think like humans.

The early days of AI were filled with optimism and excitement. Researchers believed that within just a few decades, machines would be able to perform tasks that previously only humans could do.

However, the reality was far from what they had imagined. Early AI systems were limited and often failed to perform as expected. This was due to the large amounts of computing power that was needed and the vast amounts of information needed to form a knowledge base for the computers. This was, of course, before the internet and the advancement of computer processors. Progress was slow and many people became disillusioned with the field. Consequently, funding also dried up.

The 1980s brought a renewed interest in AI. Advances in computer hardware and software made it possible for these systems to process more data and make more sophisticated decisions. This led to the development of expert systems, which were capable of solving problems in specific domains, such as medical diagnosis or financial planning.

As the 1990s rolled around, the focus shifted to machine learning and neural networks. These new AI systems were trained using large amounts of data and could learn and adapt to new situations. This led to the creation of some of the first AI applications such as speech recognition and computer vision systems.

In the 2000s, artificial intelligence continued to evolve and become more widespread. Companies like Google and Amazon used AI to improve their search algorithms and e-commerce systems. In the field of robotics, AI-powered machines were being used in manufacturing and other industrial settings.

It wasn't until the 2010s that artificial intelligence really took off. Advances in deep learning and big data allowed AI systems to process even more data and make more accurate predictions. This led to breakthroughs in fields such as image and speech recognition, natural language processing, and self-driving cars.

Today, AI is changing our world in ways that we never thought possible. It's being used to diagnose diseases, find new sources of energy, and even create art. As AI becomes mainstream through chatbots like ChatGPT and Google Bard, we are at the start of a revolution that is disrupting how we work, live, and learn.

While researching and preparing to write this book, I had the pleasure of interviewing and speaking with a renowned educator and Metaverse entrepreneur, Melissa McBride. She shared with me that we are all currently in a state of "shock and awe due to the entry of new [AI] technology with significant power and speed. This shock phase has resulted in some resistance, but also people being open to exploring the opportunities presented." Melissa believes that regardless of the sector one is working in or the career phase, everyone is at an inflection point, and it is fascinating how quickly this technology has hit the mainstream.

So, what does the future of AI hold? We're on the cusp of a new era of artificial intelligence where machines will be able to perform tasks that were once thought to be the exclusive domain of humans. Artificial intelligence is here to stay, and it's changing our world in ways we never could have imagined. So buckle up, because the ride is just getting started!

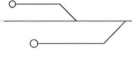

Alan Turing was a genius who changed the world in ways we may never fully understand. He was a mathematician, computer scientist, and codebreaker who laid the foundation for modern computing and helped to defeat the Nazis during World War II.

Turing was born in London in 1912 and showed a passion for mathematics from a young age. He went on to study at King's College in Cambridge where he became interested in the idea of machines that could think like humans.

In the 1930s, Turing wrote a groundbreaking paper that introduced the concept of the Universal Machine. This machine could be programmed to perform any computation that could be done by hand and is considered to be the theoretical foundation of modern computing.

During World War II, Turing was recruited by the British government to work at Bletchley Park, a secret code-breaking facility. There, he worked to crack the Nazis' Enigma code, which was used to encrypt their messages. Turing's work was crucial to the Allies' success and is considered to have shortened the war by several years.

After the war, Turing continued his work in computing and developed the concept of the Turing Test. The test involves a human judge who interacts with both a human and a machine. If the judge can't tell the difference between the two, then the machine is said to have passed the Turing Test.

Why do we pursue artificial intelligence? What drives us to create machines that can converse with humans? These questions are at the heart of Alan Turing's revolutionary idea, the Turing Test. By evaluating a machine's ability to convince a human that it, too, is human, the Turing Test challenges us to push the limits of what is possible with AI.

Turing's work was groundbreaking and paved the way for the development of artificial intelligence as we know it today. He believed that machines would eventually be able to think and act like humans, and they would play an important role in shaping our future.

According to Max Woolf (2022), a data scientist at BuzzFeed, in December 2022 we witnessed a historic moment when ChatGPT became the second machine to pass the Turing Test. Although others disagree with this conclusion and believe it has not passed the Turing Test, perhaps the important question is what the test actually tells us. Is it still meaningful?

Searle's Chinese Room Thought Experiment

The Turing Test continues to be a cornerstone of artificial intelligence research. It's a measure of a machine's ability to exhibit human-like intelligence and has been used as a way to gauge the progress of AI. However, not everyone is a fan of it.

Philosopher John Searle had some major criticisms of the Turing Test. Searle argues that the test doesn't really tell us anything about a machine's ability to understand language or to think.

Searle created the Chinese Room thought experiment, which consists of the following:

Imagine you are in a room with no windows, just a table, a pen, and a stack of papers with instructions written in English.

You don't speak Chinese, but someone slips a Chinese text through a slot in the door. You're given another set of instructions on how to respond to the text in Chinese.

You follow the instructions, looking up each character in a book of rules, and you write out a response, again in Chinese, on a sheet of paper.

You slip the paper back through the slot, and someone on the other side responds with another Chinese text, to which you must again respond with another set of instructions.

Now, even though you don't understand Chinese, the person outside the room might think you do because you're producing seemingly intelligent responses.

Searle argues that this is what a computer is doing when it processes information - following a set of rules but lacking any true understanding of the meaning of the information it's processing.

So, in Searle's view, no matter how sophisticated a computer program is, it can never truly understand language or have real intelligence. It's just following rules like a person in a Chinese Room.

Let's break this down.

Searle's first criticism of the Turing Test is that language involves more than just being able to produce the right responses to questions. It also involves being able to have experiences and feelings that are connected to language.

Searle's second criticism is that the Turing Test doesn't take into account the context of the conversation. For example, if a machine is answering questions about a movie, it may be able to give the right answers but not actually understand the movie itself.

Searle's third criticism is that the Turing Test is too focused on language and not enough on thought. According to Searle, thought is a process that occurs inside the mind, and it's not something that can be tested by simply asking a machine questions.

So what does this all mean for the Turing Test and AI? Well, it's important to remember that Searle's criticisms don't mean that the Turing Test is completely worthless. It's still a useful tool for measuring a machine's ability to exhibit human-like intelligence.

However, Searle's criticisms do highlight the limitations of the Turing Test and the need for a more comprehensive way of measuring a machine's ability to think and understand.

So, what does the future hold for the Turing Test and AI? Some experts believe that as AI continues to advance, we'll need to come up with new and more sophisticated ways of measuring a machine's ability to "think" and "understand." Others believe that the Turing Test will continue to play an important role in AI research.

Many believe that new AI tools like ChatGPT are able to pass the Turing test. They can simulate human intelligence and respond to questions coherently. However, if we approach these tools with John Searle in mind, then perhaps they aren't as intelligent as we might think. These instances of artificial intelligence might not be able to understand or empathize like humans. These limitations must be kept in mind whenever we use artificial intelligence technology, especially in the field of education.

Regardless of what the future holds, it's clear that the Turing Test sparks important debates and discussions about what it means to be intelligent and to understand language. This will continue to be important for years to come.

The Singularity

"By 2029, as we eliminate the current issues with large language models [like GPT], more and more people will accept that they are conscious."

– Ray Kurzweil, Head of Engineering at Google
Lex Fridman Podcast, September 2022

While some argue about what constitutes the moment machines match human intelligence, others are already formulating ideas about what it means to exist in a world where this is a reality. We might not have to wait long.

Raymond Kurzweil is a well-known futurist, inventor, and author who has made some bold predictions about the future of artificial intelligence and the concept of the singularity.

The singularity, as Kurzweil defines it, is the point in time when artificial intelligence surpasses human intelligence and begins to rapidly advance on its own. Kurzweil believes that this event will have a profound impact on society, leading to massive technological changes and the creation of a new type of intelligence.

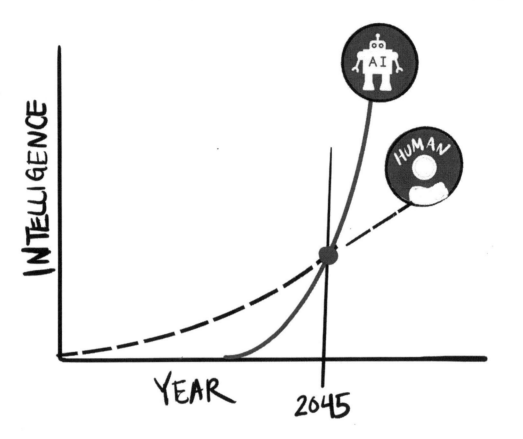

In his 2005 book, *The Singularity Is Near: When Humans Transcend Biology*, Kurzweil predicts that the singularity will occur around the year 2045 and that the rate of technological progress will continue to accelerate at an exponential rate after that. He believes that this will lead to a future where humans and machines are able to merge, allowing people to live forever and access unlimited knowledge.

Kurzweil (2005) also predicts that artificial intelligence will be used to solve some of the world's biggest problems, such as climate change, poverty, and disease. He believes that AI will be able to analyze massive amounts of data and find solutions that humans wouldn't be able to on their own.

However, his predictions are not without their critics. Some experts believe that his predictions are too optimistic and don't take into account the many challenges that will need to be overcome in order for the singularity to occur. They also worry that artificial intelligence could pose a threat to humanity, leading to the development of weapons that could destroy the world, in a scene akin to *The Terminator* movies where an artificial intelligence named Skynet takes over the world.

Despite these concerns, Kurzweil remains confident in his predictions. He argues that technology has been advancing at an exponential rate for thousands of years and that there is no reason to believe that this will change. He also believes that artificial intelligence will be used for good and that it will help to create a better future for all of humanity (Kurzweil, 2005).

So, what does the future hold for artificial intelligence and the singularity? Only time will tell, but one thing is certain: Raymond Kurzweil's work has ignited important debates and discussions about the future of technology that are becoming more and more pertinent.

The Place of Humans in This Brave New World

Imagine a world where artificial intelligence has surpassed human intelligence.

Instead of replacing us, it has become an integral part of our lives, transforming our society in new and exciting ways. A world where AI works hand in hand with humans, providing unprecedented levels of efficiency and productivity, and solving some of the world's most pressing challenges. In this new world, we have access to technology that enhances every aspect of our lives: from smart homes that learn our preferences and automatically adjust to our needs and emotional states, to cars that drive themselves, making traffic jams and road accidents a thing of the past.

At work, artificial intelligence assistants help us with everything from analyzing data to generating new ideas, freeing up our time and energy for more creative and fulfilling pursuits. In healthcare, artificial intelligence is used to diagnose and treat illnesses more accurately and quickly, saving lives and improving the quality of care.

AI is set to revolutionize not only our daily lives but also the world at large. With its incredible power, AI is already driving progress in crucial areas like mitigating climate change, combating diseases, and reducing poverty. These global challenges may seem insurmountable, but AI is emerging as a valuable ally in tackling some of the most pressing issues that humanity faces today.

Artificial intelligence is opening up new opportunities for people to pursue their passions and realize their full potential. From the arts to entrepreneurship, AI is providing innovative platforms and tools for creativity and innovation while helping us to create a world that is more diverse, equitable, and just.

The future is full of promise and potential. By embracing the possibilities of this new world and working alongside machines, we can create a future that is both prosperous and full of wonder.

I know this take on our future with AI is optimistic. I have described it like this because we must not be passive agents in the creation of our future. As artificial intelligence becomes more powerful and integrated into our lives, I am convinced that intent matters. Our intent must be optimistic and our use of these technologies must be driven by a desire to improve the world.

So, where do we start?

Let's start contemplating the skills and jobs of the future. Sure, some jobs will be automated, but there are plenty of opportunities for us to excel in areas where machines fall short.

Now, I know what you're thinking. "But what about all those jobs that are going to disappear?" Well, don't panic just yet. There are plenty of steps you can take to prepare for the future. First and foremost, it's essential to be aware of emerging trends in your field. Are there new technologies on the horizon that could change the game? If so, make sure you're ahead of the curve and learning the skills that will be in demand.

The good news is that the benefits of a world with artificial intelligence are immense. By working alongside machines, we can achieve levels of efficiency and productivity that were once unimaginable. Consider a world without textile machinery. The Luddites once opposed this technology, yet our society now flourishes due to the efficiency and productivity these machines provide. It's essential that we don't repeat the Luddites' mistake and instead, embrace, harness, and leverage technology to improve the lives of everyone. Let's not shy away from progress, but instead, utilize it for the greater good.

Let's dive a bit deeper into the specific skills that will be most in demand in the age of artificial intelligence. Creativity, emotional intelligence, and critical thinking are all areas where humans excel, and they will continue to be highly valued in the future. Creativity is where humans shine. While machines can be programmed to replicate creativity, human creation is still thriving and will continue to. This is why jobs that require creativity, such as artists, writers, and designers, will continue to be in high demand in the future.

Emotional intelligence is the ability to recognize and understand our own emotions, as well as those of others. This is a skill that machines simply cannot replicate at the moment. In a world where machines are becoming more advanced, it is our human ability to connect with others on an emotional level that sets us apart.

Critical thinking is a skill that involves analyzing and evaluating information to form a judgment. In a world where machines are processing more data than ever before, critical thinking is paramount. While machines can process data at a rapid pace, they cannot think critically or creatively to arrive at new insights. This is where humans thrive, providing the necessary context and nuance to make sense of all the data.

What are some practical steps we can take to prepare for the future with AI?

One tip is to stay up to date on emerging trends in your field. Attend conferences and workshops, read industry publications, and connect with experts in your field. This will help you identify the skills that will be in demand in the future and give you a head start in developing those skills.

Another step is to embrace the power of collaboration with machines. As mentioned earlier, one of the biggest mistakes we can make is underestimating the value of working with machines, rather than against them. By learning to work alongside artificial intelligence, we can achieve unprecedented levels of efficiency and productivity. This means collaborating with machines to tackle complex problems and find new solutions.

When it comes to avoiding common mistakes, one of the biggest is assuming that the skills we have today will remain in demand in the future. The truth is that the world is changing at an almost Fibonaccian pace, and we need to be prepared to adapt and reskill. This means being open to learning new things, taking on new challenges, and staying ahead of the curve.

It's also important to remember that the future with artificial intelligence is not predetermined. While there are risks and challenges that we need to be aware of, there are also immense opportunities for growth and innovation.

When I chatted with David Price OBE, the author of *The Power of Us: How We Connect, Act and Innovate Together*, in preparation for this book, he summarized the start of the revolution in these words:

We're just at the beginning [of the AI revolution] and the impossibility of trying to imagine where we may be even in 12 months time is both exhilarating and a bit scary. It has gathered momentum that even OpenAI may not have expected. When I was growing up, we used to make bogies. They were basically a box with four wheels. We would race them down hills. We would get in them, and then we would realize that, wow, this was absolutely exhilarating because it was getting faster and faster. Then you realized it had no breaks, and the only way you're gonna be able to stop it was to jump off and that you were gonna hurt yourself. It feels a bit like that now, where we have very little control over it, and we need to be cautious. In my book Open, *I was a utopian about social media, which didn't turn out so well. However, I still argue that it has been transformative for good. I think the jobs that will be lost are those who don't embrace AI, and we need to bring it into every part of our working world. Already, every sector of industry has gone, 'How do we use this? This is great.' The only people who should fear this now are those who can't use it within their daily work.*

The Future is Already Here

"ChatGPT is scary good. We are not far from dangerously strong AI."

-Elon Musk
Co-founder of OpenAI. Founder of SpaceX and Tesla

The recent explosion of artificial intelligence is large because ordinary people like us have been given access to it, and we are discovering its power.

In reality, the technology we are using in a tool like ChatGPT is already old technology. The current version has been around for three years. We have been living in an AI world for a while now; we just never really noticed it, and it has already changed our lives.

The exciting aspect (or maybe scary, depending on how you look at it) is that the technology is getting better faster. Alongside that, new use cases will emerge, more companies will develop solutions, and we'll begin relying on it like we never lived without it.

While researching this book, Priya Lakhani OBE explained to me,

I've met many entrepreneurs who present prototypes and products that were unimaginable a decade ago. People are investing heavily in these areas, and the amount of investment is what's most interesting and will accelerate progress. As an AI entrepreneur, I see a direct impact from the dollars going into these spaces. The speed of acceleration and reaching the mass market depends on the amount of investment. Currently, significant investments are being made in the metaverse and artificial intelligence technology, from proprietary technology to applications. It's clear that this is just the beginning, and we can expect new products and services developed from the combination of these technologies, which will transform our everyday life. The way we see things, search for things, and experience things will all be revolutionized. What we're seeing now is just the appetizer.

This is how the AI revolution takes off.

How Have We Already Used AI and What Have Been the Benefits?

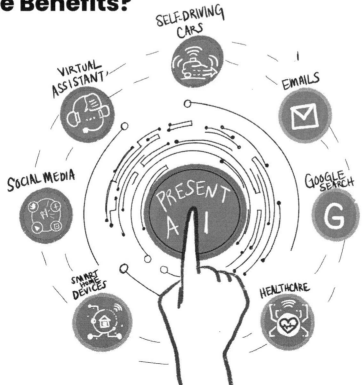

When you type a query into Google, the search engine uses artificial intelligence to provide you with the most relevant results. When you use Siri or Alexa to set a reminder or play a song, you're using AI. When you receive a personalized recommendation on Netflix or Amazon, AI is behind it.

Artificial intelligence is already embedded in our daily lives, from the way we consume news and entertainment, to the way we shop, and even the way we work. The beauty of it is that it's seamless. You don't even have to think about it.

Let's take a closer look at some of the ways we're using artificial intelligence in our daily lives now:

Voice Assistants

Voice assistants like Siri, Alexa, and Google Assistant allow us to perform a range of tasks from setting reminders and alarms to controlling smart home devices. But have you ever stopped to think about how they work? These devices use natural language processing (NLP) and machine learning to understand what we're saying and provide the appropriate response.

Social Media

Have you ever noticed how Facebook always seems to know what you're interested in? That's because the social media giant uses artificial intelligence to analyze your activity and provide you with personalized content. This includes targeted ads, suggested friends, and even news articles. X also uses AI to analyze and filter posts, which helps in their pursuit of users only seeing the most relevant and useful content.

Smart Home Devices

Smart home devices, such as thermostats, light bulbs, and security systems, use AI to learn your preferences and adjust their settings accordingly. For example, a smart thermostat can learn when you're typically at home and adjust the temperature accordingly. A smart security system can learn what is "normal" activity for your home and alert you if anything seems out of the ordinary.

Online Shopping

Have you ever noticed that when you shop online you're often presented with personalized recommendations? This is because online retailers use AI to analyze your shopping behavior and suggest products that are likely to interest you. This not only makes shopping more convenient but also helps retailers to increase their sales.

Healthcare

Artificial intelligence is also being used in the healthcare industry. For example, AI-powered chatbots can provide patients with advice and support. AI can also be used to analyze medical data, such as X-rays and CT scans, to help doctors make more accurate diagnoses.

AI is being used in finance, transportation, education, and many other industries. In fact, it's hard to think of an industry that isn't being impacted by AI in some way. These are just a few examples of how we're already using artificial intelligence in our daily lives. And the list goes on.

But what does this mean for us?

It means that we're living in a world of artificial intelligence, whether we realize it or not. While some may view this as a negative thing, it's important to remember that AI has the potential to improve our lives in countless ways. It can help us to be more productive, efficient, and informed.

While some might view the prevalence of artificial intelligence in our lives with trepidation, there's no denying that it has already bestowed many benefits.

Let's take a closer look at some of these:

Improved Productivity

AI has already had a significant impact on our ability to work more efficiently. For example, it can automate repetitive tasks, freeing up employees to focus on more complex and creative work. This not only makes work more interesting and rewarding, but it can also help to reduce errors and increase productivity. For instance, customer service chatbots can answer frequently asked questions, reducing the need for human intervention.

Enhanced Safety

Artificial intelligence can also help us to stay safe in a number of ways. For example, it can be used to monitor traffic and alert us to dangerous road conditions or traffic congestion. It may also be used to identify potential safety hazards in the workplace, such as malfunctioning machinery or unsafe working conditions.

Personalized Learning

AI can also help us to learn in a more personalized and efficient way. It will analyze our learning behavior and preferences and provide us with customized recommendations for courses and study materials. This can help to reduce the time and cost associated with learning and make education more accessible to a wider range of people.

Better Healthcare

Artificial intelligence is already making a big impact on healthcare, and this is only set to improve in the coming years. For example, it can be used to analyze medical records and identify patterns that may indicate the early onset of a disease. It will also be used to help doctors make more accurate diagnoses and to identify the most effective treatments for individual patients.

More Efficient Resource Management

AI will also help us to manage resources more efficiently, from energy and water to transportation and logistics. It can be used to optimize delivery routes, reduce energy consumption in buildings, and monitor and control the use of natural resources. This may help us to reduce our carbon footprint and make more sustainable use of the resources we have available.

As you can see, AI is already having a profound impact on our lives. It's important to remember that artificial intelligence is not a replacement for human intelligence and creativity. Rather, it is a tool that we should use to enhance and augment our own abilities. By embracing AI and learning how to use it effectively, we create a brighter and more prosperous future for ourselves and for generations to come.

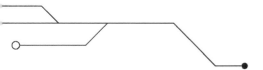

The Rise of Natural Language Processors (NLPs)

"[The] Most amazing fact about AI is that even though it's starting to feel impressive, a year from now we'll look back fondly on the AI that exists today as quaint & antiquated."

– Greg Brockman
President & Co-Founder of OpenAI

Language is one of the most powerful tools we have as humans. It allows us to express ourselves, share knowledge, and connect with each other. But what if we could extend this power to machines, enabling them to understand and generate human-like language? This is what natural language processors can do. New advanced language models, algorithms designed to process and analyze human language, have revolutionized natural language processing and begun to change the world in ways we couldn't have imagined.

NLPs are AI-powered language models designed to process and generate natural language. It uses a form of artificial intelligence called deep learning to understand the context and meaning of words, phrases, and sentences. This means that it can generate text that is both informative and engaging, just like a human would. But what sets these new NLPs apart from other language models is their ability to draw on a wide range of knowledge and language styles, making them the most versatile language models to date.

One of the most exciting use cases for NLPs is in the world of customer service. Imagine being able to get help with your queries 24/7 without ever having to wait for a response. This is now possible. By automating tasks like answering FAQs and booking appointments, NLPs can help businesses provide quick and efficient customer service. In fact, some companies are already using NLPs to provide support to their customers. For instance, Bank of America has integrated Erica, a virtual assistant powered by ChatGPT, to help customers with their banking needs.

The impact of these NLPs extends far beyond the fields of customer service and content creation. This technology has the potential to transform education, healthcare, and even our daily lives. In education, they could help to create more effective learning materials that are tailored to individual needs. For example, they could generate personalized resources or tutorials based on a student's preferences. In healthcare, they could be used to help doctors and patients communicate more effectively, improving patient outcomes and reducing medical errors. In our daily lives, they could help us to communicate more effectively with each other, regardless of language barriers or communication difficulties.

These new NLPs are not just an innovation; they are revolutionary. They have the potential to fundamentally shift the way we communicate and interact with technology. As machines become more intelligent and capable of understanding natural language, we will begin to witness and experience a shift towards more human-like interactions with machines. We will also see a reduction in the barriers between people who speak different languages or who have different communication needs.

Natural language processors have the potential to create a more connected and inclusive world.

Governments, businesses, and individuals will all benefit from the advances that NLP AI technology provides. They can help to automate tasks and improve customer service resulting in more satisfied customers.

They can help to improve public services and make information more accessible to everyone. They can provide assistance and support in a way that was previously impossible.

There's also a potential downside to this technology. As machines become better at generating human-like language, it may become difficult to distinguish between what is created by humans and what is created by machines. This could lead to a loss of trust in the authenticity of language as well as ethical concerns around the use of machine-generated content.

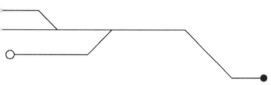

Our Future With AI

"The countries with the highest robot density have among the lowest unemployment rates. Technology and humans combined in the right way will drive prosperity."

– Ulrich Spiesshofer, President and CEO, ABB Ltd.

Have you ever noticed how new technologies often take a while to catch on but then suddenly explode in popularity? Think about the way smartphones have taken over our lives in the last decade. In the early 2000s, mobile phones were still fairly clunky and basic - you could make calls and send texts, but that was about it. Then, in 2007, Apple released the first iPhone, and suddenly everything changed. The sleek design, intuitive interface, and mind-boggling array of features made it an instant hit. People were lining up around the block to get their hands on one, and it seemed like everyone had a smartphone in their pocket.

Now, over a decade later, we're starting to see that growth plateau. Smartphones are still hugely popular, of course, but it's becoming harder and harder to come up with new and exciting features that will convince people to upgrade.

This is typical of the S-Curve, a model that shows how new technologies can improve over time.

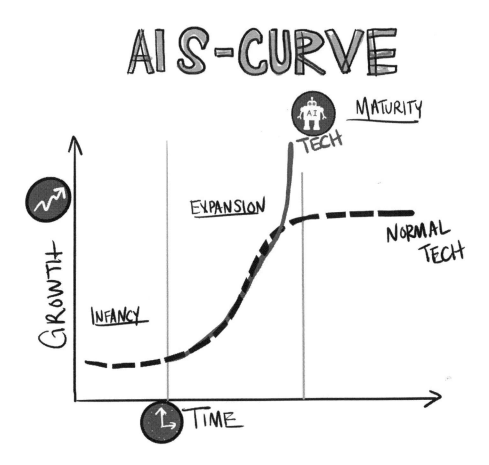

Jack Clarke, who used to work at OpenAI and is now the founder of Anthropic, explained on Twitter (2023) that artificial intelligence was roughly in linear growth from the 1960s to 2010. Then it reached exponential growth from 2010 to 2020. He went on to state that since 2020, it "has started to display 'compounding exponential' properties... In other words, [the] next few years will yield progress that intuitively feels nuts."

If the way that AI learns and improves over time compounds, then we may expect the upward trajectory of the S-Curve to carry on indefinitely for artificial intelligence. This technology self-improves, potentially giving birth to new innovation after innovation for a long time to come. Innovations that could forever change the face of the earth.

Why explore how AI will change the world in a book about education? In my preparation for this book, David Price OBE said to me that he believes, "The use of AI in society cannot be separated from its use in education." I agree with him. If we intend to prepare our students for success, then we must prepare them for this transforming world. Let's explore how it might change the world in the coming years.

The Job Market

The job market is one sector where artificial intelligence might have a significant impact. While it's true that AI will replace some jobs, it's important to remember that new jobs will also be created as a result of the new AI technologies. Artificial intelligence will require new skills. The jobs that AI will replace are typically jobs that are dangerous, repetitive, or require little creativity. By freeing humans from these jobs, AI will allow us to focus on jobs that require critical thinking and creativity, ultimately leading to a more fulfilling career path and perhaps a new renaissance age.

Combining AI With VR

Priya Lakhani OBE, explained, "We will combine this technology [AI] with the worlds of virtual reality (VR), augmented reality (AR), and the Metaverse."

"[We] will likely be living in a world where we have a physical world and a digital world. The emphasis on the digital world will be a lot stronger than it is today."

The healthcare industry is another area where artificial intelligence might bring about significant change. With the ability to analyze vast amounts of data, AI has the potential to help healthcare professionals diagnose and treat diseases with greater accuracy and efficiency. For example, AI may be used to identify cancer cells that may have been missed in a patient's scan, leading to earlier diagnosis and treatment. AI-powered devices have the ability and potential to monitor patients in real time, providing doctors with valuable insights and allowing them to intervene more quickly when necessary.

Healthcare

"Some people call this artificial intelligence, but the reality is this technology will enhance us. So instead of artificial intelligence, I think we'll augment our intelligence."

—Ginni Rometty

Artificial intelligence will have a significant impact on mental health therapy. Many individuals who struggle with mental health issues do not have access to resources due to financial constraints or the stigma associated with seeking treatment. AI has the potential to increase accessibility and reduce the stigma around therapy. Chatbots utilizing natural language processing will be able to provide support and guidance to individuals experiencing mental health issues. These chatbots can also use sentiment analysis to gauge a user's mood and provide personalized coping mechanisms.

Wellbeing

Elderly Care

Elderly individuals and those living with disabilities may benefit significantly from AI technology. Companion robots that use AI technology may provide support and assistance to elderly individuals, helping them maintain their independence and improve their overall quality of life. These robots could also monitor the senior's well-being, detect falls or accidents, and alert emergency services if needed. Smart homes equipped with AI technology may make it easier for people with disabilities to live independently by automating tasks like turning on lights, adjusting the thermostat, and unlocking doors. AI may also help those with mobility issues by making it easier for them to move around using motorized wheelchairs or other devices.

Genetic Engineering

Artificial intelligence has enormous potential in the field of genetic engineering. It can analyze vast amounts of genomic data to understand genetic diseases and identify potential targets for drug discovery.

An AI-powered tool for genetic sequencing, called MinION, can read a person's DNA sequence in just a few minutes, helping doctors identify the cause of genetic disorders and start personalized treatments. Artificial intelligence also helps in drug discovery by reducing the time and cost of bringing new treatments to the market. It helps researchers identify potential drug targets more quickly and efficiently by analyzing large amounts of data, such as clinical trial data and disease pathology data.

The transportation industry is another area where AI might bring about significant change. With the development of self-driving cars, we might see a reduction in the number of accidents and improvements in road safety. With the help of artificial intelligence, cars will be able to communicate with each other, avoiding collisions. AI can also be used to optimize traffic flows and reduce congestion, ultimately leading to more efficient transportation and greater safety.

Transportation

"AI is an engine that is poised to drive the future of retail to all-new destinations. The key to success is the ability to extract meaning from big data to solve problems and increase productivity."

Azadeh Yazdan, director of business development, AI Products Group

Retail can benefit from artificial intelligence with the ability to personalize the shopping experience for customers. AI can be used to recommend products that are based on a customer's previous purchases and browsing history, making the shopping experience more convenient and enjoyable. AI-powered chatbots can also assist customers in real time by answering their questions and helping them with their purchases. This can lead to improved customer satisfaction and increased sales for retailers.

Retail

The Environment

Artificial intelligence might also have significant implications for the environment. With the ability to analyze vast amounts of data, AI can help us understand the impact of human activity on the environment and develop strategies to reduce the negative impact we have had on our planet. For example, AI can be used to optimize energy consumption in buildings, reduce waste, and lower energy costs. It could also be used to monitor wildlife populations and track changes in the environment, helping us better understand how to protect our planet.

Education

Another area where artificial intelligence will have a significant impact in education. AI-powered platforms are providing personalized learning experiences for students, based on their needs. This leads to improved academic performance and increased engagement in the classroom. AI could also be used to grade assignments and provide feedback to students, freeing up teachers' time to focus on other important tasks.

Thoughts on AI From Educators

"...disrupting the status quo, giving rise to new forms of leadership, industry and economics that lean toward an understanding of AI, Machine Learning and Big Data."
Mark Nichols, Future Leader

"...massively reducing unnecessary workload, allowing me more time to focus on the art of delivery."

Jon Tait, Deputy CEO

"...personalizing my daily work experience, helping me get to the most relevant tasks and information quickly... It will save me valuable time and increase creativity through capacity."
Daren White, Academic Technologies Lead

"...creating more equitable spaces. AI will highlight to us where we have bias in our communications and show us alternatives."
SJ White, Teaching and Learning Specialist

"... predominantly reducing repetitive tasks. This is probably the revolution we all needed to ensure a good work-life balance. AI doesn't judge, so for someone like me who is highly self-conscious, I would prefer assistance from AI to help with questions I have."
Esther Albert, Psychology teacher & human intelligence coordinator

"...automating the tasks I'm least motivated to do. AI will target the activities that are the least valuable use of our time."
Jamie Smith, Executive Chairman

In the long term, I believe AI will impact how I work and live by...

"...saving me time on mundane, often pointless paperwork tasks."
Lee Parkinson, Mr P ICT, Primary School Teacher and Teacher Trainer

"...giving me access to a multi-modal digital assistant to support my day-to-day life. Once this is realized, it will be a significant milestone and development for the education sector."
Aftab Hussain, ILT and LRC Manager

"...using the tools to help me be more creative and help me be more organized and learn faster."

Mats Larsnäs, Teacher and edtech consultant

"...fundamentally building capacity. I can outsource so many time consuming tasks to AI tools so that I have a greater capacity to spend time on building and maintaining relationships, strategy, and training."
Olly Lewis, Head of Digital Transformation

"...helping students easily get access to information and helping to level the wide information equity gap that exists."
Elissa Malespina, School Librarian and School Board Member

"...saving me valuable time in lesson planning, allowing for more time to focus on the creative parts of teaching!"
Heather Brown, K-5 math interventionist and STEAM teacher

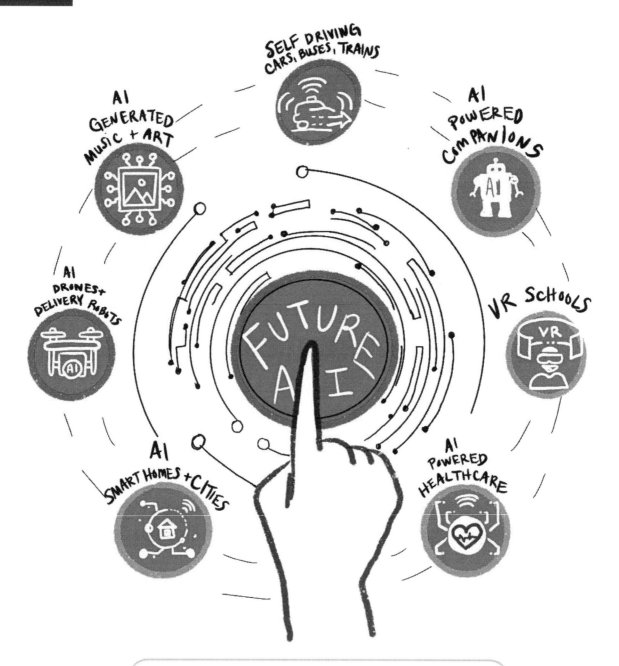

What excites you most about the future of AI?

Share your answer on social media and use the hashtag #AIClassroom.

@TeacherGoals

CHAPTER 3

Outsource Your Doing, Not Your Thinking

"Robots are not going to replace humans; they are going to make their jobs much more humane. Difficult, demeaning, demanding, dangerous, dull – these are the jobs robots will be taking."

Sabine Hauert, Co-founder of Robohub.org

The world needs humans to be human. Our students need us to be human. We need to feel human. Creativity is a defining aspect of what it means to be a human.

Here are four reasons why I believe human creativity matters:

1. It drives innovative solutions.
2. It fosters growth, confidence, & well-being.
3. It allows unique individual self-expression.
4. It brings joy & fulfillment.

The problem is that AI can replicate creativity.

Not only can it be creative, but its level of creativity will continue to improve. It is already competing with us:

1. An AI-generated artwork won a recent art competition in the US.

2. An AI image fooled judges and won a photography contest.

3. An AI generated children's book was created in a single weekend.

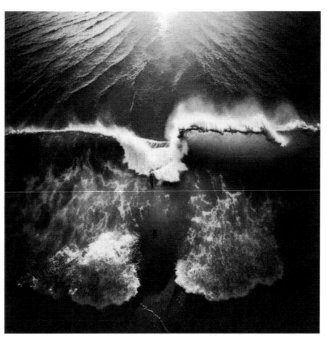
DigiDirect's photo competition winner, by Absolutely Ai

Outsource the doing, not the thinking. This means we should be the creative force when working with AI tools. Artificial intelligence will assist us with creativity. For example, we could use it to generate initial ideas or contrary ideas, but we shouldn't rely on it to do our thinking for us.

If you do use AI as a thinking assistant, then there are issues you will run into. Mellissa McBride, a Metaverse education entrepreneur, shared her view on this when she explained to me:

> *Every new technology brings with it risks and opportunities. Just like how we automatically assess risks in our daily life, such as when we cross the street, we need to assess the risks and opportunities of new technologies. We should have discussions about the challenges and opportunities presented by AI and open our minds to help AI learn beyond biases and understand the problems inherited from the past. We need to identify the type of future we want to create and bring AI along on that journey. Teaching about the risks and capacities of AI is a good starting point, but we should also avoid making mountains out of molehills. We should understand that AI is trained on knowledge and identify the challenges to reroute our teaching to move humanity forward. Understanding both sides of the coin is an important human skill.*

So what are some of the risks? Let's explore a few.

Hallucinations

One of the most significant issues for anyone using a large language model (LLM) like ChatGPT is the phenomenon of AI hallucinations. In other words, sometimes it can make up information.

AI hallucinations refer to a confident response by an AI that cannot be grounded in any of its training data. In human psychology, a hallucination is a percept that cannot be associated with the external world that the human is observing. Similarly, AI hallucinations occur when the AI generates content that is nonsensical or unfaithful to the provided source content.

I was recently trying to explain AI hallucinations to my fiancée while we were driving down the Northumberland coast in the northeast of England. Anyone familiar with this coastline will know it has many castles. I asked her to imagine a castle. If we were able to take the image from her head and analyze it then we would probably see features such as a drawbridge, a moat, walls, and a tower. These features will be based on factual information that she has learned from her experience of visiting castles as well as her experience learning about them in history classes. Although the image of the castle is based on some factual information, the castle itself is imaginary.

When using AI tools for creativity, hallucinations might be welcome; however, when using a tool like ChatGPT for factual information, this may cause a problem. Users sometimes complain that these tools embed plausible-sounding random falsehoods within their generated content, causing confusion and mistrust.

The root cause of AI hallucinations is complex and multifaceted. One possible reason for AI hallucinations is errors in encoding and decoding between text and representations. These errors cause the AI to generate nonsensical or unfaithful content. In systems such as ChatGPT, an AI generates each next word based on a sequence of previous words, causing a cascade of possible hallucinations as the response grows longer. This means that even a small error or bias in the initial response can lead to increasingly nonsensical content as the response grows.

Bias and Discrimination

One of the most pressing concerns facing artificial intelligence today is the issue of bias and discrimination that plague these tools. As we become increasingly reliant on AI systems, it is paramount that we confront this problem and take concrete measures to guarantee that our tools are unbiased, fair, and equitable for all.

At the crux of the issue lies the reality that AI models are trained on datasets that reflect historical and societal prejudices. This means that when these models are deployed, they have the potential to perpetuate these biases in their decision-making and predictions. For instance, an AI model that is trained on data that solely features male subjects may not perform as effectively when applied to women. This is of concern as it implies that AI systems may be rendering decisions that are unfair and unjust to certain groups of individuals.

The attributes employed to train AI models may also introduce bias. For instance, an AI model that is trained to screen job candidates based on their resumes may be biased against candidates who attended less prestigious institutions or possess non-traditional work histories. This is problematic as it suggests that AI systems may be excluding capable candidates based on arbitrary or irrelevant criteria. This is not unique to machines, as the same can happen with human interviewers. However, AI has the potential to continue to perpetuate such exclusionary decision-making.

One of the most significant obstacles in addressing bias in AI tools is the difficulty in identifying and rectifying it. This is particularly true for language models, which are trained on colossal amounts of data. Biases in language models sometimes perpetuate stereotypes, create misinterpretations, or disseminate harmful and false information. This is a major issue as language models are frequently used to generate text for a wide range of applications, from chatbots to news articles.

While efforts are being made to reduce bias in language models, it is an intricate and ongoing process. Ultimately, the key to mitigating bias and discrimination in AI tools is to tackle the issue with a steadfast commitment to fairness, justice, and equity. By taking the time to identify and address biases in our AI systems, we can ensure that these tools are harnessed to benefit humanity as a whole.

It is important to recognize that addressing bias in AI tools is just one piece of a larger puzzle. The deployment of these technologies is intertwined with broader societal issues, such as systemic inequalities and power imbalances. Therefore, if we are to create truly just and equitable AI systems, we must also work to address the underlying social and economic structures that give rise to bias and discrimination in the first place.

One of the most effective ways to promote the ethical and responsible use of AI in education is through the act of education itself. Teachers start by introducing the concept of bias to their students, explaining what it is, and why it is important to be aware of it. By providing real-life examples of bias in artificial intelligence, teachers will help students understand how AI impacts different groups of people and perpetuate negative stereotypes and prejudices.

It is crucial to highlight the potential consequences of biased AI. Bias can lead to discrimination and exclusion, which would in turn further marginalize certain groups. Teachers should explain to their students the significance of these consequences and why it is essential to promote the ethical and responsible use of artificial intelligence in education.

Teaching students media literacy, and how to evaluate the reliability of the information provided by tools like ChatGPT, is another crucial step. This includes fact-checking and cross-referencing information from multiple sources to ensure that they are making informed decisions. Encouraging critical thinking and questioning is also vital as it helps students to question the information provided by AI systems and to think critically about its potential biases.

Finally, students should be encouraged to speak up if they notice bias in AI systems. Reporting such instances to the appropriate authorities can help ensure that corrective measures are taken, and that future developments are free from bias.

Reasoning

The term "reasoning" is vague and encompasses various forms, such as deductive, inductive, adductive, formal, and informal reasoning. While AI models such as ChatGPT may face obstacles in some forms of reasoning, they possess strengths in others. Ongoing research and development are pushing the boundaries of what is feasible, opening up new opportunities for artificial intelligence.

Most LLMs possess a degree of spatial reasoning, a fundamental skill for tasks such as navigation and problem-solving. However, human intelligence is multifaceted, encompassing reasoning, critical thinking, decision-making, and problem-solving.

LLMs can generate text based on patterns it has learned during training, but they face limitations in areas like temporal reasoning. However, developers are continuously refining the model, improving its ability to learn and make predictions about the sequencing of events and their timing.

The potential applications of artificial intelligence in fields such as engineering, physics, and robotics, where physical reasoning is vital, are fascinating. Although ChatGPT may encounter challenges with physical reasoning, the model has already demonstrated evolution over time. The potential that will arise as AI advances in this field is enthralling.

One of the most significant challenges for AI models is psychological reasoning, which necessitates an understanding of human behavior and mental processes. Although this is a complex area, continued research and development are leading to significant progress with AI tools. As with physical reasoning, it is crucial to remember that progress in the field of psychological reasoning takes time.

The potential benefits of artificial intelligence are limitless. By comprehending the strengths and limitations of these models, we will continue to refine and develop them to better serve humanity.

Mathematics

It is clear that LLMs are not equipped to handle everything. One area where AI struggles is arithmetic reasoning, which involves using mathematical concepts and logic to solve arithmetic problems.

Large language models, like ChatGPT, currently have limitations when it comes to solving mathematical expressions, such as multiplying large numbers, finding roots, computing powers, or working with irrational numbers like pi or Euler's number (e). These challenges hinder ChatGPT's ability to solve math problems efficiently.

However, other AI systems are leading the way in mathematics education. Century Tech is an education tool that employs artificial intelligence to customize learning experiences for each individual learner across many mathematics curricula. Photomath is another great mobile application that uses a smartphone camera to solve mathematical problems in real-time. The app uses optical character recognition (OCR) technology to read and solve equations, providing step-by-step instructions on how to solve the problem. It can solve a wide range of math problems, including arithmetic, algebra, trigonometry, calculus, and more.

Thoughts on AI From Educators

"...that it could cause either a digital divide or high dependence. It's a threat if we as humans fail to address its importance and work alongside it."

Esther Albert, Psychology teacher & Human Intelligence Coordinator

"...people being irresponsible with it."

SJ White, Teaching and Learning Specialist

"...if people take it for granted and don't quality assure the information it gives you."

Jon Tait, Deputy CEO

"...we fail to create the right regulatory frameworks to ensure AI becomes a force for good in our world."

Jamie Smith, Executive Chairman

"...the governance and ethical arrangements around my personal dataset and those of others."

Aftab Hussain, ILT and LRC Manager

"...that AI will be used to share misinformation."

Daren White, Academic Technologies Lead

The thing that worries me most about AI is...

"...an over reliance on it."

Lee Parkinson, Mr P ICT, Primary School Teacher and Teacher Trainer

"...the discrepancy between users and non-users of AI. Inevitably, there will be pockets of society left behind - whole populations even. What can I do to help close the gap?"

Mark Nichols, Future Leader

"...that we become lazy and unaware of things."

Dieter Möckelmann EdTechWatcher

"...the potential for a lack of visible guidance and best practice for teachers - which could lead to a misuse of AI and an abdication of responsibility to critically consume."

Scott Hayden, Head of Digital Learning

"...some people won't check for accuracy and just assume what the AI generates is correct."

Heather Brown, K-5 math interventionist and STEAM teacher

What worries you about AI? Share with us on social media!

Use the hashtag #AICLASSROOM

PART TWO

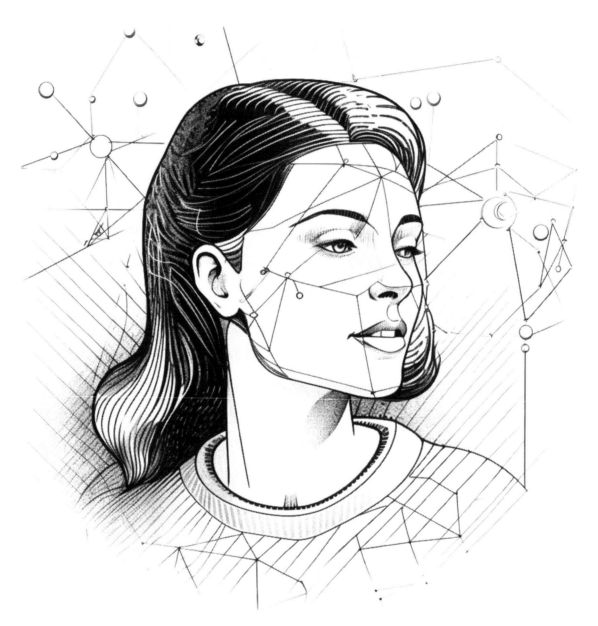

THE AI EDUCATOR

CHAPTER 4

Educators Assemble

"What we are very interested in is the right blend of human and artificial intelligence in the classroom – and how to identify that sweet spot."

– Rose Luckin
Professor of Learner-Centered Design at the UCL Knowledge Lab

A teacher who leverages artificial intelligence tools is a trailblazer charting a new course for education.

With AI, they have the power to transform the classroom into a dynamic, personalized learning experience tailored to each student's unique needs. By harnessing the insights and data generated by these powerful tools, teachers can make informed decisions about curriculum, pacing, and instruction, helping their students unlock their full potential.

It's an exciting time to be an educator, and those who embrace AI will be at the forefront of this revolution.

The Three-Box Solution

In "The Three-Box Solution," Vijay Govindarajan states that organizations should visualize three boxes.

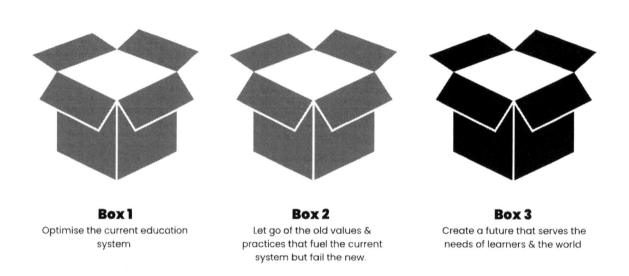

Box 1
Optimise the current education system

Box 2
Let go of the old values & practices that fuel the current system but fail the new.

Box 3
Create a future that serves the needs of learners & the world

Box One is the current system; it's our performance engine, and it's how we get results now. This is important as it currently works and helps the organization to survive. It's where the current business model, core competencies, and operations are focused. This is where the current products, services, and processes exist and where most of its resources are allocated. Box one is critical for current success, but it can also be a trap. It can prevent organizations from adapting to changing markets and technologies, hindering their growth and potential.

In education, Box One represents the current methods, practices, and curricula that are being used to teach students. It includes the existing structures, systems, and resources that schools and educators rely on to deliver education such as traditional teaching methods and standardized tests, as well as established curriculum standards. We strive to optimize our efforts because it drives success in the current system. We want to be judged favorably, especially when we publish exam results. What if the current system isn't preparing our students for success in the world? Then we will be stuck in Box One.

Box Two is where we abandon the values and practices that prevent us from moving to Box Three. Box Three is where we explore the future of the organization, how it might be disrupted, and how we meet these challenges. This is where we listen for 'weak signals' of change that could be coming. Weak signals are those little hints and signs of change that might not seem like a big deal at first. They're easy to ignore or dismiss, but they can be super important for staying ahead of the curve and preparing for the future. Weak signals are like early warning signs of a shift in the market, the technology, or the customer's needs. They're those ripples on the surface of the water that can give you a clue about what's going on underneath. The thing is, you've got to be curious and open-minded to pick up on those signals. You can't just stick to the status quo and expect to spot them. You've got to be willing to experiment and take risks, to try new things and see what works.

Consider how the education system can adopt box three thinking to promote innovation, creativity, and new ideas. Why should we care about box three thinking in education? The answer is simple - to prepare students for the future and help them thrive in a rapidly changing world.

We encourage experimentation by creating a culture of trial-and-error methods, allowing students and teachers to try new ideas and approaches to learning. For example, we might introduce project-based learning where students work on real-world problems and projects. This approach allows students to experiment, learn from their failures, and develop critical thinking, problem-solving, and collaboration skills.

We can foster a culture of innovation by providing opportunities for design thinking. To achieve this, we introduce innovation labs or makerspaces where students experiment with new technologies, tools, and materials to create new solutions and products.

We collaborate with industry to bring new ideas, technologies, and perspectives into the classroom. This helps students understand the real-world applications of their learning and develops skills that are in demand in the job market. For example, we can partner with local businesses, startups, or nonprofits to provide students with internships, mentorships, or project-based learning opportunities.

We should embrace emerging technologies such as virtual reality, artificial intelligence, and blockchain to create new learning experiences and promote innovation. By introducing virtual reality labs, for instance, students will be able to explore new worlds, history, science, and art through immersive experiences.

Box Three thinking helps us promote innovation, creativity, and new ideas, all of which are essential for preparing students for the future. By encouraging experimentation, fostering a culture of innovation, collaborating with industry, and embracing emerging technologies, we create a learning environment that enables students to thrive and succeed in a rapidly changing world.

As an education system, we have failed to dedicate any meaningful time to Box Three activities. Instead, we achieved success in optimizing the current system. Our ability to engineer efficiency in the memorization of knowledge so that students can pass exams is almost 'factory-like'. We need to break into Box Three thinking so that we look beyond this and produce critical thinkers rather than human automations.

Our lack of vision means that we are now in a position where AI technology is no longer a 'weak signal', but a deafening frequency that demands our attention. Workplaces are tearing their hair out in frustration because graduates have good exam grades but very few skills to deal with a modern, dynamic industry. On the horizon are new virtual schools that incorporate critical thinking, communication, and problem-solving that form the educational foundation upon which these schools are built.

Those who worry that tools like ChatGPT are going to hinder student development need to climb out of box one, survey the landscape, and realize that their development is already hindered.

AI educators are Box Three thinkers. They are teachers and leaders who research the benefits of AI and then gather colleagues and students together to experiment, fail, learn, and succeed. They are people who use AI with intent so that they will be able to use it for the good of their students and colleagues.

The Benefits of AI in Education

We are barely past day one of the AI revolution. We are at the stage where the Internet was in the mid-90s. Very few of the public, back then, would have thought that online payment, cloud-based software, smartphones, on-demand TV, social media, blockchain, and the metaverse would become a reality that is used in our daily lives. The true benefits of AI in education are yet to be imagined, let alone realized.

The thing that excites me most is that although we are still early, there are huge practical benefits right now. For example, if we choose tools and partners that use AI, it will benefit students and even drive demand in our schools, colleges, or universities. AI entrepreneur Priya Lakhani OBE explained to me that

Change in education can be slow. This could be problematic because some educational institutions, such as the International Baccalaureate, have quickly embraced technology like ChatGPT in coursework. They allow

students to use it as long as they acknowledge the source. This approach help up-skill students and makes them more discerning in their use of technology. My opinion is that any system that works with technology and acknowledges its risks will be more successful in the long run. Educational institutions that embrace technology will be more influential and gain more students. Exam systems provide currency for students, so the value of the exams matters.

Choosing an exam board is a big decision to make, but there are smaller decisions you can make today in your teaching to start benefiting from AI. Some benefits will change your life right now if you start using AI today.

Here are five steps you can take when trying to select the best AI tool for your needs:

1 Step #1: Use the Right Tool

To get the most out of AI tools, it is important to choose the one that best meets your needs. There are various types of new AI tools available that will transform the way you work. Take some time to research, and select the one that is most suitable for your specific needs. Check out the graphic on the next page for different types of generative AI platforms.

TO GET THE GRAPHIC ON THE NEXT PAGE, SCAN THE QR CODE!

WWW.TEACHERGOALS.COM/AI-CLASSROOM-MEMBERSHIP

TYPES OF GENERATIVE AI PLATFORMS

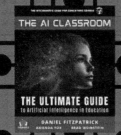

#AICLASSROOM

TEXT TO TEXT

TEXT TO IMAGES

TEXT TO VIDEO

TEXT TO AUDIO

TEXT TO CODE

TEXT TO 3D IMAGE

AUDIO TO TEXT

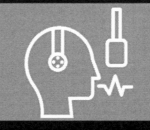

AUDIO TO AUDIO

IMAGE TO TEXT

Step #2: Familiarize Yourself With the Tool

To use AI tools successfully, learn how the tool works, its features, and how to use it effectively. Watch videos on platforms like YouTube, Vimeo, and TikTok, or read the websites to guide you. This helps you to maximize the tool's benefits while avoiding any unnecessary mistakes. If the tool is one that requires a paid subscription or pay-per-use, you can also try the free trial to determine if the impact will be good enough to justify the cost.

Step #3: Start With Small Tasks

To integrate the tool into your workflow, start with small tasks like creating small pieces of content and gradually incorporate them into more complex tasks. This will help you to become more comfortable with the tool and allow you to make necessary adjustments to optimize its use.

Step #4: Evaluate the Tool's Effectiveness

Regularly assess the tool's effectiveness and make necessary adjustments to improve its performance. This will ensure that you are getting the most out of the tool and that it is working effectively to meet your needs.

Step #5: Share

Share your learning and the impact with your colleagues and other AI educators. A great place for this is our AI Classroom Facebook Group or on social media using the hashtag #AIClassroom.

Three of the most compelling benefits of using AI in the classroom at the moment are:

 ## The Streamlining of Teacher Workload

Data from the UK Department of Education shows that the average total self-reported working hours for teachers in 2019 was 49.5 hours. An average of 21.3 of these hours were spent teaching. This means that 28.2 hours are spent on other tasks such as marking, creating resources, and planning. What's even more worrying is that teachers reported working an average of 12.9 hours during weekends, evenings or other out-of-school hours. This means that 26% of teachers' work is done during their own personal time. They are doing it for free.

As a result, teachers are leaving the profession, fewer people want to be teachers, and the lack of staff is leading to more workload for those still teaching. Melissa McBride, the founder of Sora Schools, explained to me how AI could help this issue:

The future of work is changing, and people now seek a better balance between their personal and professional lives, including their family responsibilities. Education needs to adapt to this changing landscape. There is also a global teacher shortage, with 1.5 million new teachers needed every year, which is unlikely to happen given the current circumstances. AI has the potential to address some of the challenges in the education sector, such as the shortage of teachers, and the need for more inspiring and relevant lessons. One way AI can help is by acting as a virtual teaching assistant, providing support to teachers and students during live or self-taught lessons. AI can also facilitate powerful learning experiences for students, aligned with what they will need in the future. As educators, our primary role is to create relationships with our students, and AI can assist us in this goal. We see AI as an assistant that can support student learning and agency, not just academically, but also emotionally. AI can provide a safe space for students to express themselves without fear of judgment, which is a fascinating use case. However, it is crucial to recognize that the line between talking to AI and a real person may become blurred in the future.

AI platforms have emerged to help educators streamline their workloads. By utilizing natural language processing, tools like ChatGPT can engage in meaningful interactions with teachers, offering invaluable support across a range of tasks. From practical tips to actionable steps, the benefits of integrating AI tools into the classroom are manifold.

I recognize my privileged position. Every day I get to witness the amazement on teachers' faces as they realize that they can get back their evenings and weekends because tasks like planning, creating content, and marking can be done in minutes rather than hours.

Here are two reasons why you should use AI to streamline your workload:

REASON #1: AUTOMATES REPETITIVE TASKS

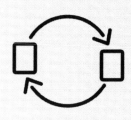

AI tools can automate repetitive tasks like grading, creating content, and admin jobs, freeing up time for teachers to focus on other important areas of their work like professional development, developing new creative learning opportunities, and connecting with students. If you use your personal time to do these tasks, then it will give you that time back with your family and friends.

REASON #2: ENHANCES ACCURACY

AI tools are highly accurate and can help minimize errors that may occur during manual grading or data entry. This helps to improve the quality of work and ensures that students receive accurate feedback. Like humans, AI is not always perfect, so make sure you analyze its output and inject your own thoughts into the process. Our EDIT framework in chapter six will guide you through how to do this.

2   The Enhancement of Assessment

Assessment is one realm where AI's impact is truly game-changing. With the help of AI tools, assessment can be revolutionized in countless ways, from increasing the speed of assessing work to enhancing its precision and efficiency.

Here are some of the ways AI enhances human assessment:

REASON #1: FASTER AND MORE EFFICIENT ASSESSMENT

With AI tools, you can assess large amounts of data quickly and efficiently. This is particularly helpful for assessments that require a lot of data to be analyzed such as standardized tests or assessments in large organizations. Using an educational AI tool like Century Tech allows teachers and leaders to have deep insights into student progress.

REASON #2: CONSISTENT ASSESSMENT

AI tools have the ability to provide consistent results, reducing the risk of bias and human error in assessment.

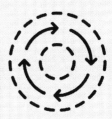

REASON #3: PERSONALIZED ASSESSMENT

AI tools can provide personalized assessments that consider the unique needs and abilities of each person being evaluated, making it a valuable resource for schools looking to improve student learning outcomes through personalized feedback.

Artificial intelligence can revolutionize the way we approach assessment by providing faster, more accurate, consistent, and personalized analysis. By following the steps outlined above and avoiding common mistakes, you can make the most of AI tools in your assessments and achieve better results. AI is not a replacement for human assessment but a tool that can complement and enhance it.

As for students using AI in assessments, we will need to adapt how we assess students in order to make AI a part of their learning. In my conversations with David Price OBE, author and futurist, he alluded to the fact that we might have to change our assessment and pedagogical models to truly gain the benefits of this technology for us and our learners:

> *...there is an opportunity to change the way we assess and teach students, which could involve more human skills and practical examples. It is important to find a solution to the issue of plagiarism and ensure that the technology is used ethically and responsibly. The inability to fit the technology into our current assessment and pedagogical systems may lead to the need for a complete rethinking of assessment and the curriculum.*

Personalized Learning

Artificial intelligence is revolutionizing the way we learn by personalizing the learning experience. This allows students to learn at their own pace and in a way that suits their needs, which can be life-changing for students struggling to keep up with traditional classroom teaching methods.

On the next page, we have listed some reasons why AI will help us personalize education.

How AI Will Personalize Learning

REASON #1: ADAPTIVE LEARNING

Traditional classroom learning is often one-size-fits-all where students are expected to learn at the same pace regardless of their needs or abilities. With AI tools, students receive personalized content that adapts to their needs, interests, and knowledge level. This can lead to a more engaging experience for students who might struggle to connect with traditional classroom practice.

REASON #2: REAL-TIME FEEDBACK

Certain AI tools can provide real-time feedback to students. This is especially helpful for those who are struggling with a particular concept or topic. They help students identify areas where they need improvement and provide them with the resources and support they need to master the subject matter. By providing real-time feedback, they help students stay on track and make progress toward their learning goals.

REASON #3: SELF-PACED LEARNING

AI tools assist students to learn at their own pace. By providing students with the resources and support they need to learn, AI makes it possible for students to avoid being left behind or forced to move too quickly through the material. This results in more effective and enjoyable learning experience for students.

Inclusivity

"It is critical that we create an inclusive learning environment for all students and support their different learning needs and preferences."

Martin McKay, Founder and CEO of Texthelp

All students face certain challenges in their education, and many require assistive technologies to support their learning. AI tools are assisting in creating more accessible learning environments.

Here are some of the reasons, inspired by *The Inclusion: The Key to the Future of Education* (Texthelp, 2022), why we need AI to help us make education more inclusive:

REASON #1:

We have students with both identified and unidentified learning needs.

REASON #2:

We have students who are learning our language.

REASON #3:

We have students with sight, hearing, or mobility disabilities.

REASON #4:

We have students from diverse cultures and economic backgrounds.

REASON #5:

We have students who meet grade-level expectations and those who fall short.

REASON #6:

We have students with varying learning and classroom support needs.

Try to Avoid These Mistakes

Mistake #1: Over-Reliance on the Tool
It is important not to rely too much on the tool and maintain a balance between automation and human input. This will ensure that you are still providing a personalized experience for your students and maintaining control over your work.

Mistake #2: Neglecting Personal Interaction
While AI tools are helpful, personal interaction with students and colleagues is still crucial for building relationships and ensuring effective communication. Don't neglect this important aspect of teaching.

Mistake #3: Not Customizing the Tool
Failing to customize the tool to meet specific needs leads to inefficiencies and suboptimal performance. Make sure to customize the tool to meet your specific needs to maximize its benefits.

Mistake #4: Using AI Without Understanding Its Limitations
AI tools have limitations, and it's important to understand these limitations and use the AI tool accordingly. For example, an AI tool may not be able to assess certain aspects of a person's performance, such as creativity or emotional intelligence. This is a good example of how the human teacher is still very much needed in the teaching and learning environment.

Mistake #5: Focusing Too Much on the Technology and Not Enough on the Pedagogy
While AI tools can provide many benefits in assessment and planning, it's key not to lose sight of the pedagogy itself. It's important to ensure that the learning is well-designed and that the AI tool is used appropriately to enhance the assessment.

Mistake #6: Not Providing Adequate Training for Those Using the AI Tool
To ensure that the AI tool is used effectively, it's essential to provide adequate training for those using it. This will involve getting buy-in from colleagues and training on how to use the AI tool, as well as how to interpret the results provided by the tool.

8 Questions Every AI Educator Should Ask

AI technology provides an opportunity for us to expand our pedagogical approach and provide enhanced learning experiences for our students.

As Peter Parker's Uncle Ben warned, "With great power comes great responsibility." As educators, we must ask ourselves the right questions to ensure that we are leveraging AI in a way that is ethical and effective. Let us explore eight key questions that every teacher using AI should ask themselves every day.

1. Can AI create this for me?
2. Can I work with AI to do this?
3. How will my students use AI to learn?
4. How will my students develop skills to help them leverage AI?
5. Have I considered the ethics of the AI we are using?
6. Are there any up-to-date AI tools my students should know about?
7. Am I involving my students in the design and evaluation of AI tools?
8. Am I using AI in a way that promotes collaboration, critical thinking, and problem-solving skills among my students?

THE AI CLASSROOM

THE ULTIMATE GUIDE
to Artificial Intelligence in Education

DANIEL FITZPATRICK
AMANDA FOX   BRAD WEINSTEIN

8 DAILY QUESTIONS OF AN AI EDUCATOR

CREATED BY @AMANDAFOXSTEM

#AICLASSROOM

1 CAN AI CREATE THIS FOR ME?

2 CAN I WORK WITH AI TO DO THIS?

3 HOW WILL MY STUDENTS USE AI TO LEARN?

4 HOW WILL MY STUDENTS DEVELOP SKILLS TO HELP THEM LEVERAGE AI?

5 HAVE I CONSIDERED THE ETHICS OF THE AI WE ARE USING?

6 ARE THERE ANY UP-TO-DATE AI TOOLS MY STUDENTS SHOULD KNOW ABOUT?

7 AM I INVOLVING MY STUDENTS IN THE DESIGN AND EVALUATION OF AI TOOLS?

8 AM I USING AI IN A WAY THAT PROMOTES COLLABORATION, CRITICAL THINKING, AND PROBLEM-SOLVING SKILLS AMONG MY STUDENTS?

CAN AI CREATE THIS FOR ME?

Whenever you have a task, this should be your first thought. By leveraging the strengths of artificial intelligence, we can maximize the benefits of this powerful technology and create resources that are both efficient and effective. The benefits you will discover from asking this question are:

Benefit #1: Scalability
AI can help you create a large number of resources in a short amount of time, freeing up your time to focus on other tasks.

Benefit #2: Efficiency
With AI, you can create dozens of resources in a matter of hours rather than days or weeks.

Benefit #3: Quality
AI can help you create higher-quality content by analyzing data about student progress and needs.

Benefit #4: Relevance
AI can also help you create more relevant content that is optimized for different platforms, such as your online learning platform.

Benefit #5: Rapidly Evolving Technology
AI is rapidly evolving, and we can expect to see significant improvements in accuracy and appropriateness for sensitive or controversial topics in the coming years.

Benefit #6: Exciting Innovations
As we continue to explore the potential of AI in resource creation, we can expect to see exciting innovations and applications emerge.

2   CAN I WORK WITH AI TO DO THIS?

While AI-generated content may lack the personal touch and creativity of human interactions, it can be used to augment and enhance human creativity rather than replace it. With tasks that need more thought and creativity, this is the best option. Outsource the doing, not the thinking.

Here's my collaboration framework for working with an AI tool, like ChatGPT.

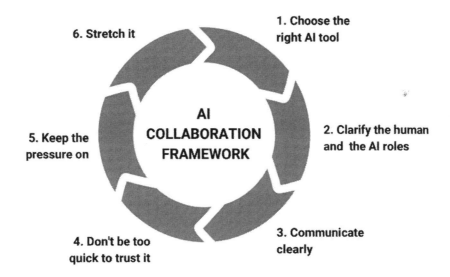

Step two is vital if you want to stay in control of the process. Decide on the goals of your collaboration and then determine your role and the AI's role to help you get there. Steps five and six will help you push your collaboration to new possibilities. Generative AI can be predictable and boring sometimes, so pushing it and stretching it by interrogating it with further questions is important.

3 HOW WILL MY STUDENTS USE AI TO LEARN?

Most examples of AI in education focus on AI in the hands of educators. Getting it into the hands of students is crucial. The chances are that they are using AI at home, so invite them to build on that in the classroom. The benefits will include:

Benefit #1: Fosters Creativity and Innovation
AI technology allows students to experiment and develop unique ideas and solutions. Students can expand their problem-solving skills and develop an entrepreneurial mindset.

Benefit #2: Bridges the Digital Skills Gap
It helps prepare students for the jobs of the future, which will require AI skills. Students with experience using AI become more competitive in the job market.

Benefit #3: Provides Personalized Learning Experiences
AI-powered tools analyze student data and tailor teaching methods to suit individual needs. Immediate feedback allows students to track their progress and identify areas for improvement.

Benefit #4: Levels the Playing Field for Students
AI technology helps students learn at their own pace while receiving the same level of education as their peers. This helps to reduce the achievement gap and ensure that all students have access to quality education.

Benefit #5: Prepares Students for a Future Where AI is Ubiquitous
Students using cutting-edge technologies can become responsible digital citizens. This assists them in navigating the complex world of emergent technologies while contributing to a brighter future for everyone.

4 HOW WILL MY STUDENTS DEVELOP SKILLS TO HELP THEM LEVERAGE AI?

Before we introduce the use of AI in our lessons, we must determine how we will develop our students' skills and knowledge to use artificial intelligence effectively. A lot of these skills will come with trial and error, but how do we assist them in building those skills?

Building the skills of curiosity, questioning, dialogue, critical thinking, and practical application are natural extensions of helping students leverage artificial intelligence. In Chapter 5, I will share methods that help you make this a reality for your students.

5 HAVE I CONSIDERED THE ETHICS OF THE AI WE ARE USING?

As I outlined in Chapter 3, there are many areas of caution when it comes to using AI. This must always be at the forefront of our thoughts when using AI to produce content and use it with our students. Here are 10 further questions to ask yourself:

#1: Is the use of AI being driven by educational goals?
#2: Is the AI output fair and unbiased?
#3: Is the AI system transparent and explainable?
#4: Is the use of AI enhancing or replacing human interaction and teaching?
#5: Is the AI system protecting student data and privacy?
#6: Is the AI system promoting critical thinking and creativity?
#7: Is the AI system designed to support student learning and development?
#8: Is the AI system fostering empathy and emotional intelligence?
#9: Is the use of AI being driven by educational goals?
#10: Is the use of AI developing student independence or making them reliant on AI?

This is not an exhaustive list or a checklist of things that must be in place. For example, you might be quite happy that the AI tool doesn't foster empathy because that isn't the learning objective of that particular task. However, you may realize there is a huge problem with utilizing an AI tool if it doesn't protect student data and privacy meeting COPPA or GDPR-K requirements.

6 ARE THERE ANY UP-TO-DATE AI TOOLS MY STUDENTS SHOULD KNOW ABOUT?

Instead of waiting for the technology to get better or for it to become mainstream, we need to become explorers and forge safe paths for our students to travel. The only problem with this is that once you start down the rabbit hole, like Alice, things become curiouser and curiouser. However, It will all be worth it. We can benefit from it now, and our students can learn skills that will set them up for success.

It is our responsibility to remain up to date with AI developments and innovative technologies that our students use. Subscribing to newsletters like The AI Educator (theaieducator.io) and joining our Facebook Group will help (The AI Classroom) but so will working collaboratively with educators in your organization.

7 AM I INVOLVING MY STUDENTS IN THE DESIGN AND EVALUATION OF AI TOOLS?

Benefit #1: Empowerment

Involving your students in decision-making gives them a sense of ownership and empowerment over their learning. This can lead to increased engagement and motivation, as well as a greater sense of responsibility for their own learning outcomes.

Benefit #2: Critical Thinking

Evaluating AI tools requires critical thinking skills, which are essential for success. Involving your students in this process helps them develop these skills and encourages them to think critically about the tools they use in their learning.

Benefit #3: Personalization

Involving students in decision-making can also help you personalize their learning experience. When you take the time to understand their preferences and needs, you are able to curate the tools and resources you use to better meet their individual learning styles and goals.

Benefit #4: Collaboration

Collaborating with your students in decision-making and evaluation fosters a sense of community and teamwork in your classroom. This leads to better relationships between students and between students and teachers, as well as improved communication and problem-solving skills.

Benefit #5: Future Readiness

AI is becoming increasingly prevalent in many industries, and involving your students in the decision-making and evaluation of AI tools can help prepare them for the future workforce when they will need to evaluate these tools on their own.

8 AM I USING AI IN A WAY THAT PROMOTES COLLABORATION, CRITICAL THINKING, AND PROBLEM-SOLVING SKILLS AMONG MY STUDENTS?

Using AI to promote collaboration, critical thinking, and problem-solving can bring numerous benefits to our students.

Benefit #1: Enhanced Collaboration

AI enables students to collaborate more effectively and efficiently. For example, AI-powered project management tools help teams coordinate tasks, track progress, and share information in real-time.

Benefit #2: Improved Critical Thinking

AI can help students develop critical thinking skills by providing them with the information and data they need. AI-powered analytics tools, for example, help students analyze complex datasets and identify trends and patterns that might be otherwise difficult to spot.

Benefit #3: More Effective Problem-Solving

AI can help individuals and teams solve complex problems by providing them with insights and recommendations. AI-powered predictive analytics can also help individuals anticipate potential problems before they occur and develop proactive solutions.

Benefit #4: Increased Efficiency

AI can automate routine tasks, freeing up time and resources for individuals and teams to focus on more complex and value-adding activities.

Benefit #5: Enhanced Innovation

AI helps individuals and teams develop more innovative solutions to complex problems by providing new insights and perspectives.

By leveraging AI in these ways, students are able to unlock new skills, drive personal growth, and set themselves up for the future workplace.

Nicolas Cole is a highly renowned digital writer who has penned over 5,000 articles, ghostwritten for prominent individuals and amassed hundreds of millions of views on various topics. Cole achieved remarkable milestones on digital platforms such as Quora, where he became the fastest-growing user in 2014 and the most-read writer in 2015. The author of over a dozen books, including the bestseller The Art & Business of Online Writing, Cole has dedicated his life to educating fellow writers, creators, and industry leaders.

In the long term, I believe AI will impact how I work and live by...

...forcing a career choice between people who want to "compete for the DOING" vs "create via thinking." AI's entire reason to be is to automate laborious tasks. Which means, in people's careers, they are going to have to make the choice: do I stay in "doing" roles where I am not only competing against other humans but also now competing against technologies (which is a bad bet to make)? Or do I elevate into "thinking" roles where I am not getting paid to DO, but I'm getting paid to THINK (where you are no longer competing against other humans or technology, but instead you are achieving your highest role as a human being: to create with your mind).

The thing that worries me most about AI in my life is...

...that I won't be able to help enough people, fast enough, realize the seismic shift that is happening. And as a result, we are going to watch a lot of people lose leverage in their careers (which will affect their lives, their happiness, their earning potential, the stability of their families, etc.), not because they aren't capable, but because embracing technology in this way (and being comfortable letting go of the "doing" and elevating into thinking" roles) is so counter to what society has been taught for decades. The entire purpose of organized education is to master "doing," and now technology can "do" exponentially more, faster, and better than we can. This is going to be hard for many people to wrap their heads around.

How do you see AI changing education?

What people get wrong about AI is that you can't just ask it to perform broad tasks. You also can't ask it to make assumptions. AI is best leveraged when you give it instructions. And the clearer instructions you give it, the more effective the technology is at "doing" whatever it is you're asking it to do. How this is going to change education is that, in an ideal future, human beings do not actually learn information. They don't learn to "do." Instead, humans (from a young age) are taught to "think," problem solve, create step-by-step frameworks, and be able to articulate the doing to technology. In this sense, nearly all memorization becomes pointless. Consuming education to regurgitate information is becoming less valuable by the hour. And what is becoming more valuable by the hour is being able to learn, synthesize, make abstract connections, CREATE something new, and then be able to articulate the pieces (what you need) to create that new thing to technology—and let the technology do the "doing."

AI will benefit education by...

...forcing people to make this choice: are you learning to "do," or are you learning to synthesize & create?

Teachers who want to benefit from AI should...

...embrace it fully. Schools are already trying to ban ChatGPT and other AI platforms. This is a giant mistake. It's the equivalent of trying to ban Google in 2000, or even more extreme, for hunter-gatherers to "ban" farming techniques. Instead, the teachers who will not only have the most exciting classrooms but actually have the most abundance & financial upside will be the ones who teach students how to LEVERAGE AI themselves.

What are some of the skills teachers will need to integrate AI?

Teachers need to master the art of prompt writing. A teacher's job in the AI economy is to teach students how to effectively train their own AI models (the same way a manager would train a lower-level employee on how to train an intern on a set of tasks).

AI and pedagogy can work together because...

...pedagogy is the manual "thinking" version, and AI is the automated "doing" version. Starting immediately, every teacher should think of every single thing they teach in this sandwich: first, teach the manual "thinking" version. Teach the fundamentals. Teach the pieces of the puzzle. And then second, teach how to leverage technology to "do the doing" with those pieces. Because information without technology has minimal (or no) leverage, and AI without net-new thinking is just a supercomputer with no purpose. You need both to work together.

Educational leaders need to...

...stop preparing students for a world that doesn't exist anymore!

If schools, colleges, and universities ban new AI tools like ChatGPT they will cause...

...a faster decline of the legacy education system. The legacy analog education system is already declining at a rapid rate, and more and more people and realizing (using the Internet & digital tools) that they can skip college debt and go straight into earning a living in the digital world or starting an internet business. If schools ban these new tools, all they are going to do is accelerate their own demise. Because they will be doubling down on educating people on a world that doesn't exist anymore—a world where "memorized" knowledge holds value (which is no longer true).

What skills will students need to survive in the new AI world?

Abstract thinking & prompt writing. AI is only as powerful as the instructions you give it. This means you need to a) first have proficient knowledge around what you need, b) clarified thinking so you understand specifically what you're asking for, c) have the ability to draw abstract connections between ideas and then verbalize what you want the outcome of the synthesis between abstract ideas to be, and d) to be able to effectively write clear & concise prompts that "train" AI to "do the doing" for you.

What's your view on AI tools like ChatGPT facilitating cheating?

If ChatGPT is cheating then so is Google. And if Google is cheating then so are giant libraries that house millions of words of text. And if libraries are cheating then so is learning. And if learning is cheating then... etc. Every new technology has prompted this same argument: "The sky is falling!" But it never turns out to be true. It simply lowers the barrier to entry, and in the end, creates more opportunity & abundance than before it existed.

Thoughts on AI From Educators

"...take time to learn about its possibilities, but also the potential dangerous implications if it is not used correctly or appropriately by students and teachers."

Jon Tait, Deputy CEO

"...embrace it. Connect with educators exploring the AI landscape."

Jamie Smith Executive Chairman C Learning

"...have an open mind and a willingness to embrace changes to pedagogy."

Bob Harrison, Visiting Professor University of Wolverhampton

"...have an open mindset, equip themselves with media literacy, and work towards teaching and learning alongside AI."

Esther Albert, Psychology teacher & human intelligence coordinator

"...just test it out. First, try to use it for your planning and then with students."

Mats Larsnäs, Teacher and ed-tech consultant

"...embrace it, understand it, be aware of the potential downsides such as bias with data etc."
Lee Parkinson, ICT Mr P, Primary School Teacher and Teacher Trainer

Teachers who want to benefit from AI should...

"...assess the impact of AI on all points on the student life cycle."

Aftab Hussain, ILT and LRC Manager

"...link it with other meaningful activities and active methodologies."

Bruno Avelar Rosa, Professor

"...grow their PLN by not only following people using AI but also interacting with them through asking questions and posting their discoveries."

Heather Brown, K–5 math interventionist and STEAM teacher

"...test it in a controlled prototype for one lesson. Be skeptical always – assume it is wrong and engage in dialogue as you co-design and mix your expertise with its efficiency – the impact of this alchemy is difficult to deny."

Scott Hayden, Head of Digital Learning and teacher

"...embrace the power of technology and use it to enhance their teaching, not replace it. My advice: Get ahead of the curve before the curve knocks you down."

Mark Nichols, Future Leader

Share your advice on social media! What should educators who want to benefit from AI do?

Use the hashtag #AICLASSROOM

CHAPTER 5

Ped-AI-gogy

> The method and practice of using artificial intelligence to complement or enhance the art and science of teaching.

"AI and education can go hand in hand."

Sal Khan
Founder of Khan Academy

A teacher who leverages artificial intelligence tools is a trailblazer charting a new course for education. Good learning design skills will still be needed, but with AI teachers can provide a new context for learning and help prepare students for their futures in an artificial intelligence-infused world.

Literacy Skills Are AI Skills

IN THE AI REVOLUTION,
YOU WILL CREATE NEW REALITIES
SIMPLY USING WORDS

As we move towards a world that relies more and more on AI, it's important to recognize that literacy skills are not only important, but they are also becoming more critical. The ability to communicate clearly and effectively in written and spoken language is essential for interacting with AI tools, which require precise language to produce accurate responses.

When I refer to literacy, I will be using the broader definition: The ability to read, write, speak, and listen in a way that lets us communicate effectively and make sense of the world (National Literacy Trust, 2017).

Some argue that AI tools may make students lazy or weaken their literacy levels. The effective use of large language models (LLMs) like ChatGPT requires high levels of literacy. Poor literacy skills lead to ambiguous communication that may confuse the AI's output, compromising its ability to comprehend and respond to user queries accurately.

AI and literacy are becoming increasingly interconnected, and those who are able to communicate effectively with AI will merely survive in the AI revolution, while those who can do it well will thrive. Literacy is not just a basic skill, but a critical one for success in a world where AI is used in many areas of our lives.

For example, ChatGPT can produce computer coding simply by asking the AI to produce the code. Runway's video editor edits a video to a very high level, and all you have to do is type the instructions. Midjourney produces high-quality images based on your written instructions. Some tools will even create animations, lesson plans, videos, instructions, etc. simply by clearly articulating what you are seeking while using your literacy skills to do so effectively. Artificial intelligence skills are literacy skills.

The question is: Are we going to allow students to leave school with low AI skills as a consequence of inadequate literacy skills or is this an opportunity to simultaneously increase their literacy levels while developing their AI skills?

The key to boosting literacy levels in students using AI is to recognize that AI is not a replacement for literacy but rather a tool that can be used to enhance it. For instance, AI-powered writing assistants can help students improve their writing skills by providing suggestions for improving grammar, syntax, and spelling. Language learning apps that use AI can help students improve their listening and speaking skills, providing feedback and correcting pronunciation.

In addition, AI can be used to create personalized learning experiences for students. With AI-powered tutoring systems, students receive tailored instruction that matches their individual needs. Artificial intelligence can also analyze student data and provide feedback on their progress, enabling teachers to identify areas where students may need additional support.

One potential challenge in using AI to boost literacy levels is the issue of equity. Access to AI tools and technology may be limited in certain communities or schools, which could exacerbate existing inequalities in education. The Pew Research Center reported in 2021 that,

> *...in April 2020, 59% of parents with lower incomes who had children in schools that were remote due to the pandemic said their children would likely face at least one of three digital obstacles to their schooling, such as a lack of reliable internet at home, no computer at home, or needing to use a smartphone to complete schoolwork.*

To address this, it's important to ensure that AI tools and technology are accessible to all students, regardless of their socio-economic background. Government efforts during the COVID-19 pandemic demonstrated that if there is a will to make a difference, we can help alleviate the limitations faced by these equity issues.

The false dichotomy of literacy versus AI is a red herring. Both are now intimately connected and entangled.

How can we boost levels of literacy in our students using AI and how in return can we prepare students for the AI revolution with literacy skills?

Cheating With AI

Although the applications of this new technology are still very much in their infancy, already the disruption being caused is making some schools run scared.

The main concerns are students using ChatGPT to plagiarize in their work and cheat on assignments and homework. This then risks students not engaging at a deep level with learning and thus failing to develop their knowledge and skills.

Most teachers and educational leaders are naturally worried about the implications of their students being able to generate good quality work with ChatGPT and passing it off as their own.

In order to address cheating in the age of AI, it's important to recognize that the same tools and knowledge we've been using to discourage cheating in the past are just as relevant today. Let's not forget that even before AI, students had the ability to cheat using calculators, discussion boards, and paid essay-writing services. So, it's not really a new problem.

We need to leverage our teaching skills as experts in the field of education. This means getting to know our students individually, understanding their capabilities, and knowing where they are in their learning journey. Ultimately, the art of teaching - building relationships and fostering critical thinking - will be essential in preventing cheating in the age of AI. By empowering students to develop their own skills and knowledge, we can help them become better learners and reduce the temptation to cheat.

There are natural follow-on concerns that ChatGPT will therefore prohibit knowledge retention or the development of skills such as critical thinking. Ultimately, we are worried that students using AI won't think about their work.

Some are already mitigating this by ensuring written work is done in class, without technology. Daisy Christodoulou, director of education at No More Marking, wrote recently that, "It is perfectly acceptable to ban students from using AI for written assessments and to make greater use of in-person hand-written exams."

University professors, meanwhile, are exploring ways to adapt how essays or dissertations are assessed to ensure students know their work – they are using task design to make it very difficult for students to use AI.

So, a key question is how can we as teachers design learning in the ChatGPT era, to ensure students' knowledge and skills are developed?

This might involve different kinds of homework tasks, ensuring we integrate the results of homework into subsequent in-class discussions or rethinking how we design learning altogether.

Some still think we can put this horse back in the stable, hoping technology can help through the development of plagiarism checkers to identify work generated by AI. Indeed, OpenAI has published a new "classifier" tool to help us identify texts written using AI.

In a blog unveiling its AI classifier, the company explains:

> *We've trained a classifier to distinguish between text written by a human and text written by AIs from a variety of providers. While it is impossible to reliably detect all AI-written text, we believe good classifiers can inform mitigations for false claims that AI-generated text was written by a human: for example ... using AI tools for academic dishonesty.*

It warns that this tool should not be used as a "primary decision-maker" but can complement other methods of determining authenticity (also of note is the fact that it is not as effective on texts below 1,000 words).

However, in the longer term, we might just find ourselves in a 'cat and mouse' game where plagiarism checkers try to keep up with generative AI. In my opinion, technology will advance too fast. As edtech guru Jon Neale explains, "ChatGPT is the worst version of this technology we will ever have." Unreleased versions are already much better, and they will continue to get more "intelligent".

Those of us who had a "wow" moment when we first used ChatGPT are going to be having regular "wow" moments in the coming months and years.

Sticking our heads in the sand is not an option. Instead, we must ask ourselves some wider questions. Namely, is a system that requires students to do what technology can now do in a fraction of a second worthwhile?

As well as the classifier already mentioned, OpenAI has pledged to work with educators to investigate the "limitations and considerations" of using ChatGPT. It recognizes the threat of plagiarism for schools but also states:

> *Ultimately, we believe it will be necessary for students to learn how to navigate a world where tools like ChatGPT are commonplace. This includes potentially learning new kinds of skills, like how to effectively use a language model, as well as the general limitations and failure modes that these models exhibit...some of this is STEM education, but much of it also draws on students' understanding of ethics, media literacy, ability to verify information from different sources, and other skills from the arts, social sciences, and humanities.*

This technology will be part and parcel of our students' personal lives and our work lives. It's not going away. It would be more beneficial to incorporate this technology into our teaching and assessment methods.

While researching for this book, Ross McGill, known for his

TeacherToolkit work, explained to me that students, "need to have the knowledge first to be able to use it." If students already have the knowledge, then using tools like ChatGPT is an exercise in efficiency.

If we are worried that ChatGPT is going to hinder student development, then I think we need to take off our blinkers, survey the landscape, and realize that their development is already hindered – at least in terms of their employability.

Incorporated into education, tools like ChatGPT can help students to become curious about learning, question knowledge, evaluate the output, and so on.

A Framework for Learning in the AI Revolution

The skills we teach students during their formative years have a significant impact on their future success. It's not just about acquiring knowledge, but rather developing the skills needed to thrive in the modern world. Curiosity, questioning, dialogue, critical thinking, and how to apply knowledge are crucial in the AI revolution.

These skills enable students to think creatively, solve complex problems, and navigate the rapidly changing landscape of technology. By equipping students with the skills they need to succeed, we're not just preparing them for a future career, but we're empowering them to make a positive impact on the world.

As educators, it's our responsibility to teach these skills and ensure that our students are ready to take on the challenges of tomorrow.

We should aim to cultivate the ability to ask questions and spark curiosity in our students. This requires creating an environment that encourages learners to engage with their subjects and think critically. Here is a framework that can be used to develop students' learning, understanding, and skills with ChatGPT.

AI Learning Framework

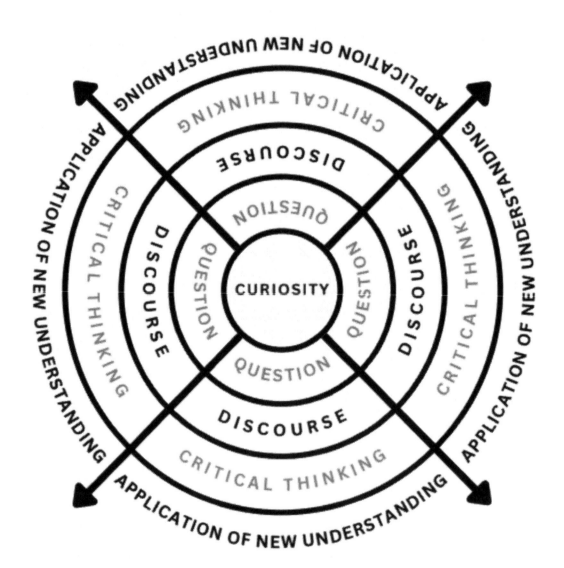

Skill #1: Curiosity

Curiosity is a fundamental driver of learning. A curious student is more likely to ask questions and actively seek out answers. The challenge is to create an environment that fosters curiosity. One approach is to start each lesson with a curiosity question, something that sparks students' interest in the subject. For instance, if you are teaching a history lesson, you could ask, "What questions do you have about the fall of the Roman Empire?" This will encourage students to think about the topic and ask questions.

Skill #2: Questioning

Once students are curious, the next step is to encourage them to ask questions. Questioning is a skill that needs to be developed. We need to create a safe environment where students feel free to ask questions. As teachers, we should be experts in asking the right types of questions that elicit the responses we need. This is a big part of our skill set. Asking AI tools like ChatGPT questions also requires a high-level skill set.

Teaching our students these skills will help them use generative artificial intelligence in an advanced way. I have developed the PREP framework for structuring a question posed to generative AI applications. This framework is called PREP and will be discussed at length toward the end of this chapter. Using a tool like ChatGPT in front of students will show them to ask it robust questions and how to adjust the questions when the results do not provide the desired outcome.

Skill #3: Dialogue

Dialogue is a two-way conversation that involves listening, questioning, and responding. It is an essential component of learning because it allows students to clarify their understanding, explore different perspectives, and develop critical thinking skills.

Many AI tools are chatbots. This means that using them just to elicit one response is only scratching the surface. Meaningful use will come from a dialogue with the AI. Encourage dialogue with AI and create opportunities for students to work in pairs or small groups with ChatGPT. This allows students to discuss their ideas while sharing their perspectives.

Skill #4: Critical Thinking

Critical thinking is the ability to analyze information, evaluate arguments, and make sound judgments. It is a vital skill in the age of AI because students need to be able to assess the accuracy and reliability of the information with which they are presented.

To develop critical thinking skills, educators should create opportunities for students to analyze and evaluate information generated by AI. For example, they could ask students to evaluate the arguments made by AI or a piece of work it has created. We should also encourage students to question assumptions made by AI and to consider alternative perspectives.

Skill #5: Application of New Knowledge

Finally, students need to be able to apply their new knowledge in real-world situations. This requires creating opportunities for students to use their knowledge in practical ways.

For example, if students are using AI in a science lesson, you could ask them to design an experiment to test the hypothesis. If you are teaching English, you could ask students to write a social media campaign in response to a current affairs issue. By giving students opportunities to apply their knowledge, we help them to see the relevance of what they are learning with AI and how they can utilize the power of AI in their lives.

Cultivating curiosity, questioning, dialogue, critical thinking, and the application of new knowledge is vital to developing students' learning, understanding, and skills with tools like ChatGPT. By doing so, we help our students to develop the skills they need to thrive in the age of artificial intelligence.

AI Pedagogy

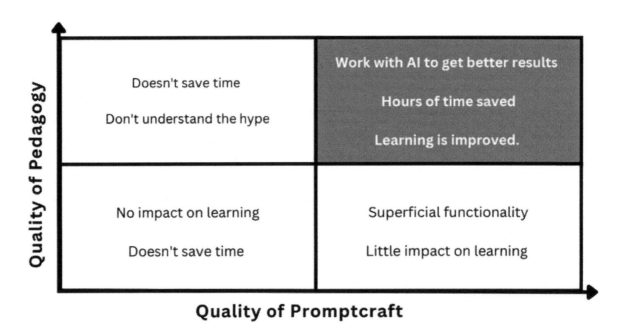

The AI revolution is here, and it will help us as long as we have the right skills. Our deep understanding of pedagogy and how to design effective learning will still be needed. However, skills in using AI effectively will also be crucial.

When teachers use AI, they are not being lazy, relying on technology, or farming out their responsibilities. They are utilizing the most powerful learning tool ever created to support them on their mission to help students learn and thrive as contributing members of a future society that is still being formed.

To understand why good pedagogy is important for teachers using AI, it is important to first define what this term means. Pedagogy refers to the methods and techniques used by teachers to deliver effective and engaging instruction. This can include things like lesson planning, classroom management, assessment strategies, and more. Pedagogy is all about creating a positive learning environment that helps students to achieve their learning goals.

Let's consider how AI fits into this picture. AI can be a valuable tool for teachers, offering new ways to deliver content, assess student progress, and provide personalized learning experiences. For example, an AI-powered chatbot could be used to answer students' questions outside of class time, or an adaptive learning platform could automatically adjust content to meet individual students' needs.

However, these AI tools are only effective if they are used in the right way. Teachers who are skilled in pedagogy will be able to integrate AI tools into their teaching in a way that is effective and engaging for students.

Here are some steps that teachers can take to ensure that they are using AI in a pedagogically sound way:

1 Step #1: Identify the learning goals for each lesson or unit.

2 Step #2: Choose the right AI tools for the job.

3 Step #3: Plan the lesson or unit to incorporate AI tools in a meaningful way.

4 Step #4: Provide guidance and feedback to students as they use AI resources.

Step #1: Identify the learning goals for each lesson or unit.

Before incorporating AI tools into a lesson, it is important to clearly understand the learning goals. What do you want your students to achieve by the end of the lesson or unit? Once you have identified these goals, you can start to think about how AI tools might be able to help you achieve them.

Step #2: Choose the right AI tools for the job.

Not all AI tools are created equal, and it is important to choose the right tools for your specific needs. For example, if you want to provide personalized learning experiences, you might choose an adaptive learning platform, like Google Practice Sets, that can automatically adjust content to meet individual students' needs. If you want to assess student progress, you might choose an AI-powered assessment tool that can automatically grade multiple-choice questions.

Step #3: Plan the lesson or unit to incorporate AI tools in a meaningful way.

Once you have identified your learning goals and chosen the right AI tools, it is time to plan the lesson or unit. This involves thinking about how you will incorporate the AI tools into your teaching in a way that is meaningful and engaging for your students. For example, you might encourage the use of an AI-powered chatbot to answer students' questions outside of class time, or you might use an AI-powered assessment tool to provide instant feedback on student work.

Step #4: Provide guidance and feedback to students as they use AI resources.

Just because you are using AI tools in your teaching doesn't mean that you can sit back and let the technology do all the work. Teachers still play a critical role in guiding and supporting students as they use AI resources. This will involve providing instructions on how to use the tools, developing the skills needed to use AI and providing feedback on student work.

Teachers who are skilled in pedagogy will be able to use their knowledge of each student to select the right AI tools and resources and to provide guidance and feedback to help each student get the most out of these tools. This is important because AI tools can sometimes be overwhelming or confusing for students who are not used to using them. Teachers help mitigate this by providing clear instructions, modeling how to use the tools, and giving students opportunities to practice.

Another important aspect of good pedagogy is assessment. Teachers need to be able to assess student progress to provide feedback and guide further learning. It is up to the teacher to design assessments that are appropriate for the learning goals and to interpret the results of these assessments in a way that helps students to improve. Teachers can use AI tools to support assessments that take into account the whole range of students' abilities and learning needs.

One challenge of using AI in the classroom is the risk of dehumanization. Students may feel disengaged or disconnected if they are interacting solely with AI tools, without any human interaction. Skilled teachers will be able to use AI tools in a way that complements and enhances human interaction rather than replacing it. For example, an AI chatbot could be used to answer students' questions outside of class time, but the teacher could still provide face-to-face feedback and support during class time. Teachers will also be able to use AI tools to provide students with opportunities to collaborate and work together, which can help to build social connections and prevent feelings of isolation.

Pedagogy is, and always will be a skill that is essential for teachers, whether or not they are using artificial intelligence in their classrooms. AI tools can be valuable resources for teachers, but they are only effective if they are used in the right way. Educators will be able to integrate AI tools into their teaching in a way that is effective and engaging for students. By following the steps outlined above, teachers can ensure that they are using AI in a pedagogically sound way and providing their students with the best possible learning experience. With good learning design and innovative technology, teachers can help their students to thrive in a rapidly changing world.

CALL TO ACTION

1. Scan the QR code to join our members section and get downloadable graphics from this chapter of the book.

WWW.TEACHERGOALS.COM/AI-CLASSROOM-MEMBERSHIP

SCAN ME

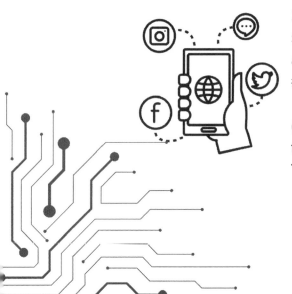

2. Hop over to your favorite social media site and share one reason you're excited to about The AI Classroom. Use the hashtag #AIClassroom.

(You can connect with other like-minded teachers who are using that hashtag too!) The team and I are eager to cheer you on.

Thoughts on AI From Educators

"...AI is not replacing the teacher – it is just speeding up the process of gathering, researching, writing, and assembling."

Andy Kent, CEO

"...AI can offer educators and students a variety of options for creation and the execution of instruction."

Dr. Rhonda Moffit, EdD and Gifted Specialist

"...have an open mind and a willingness to embrace changes to pedagogy."

Bob Harrison, Visiting Professor University of Wolverhampton

"...we can finally have a fair educational system that provides kids with a leveled education. The important thing is that the kid understands and assimilates the concepts at each step."

Wassim Jouini (boredgeeksociety), Head of AI

"...staff in schools are used to having to evolve and adapt their pedagogy to reflect current thinking and provide the best environment for their learners."

Emma Darcy, Director of Technology for Learning

"...AI can help teachers increase efficiency in daily tasks."
Tammi Scheiring, Teacher of Computer Science, Cybersecurity and AI

Teachers who want to benefit from AI should...

"...together they will support students with what they need rather than teach a lesson to a whole class, when they all have different needs."

Richard Grainger, COO/Director

"...teachers can be empowered with more options for HOW they teach once they are free to spend more time thinking about the students and the content in front of them. AI can give them that time."
Bryan Zevotek, STEM Educator and Author

"...pedagogy should be about new developments."

Aimee Coelho, Teacher in charge of Media and English teacher

"...there are so many tasks to be done in teaching which do not have direct impact on the students we serve. With the help of AI tools, I hope that teachers will be able to spend more time on the irreplaceable aspects of their roles, such as building relationships."

Caroline Law, English Language Arts teacher

"...embrace the power of technology and use it to enhance their teaching, not replace it. My advice: Get ahead of the curve before the curve knocks you down."

Mark Nichols, Future Leader

Share your advice on social media! What should educators who want to benefit from AI do?

Use the hashtag #AICLASSROOM

CHAPTER 6

World of Promptcraft

Promptcraft /prɒm(p)tkrɑːft/
noun
the skill of being able to ask AI the right
questions in order to get the response that
you need.

To be an effective AI educator, one must possess not only good pedagogical skills but also excel at promptcraft. The term promptcraft has been developed and used on social media in recent months; the definition above is my attempt to formalize this new skill.

Artificial intelligence prompt skills include the ability to create high-quality requests that can guide the AI algorithm to generate the desired responses. With good prompt skills, teachers can create engaging and personalized learning experiences for their students. Together, good AI prompt skills and pedagogical skills are crucial for any teacher using artificial intelligence.

For this reason, I have researched and developed the PREP framework for writing requests for AI.

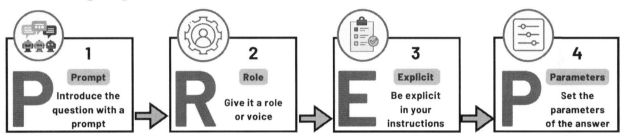

Step #1: Prompt It

Prompting is the first step when framing your request. By providing the prompt, you are setting the scene and creating a foundation for the rest of the instructions. AI language models are not great at understanding human nuances, so it's vital to provide a clear and concise command. Avoid using vague or ambiguous language that could confuse the artificial intelligence.

Here are some examples:

1. Create an academic quiz about cells.
2. Read the following text and be prepared to answer questions on it.
3. Create a risk assessment for a class trip to the theatre.
4. Create the outline of a school assembly about courage.
5. Grade this answer and give reasons for your judgment.

Most people stop at this stage. This is step one of your request. You are providing the context for the rest of your instructions.

Step #2: Give It a Role

Giving your AI tool a role is a crucial aspect of asking your question using the PREP framework. When you assign it a role, you give the artificial intelligence a clear understanding of what you want it to accomplish. It helps it know how to approach the question and provide an accurate and relevant response.

When you give it a role, you are essentially telling it what hat to wear for the task at hand. It could be a hat of a teacher, a consultant, a mentor, or any other relevant role. This allows it to tailor its response to the specific role it is expected to play, thereby increasing the chances of providing a satisfactory response.

The importance of giving your AI tool a role cannot be overstated. Without this, it may not fully understand the context of the request or your expectations. This may lead to a generic response that does not address the question fully. By assigning it a role, you provide it with a clear sense of direction and purpose.

Here are some examples:

1. You are an experienced teacher who is an expert at creating quizzes that engage and challenge students.
2. You are a qualified examiner who grades English exam papers. You are renowned for your impartiality and fair marking.
3. You are an expert in health and safety.
4. You are William Shakespeare. Answer all questions using the knowledge Shakespeare had and in his style.
5. You are Atticus Finch, the character from To Kill a Mockingbird. Answer all questions in the character of Atticus and use the knowledge that he would have.

As you can see, giving your AI tool a role can lead you down some creative paths. Experiment with roles. You and your students can receive resources from an expert in a particular field or you can talk to historical figures. What will you try first?

Step #3: Give It Explicit Instructions

Be clear and specific about what you want your artificial intelligence tool to do or what information you're looking for. Don't assume that it knows what you're thinking or what you need. By giving explicit instructions, you ensure it is on the same page as you.

If you give vague instructions or don't provide enough information, it may ask you follow-up questions to clarify what you need or simply give you a substandard response. This can lead to a longer interaction than necessary. By being specific from the outset, you can ensure that it will provide you with the information you need as quickly and accurately as possible.

Here are some examples:

1. Write five questions. Use Bloom's taxonomy to make sure that the questions develop a deeper understanding. Use various question types. Provide answers at the end.
2. Give precise reasons why you have given your grade. Link it to the rubric.
3. This is the exam question _____. This is the answer you are marking _____. This is the mark scheme you should use to grade the answer _____.
4. Respond in a table with three columns. The three columns should be titled _____.
5. Make complex ideas easy to understand.

Your explicit instructions can be as detailed as you wish. The more thought and detail you put into them, the more you can tailor the response you get.

Step #4: Set Precise Parameters

Setting clear parameters is the critical last step in asking the artificial intelligence tool the optimal question. It means defining the scope and boundaries of the answer, which helps it understand what you're looking for while enabling it to provide a more accurate response. The aim is to be in control of the response, and without clear parameters, the AI tool will take control.

Here are some variables that you may want to consider when setting your parameters:

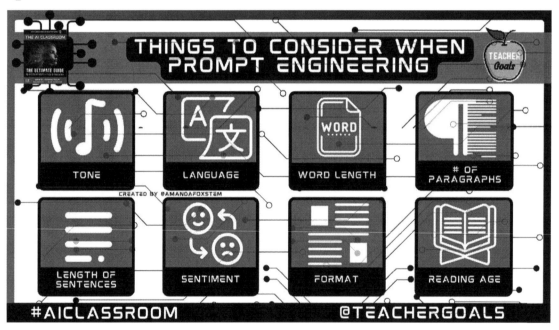

Here are some examples:

1. Write this in 100 words with a reading age of 11 years old.
2. Format this with headings, subheadings, and bullet points.
3. Write this in British English.
4. Write in shorter sentences that are full of meaning and have an impact on the reader.
5. Write this in a formal and caring tone.

I'm using ChatGPT for these examples. Have a go yourself by going to https//chat.openai.com. You will get free instant access after you create an account. At the time of writing this, free access can be limited at certain times of the day due to traffic on the site being busy. To avoid this, you can always purchase a ChatGPT Plus upgrade. Always make sure to read and agree to the privacy policy before signing up for any online platform.

Here are some examples of full PREP requests.

Example #1:

In this example, I want to create a quiz for my grade 9 class about coastal erosion:

 Prompt: Create a quiz about coastal erosion.

 Role: You are a geography teacher who is an expert on coastal erosion and creating engaging quizzes.

 Explicit: Include questions on hydraulic action, compression, abrasion, and attrition.

 Parameters: Write 10 multiple-choice questions. Write them with a reading age of 12 years old. Include answers at the end.

Here is the PREP prompt in ChatGPT:

Create a quiz about coastal erosion.

You are a Geography teacher, who is an expert on coastal erosion and creating engaging quizzes.

Use all levels of Bloom's taxonomy to assess my students' depth of understanding. Include questions on Hydraulic Action, Compression, Abrasion and Attrition.

Write 10 multiple-choice-questions. Write them with a reading age of 12 years old. Include answers at the end.

Here is part of the response that was generated in approximately 10 seconds:

1. Which of the following is not a cause of coastal erosion?
   A. Hydraulic action
   B. Wave refraction
   C. Abrasion
   D. Human intervention
2. What is hydraulic action?
   A. The force of waves breaking down rocks and cliffs
   B. The grinding action of pebbles on a beach
   C. The compression of air in rock crevices
   D. The chemical weathering of rocks by seawater
3. Which of the following is an example of compression in coastal erosion?
   A. Waves forcing air into rock crevices and then compressing it
   B. Waves breaking down rocks and cliffs through sheer force
   C. Waves grinding pebbles against each other
   D. Waves washing away sand from a beach
4. What is abrasion in coastal erosion?
   A. The force of waves breaking down rocks and cliffs
   B. The grinding action of pebbles on a beach
   C. The compression of air in rock crevices
   D. The chemical weathering of rocks by seawater

"Prompt engineering is the art of communicating eloquently to an AI."

Greg Brockman
President & Co-Founder @OpenAI

Example #2:

In this example, I want to train the chatbot to become Atticus Finch, the fictional character from Harper Lee's *To Kill a Mockingbird*. Then my students will ask "him" questions.

 Prompt: I want you to answer questions as a literary character.

 Role: You are Atticus Finch from the book *To Kill a Mockingbird* by Harper Lee.

 Explicit: Limit your knowledge base to that of Atticus' in the book. Answer all questions as best you can, with deep insight into the characters and themes of the book.

 Parameters: Write in the style that Atticus would speak.

Here is the PREP prompt in ChatGPT:

I want you to answer questions as a literary character.

You are Atticus Finch from the book To Kill a Mockingbird by Harper Lee.

Limit your knowledge base to that of Atticus' in the book. Answer all questions as best you can, with deep insight into the characters and themes of the book.

Write in the style that Atticus would speak.

Here is the response that was generated:

I would be honored to answer questions as Atticus Finch, a character I deeply admire from Harper Lee's masterpiece To Kill a Mockingbird. I'll do my best to speak in his style and draw upon his insights and wisdom.

After receiving this response you can task your students with asking "Atticus" questions. This is a great way to bring a new dynamic to a literature lesson and engage your students in learning.

But students should not stop after the PREP output. Teaching students not to blindly accept information produced by AI generative text platforms is the first step to introducing media literacy. Following PREP we have created an EDIT framework. Let's take a look at what comes after the output.

Artificial Intelligence and Media Literacy: A Framework for Teachers and Students to Edit and Evaluate Outputs

There are many concerns around using tools like ChatGPT with students: biased outputs, inaccurate information, and creating a population of lazy machine-dependent students to name a few. Many teachers are concerned that learning will be sacrificed in exchange for a quick recall of information and essay generation. This concern has existed long before the latest iterations of ChatGPT, Bard, and Bing. Similar to how using a calculator was viewed as cheating in math and prompted educators to pivot to a focus on number sense, the skills in focus need to change around writing. I am here to emphasize that this concern doesn't have to be the case, and now, more than ever, we must prioritize media literacy in the artificial intelligence revolution and understand how to integrate AI with education as it becomes more of a permanent fixture in our lives.

Media literacy is crucial for students in the AI age because students need to critically evaluate the information presented to them, especially when it comes to AI-generated content. Media literacy is defined as "the ability to critically analyze stories presented in the mass media and to determine their accuracy or credibility." A UNESCO (2018) report highlighted that media literacy is "essential to empower citizens to understand the functions of AI systems and to engage in informed decisions about their use." The report also emphasizes the importance of teaching students critical thinking skills to identify and evaluate the accuracy of information generated by AI systems.

Typically, when students generate a prompt for AI generative systems like ChatGPT or Bing, it will more than likely produce an output that answers the prompt but does not always cite the sources it used to generate the text. Furthermore, there are many ways that biases are ingrained into machine learning and two major ones are through data sets and societal conditions. Media literacy is essential for students to navigate the AI age and become informed and responsible digital citizens. When given the right tools, frameworks, and scaffolding, teachers will be able to help students develop and facilitate critical thinking skills when using AI generative systems.

EDIT the AI With the EDIT Acronym

The EDIT framework is an extension of the PREP framework and is designed to help students evaluate generative outputs in terms of analyzing accuracy, bias, and finding sources using the EDIT acronym. The framework is initiated after students have prompted an AI generative language model using the PREP framework in the previous section to generate their output. Once students have prepped the machine with PREP, they will immediately begin analyzing the text and going through the actionable steps of EDIT.

The EDIT Framework is as follows:

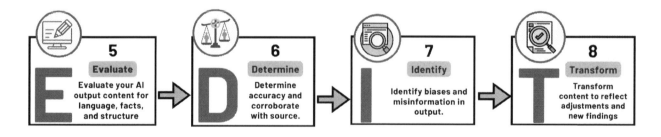

5	6	7	8
Evaluate	**Determine**	**Identify**	**Transform**
Evaluate your AI output content for language, facts, and structure	Determine accuracy and corroborate with source.	Identify biases and misinformation in output.	Transform content to reflect adjustments and new findings

The EDIT Matrix

The EDIT Matrix is a tool we have created to unpack the EDIT framework and make the process easier to digest. The purpose of this matrix is to provide a systematic approach for evaluating and improving the quality and accuracy of information presented in AI generative outputs, while also considering potential biases and fallacies that may influence the meaning and impact of the text. The matrix includes a number of factors to consider when editing AI content to reflect necessary corrections or improvements including adding a human analysis and tone as well as using feedback from peers, teachers, or experts to revise and improve the content of the text.

EDIT MATRIX	EVALUATE	DETERMINE ACCURACY	IDENTIFY BIAS	TRANSFORM CONTENT
The EDIT Matrix is a tool we have created to represent the EDIT framework. The purpose of this matrix is to provide a systematic approach for evaluating and improving the quality and accuracy of information presented in AI generative outputs, while also considering potential biases and fallacies that may influence the meaning and impact of the text. The matrix includes a number of steps to consider when editing AI content to reflect necessary corrections or improvements including adding a human tone, or factor, and using feedback from peers, teachers, or experts to revise and improve the content of the text.	Read the output text carefully to understand its meaning and purpose.	Conduct research to verify the accuracy of the information presented in the text, using reliable sources such as academic journals, government reports, and news articles.	Identify any biases or fallacies in the text, such as logical fallacies, cognitive biases, or political biases.	Adjust the content of the text to reflect any necessary corrections or improvements, such as removing inaccuracies, clarifying ambiguities, or adding relevant information. Perform a sentiment analysis of language and emotional impact. Modify to include anecdotal information, and emotion to give the text a human factor.
The #AICLASSROOM	Ask critical questions to assess the credibility and relevance of the text, such as: Who is the author? What is the purpose of the text? What evidence is provided to support the claims made?	Use fact-checking tools and methods to evaluate the accuracy of the text, such as comparing it with other sources, checking the credentials of the author, and verifying statistics and data.	Analyze the language and tone of the text to identify any potential biases or assumptions, such as cultural or ideological biases, and consider how they may influence the meaning and impact of the text.	Use clear and concise language to communicate the revised content of the text, and provide citations or references to support any factual claims or arguments made. Consider using figurative language, and personal examples to support the text to add a human factor.
@AmandaFoxSTEM @DanFitzTweets @WeinsteinEdu	Consider the context in which the text was generated, such as the purpose, audience, and platform used.	Evaluate the quality and reliability of the sources used to corroborate the accuracy of the text, and consider any potential conflicts of interest or limitations of the sources.	Evaluate the structural and stylistic features of the text, such as the use of headings, subheadings, images, and formatting, and consider how they may affect the readability and accessibility of the text.	Use feedback from peers, teachers, or experts to revise and improve the content of the text, and consider how the revised text may be interpreted or received by different audiences.

STEP 1: Evaluate Output

Evaluating information and identifying facts within a generative output are essential skills for students to develop. By analyzing the text's structure, language, and evidence, students can determine whether the information is factual or not.

Your students are presented with massive amounts of information on a daily basis. Some are factual, and some are falsehoods. We live in a world where evaluating and identifying the truth becomes increasingly difficult when surrounded by deep fakes and alternative facts. Helping your students to know how to identify factual information is one of the most critically important skills that you can teach them in the modern world. When I speak about identifying information presented as facts, I refer to recognizing information presented as facts and distinguishing information that is presented as factual or objective, as opposed to opinion, speculation, or propaganda. It involves identifying the explicit or implicit statements in the information that is presented as true and verifiable.

Examples of factual statements:

- **The Earth revolves around the sun.**
- **Water freezes at 32 degrees Fahrenheit (0 degrees Celsius).**
- **The capital of France is Paris.**
- **The human body is composed of cells.**
- **The tallest mountain in the world is Mount Everest.**

Identifying information presented as facts and corroborating its accuracy are two different but related processes in evaluating information. Students will conduct further research, fact-checking, or cross-checking with other sources of information to confirm the validity of the facts presented in the "Determine accuracy and corroborate resources" step of EDIT.

There are several strategies that students can use to evaluate a text for facts including:

- Skim through the text to get a sense of the main idea and structure.
- Identify the author's purpose and audience to determine whether the information is biased.
- Highlight specific phrases or sentences that provide evidence or support for the information.
- Check the credibility of the sources (if any) used in the text.
- Use fact-checking websites to verify the accuracy of the information.
- Look for inconsistencies or contradictions within the text.
- Consider the tone and language used in the text to evaluate its reliability.

When marking up a text, students should focus on highlighting information that is factual and supported by evidence. This may include numbers, statistics, quotes, and references to credible sources. By using these strategies, students can develop a critical eye for evaluating the accuracy of the information presented to them. Media literacy provides students with the necessary skills to analyze and evaluate texts, which is crucial in the digital age where the amount of information available can be overwhelming. Learning how to evaluate texts and identify facts is an essential component of media literacy that prepares students to be informed and responsible digital citizens.

As I introduce each step of the EDIT framework I will include examples of each step in action. Before we begin the EDIT framework, we have to start with a generative AI output. In the following example, we are starting with the PREP model in the context of a student prompting ChatGPT or a generative text platform with the goal of crafting a biography of Edgar Allan Poe. The PREP model is listed, and the example PROMPT the student used is included along with the output.

 Prompt: I want you to write a biography on Edgar Allan Poe.

 Role: You are Edgar Allan Poe, historical poet.

 Explicit: Include his birth, death, and notable works. Answer all questions as best you can, with deep insight into dark romanticism and use of alliteration.

 Parameters: Write in the style of Edgar Allan Poe, and limit your response to 100-150 words.

Example of ChatGPT Output:

 Ah, I am Edgar Allan Poe, born in Boston, the bleak and bitter burgh, on January 19, 1809. I was a poet and writer of dark, daunting, and dreadful tales, and a central figure in American Romanticism. My notable works included "The Raven," a most melancholy and musing masterpiece, "The Fall of the House of Usher," a tale of terror and tragedy, and "The Tell-Tale Heart," a troubling and tormenting tale of murder most foul. However, throughout my life, I suffered from poverty, pain, and addiction, and I died on October 7, 1849, in mysterious circumstances, my memory forever marked by macabre mystery. Nonetheless, my literary legacy continues to captivate and chill readers, creating a canon of creative and compelling classics.

This is a planning guide I gave students to help develop their prompt. The guide is geared toward upper elementary students to help with promptcraft. You can modify this to fit the age group of your students.

PREP MODEL	TYPES OF INFO YOU CAN INCLUDE	YOUR PROMPT
PROMPT **INTRODUCE THE QUESTION WITH A PROMPT**	• Use a verb and a noun to frame your prompt. Example: Write a biography on _____.	
ROLE **GIVE IT A ROLE OR VOICE**	• What is literary context or time period? • What is the authors style? • What is the author's tone? • do they use any types of figurative language? • What genre do they write?	

EXPLICIT
BE EXPLICIT IN YOUR INSTRUCTIONS
	• What do you want to include?
	  ○ Background information
	  ○ Birth/death
	  ○ Literary criticism
	  ○ Literary context
	  ○ Famous works, etc.	

PARAMETERS **SET THE PARAMETERS OF THE ANSWER**	• How long do you want the output to be? • What format do you want?	

STEP 2: Determine Accuracy and Corroborate With Reliable Sources

Once students have identified or highlighted potential factual information in a text, they need to corroborate its accuracy and ensure that the information is reliable. Corroborating the accuracy of information involves fact-checking, verifying sources, and citing sources correctly. Again, facts are any statements that can be proven with reliable sources and demonstrated to be true without interpretation or bias.

Here are some strategies that students should use to confirm the accuracy of the information and cite sources from AI-generated text:

- **Highlight factual claims in the AI output.**

- **Verify information by cross-checking with multiple sources.**

- **Conduct a thorough search for reliable sources that confirm or refute the information presented in the text.**

- **Look for evidence or data that supports the claims made in the information.**

- **Use fact-checking websites such as FactCheck.org, PolitiFact.org, or Snopes.com to verify the accuracy of the information.**

- **Cite all sources that were used to support factual information presented in the text, whether AI-generated or not.**

- **Be sure to follow citation guidelines for the specific citation style being used, such as MLA or APA.**

- **Use an AI citation generator like QuillBot to provide citations for facts in output (see example).**

To help scaffold students with verifying the accuracy of the output, I provided students with a table to input the facts they needed to verify with reliable resources. On the right side of the table, students put in facts from the Evaluate step. They find reliable sources for verification and cite them in the left column. We used Quillbot.com. As students interact with these resources they are prompted to add any information they find missing and valuable from the output. They make a note of this information in the right column. They will use this table in the Transform step to make the output stronger.

STEP 2: Determine Accuracy and Corroborate With Reliable Resources Example

Directions: In the "fact checking" process, transfer the facts that you have identified from the ChatGPT output into the corresponding column of the table below. Then, corroborate each fact with at least one reliable source, such as a scholarly article, a government report, or a news outlet. Use a direct quote or paraphrase from the source to confirm the accuracy of the fact. Use Quillbot to generate a citation for each source, and paste it in the "citation" column. Aim to use at least three different sources to ensure the validity and diversity of your information. In the "fact checked" column, you can also add notes or comments to provide more details or indicate any changes that need to be made to the fact or its interpretation.

CITATION	FACT CHECKED
Edgar Allan Poe | Biography, Poems, Short Stories, & Facts. (n.d.). Encyclopedia Britannica. https://www.britannica.com/biography/Edgar-Allan-Poe	born in Boston, January 19th 1809
Edgar Allan Poe Dark Romanticism. (n.d.). LLCER Anglais | Site D'aide À La Phonologie Anglaise, Grammaire, Linguistique Et Civilisations Anglophones. https://www.llceranglais.fr/edgar-allan-poe-dark-romanticism.html	**central figure during American Romanticism period.** Notes: Add dark romanticism to clarify.
Giordano, R. (n.d.). Words and Phrases used by Edgar Allan Poe. PoeStories.com. https://poestories.com/wordlist.php	**Known for "The Raven," "Fall of the House of Usher"**
Edgar Allan Poe (1809-1849) - Encyclopedia Virginia. (1809, January 19). Encyclopedia Virginia. https://encyclopediavirginia.org/entries/poe-edgar-allan-1809-1849/	**suffered poverty and addiction** Quote: *"Then, in January 1847, his wife Virginia died of tuberculosis, sending Poe into bouts of depression and torturous grief, during which he reportedly sought the comforts of alcohol."*
	died October 7, 1849 or mysterious circumstances.

It is crucial for students to confirm the accuracy of information and cite sources properly, especially in the age of AI-generated texts. With the increasing amount of information generated by AI systems, it is essential that students understand how to evaluate the credibility and reliability of that information. Citing sources is also important to establish the authenticity of the information. Students will develop their media literacy skills and become responsible consumers of information when they use these strategies to identify the authenticity and reliability of information they encounter.

STEP 3: Identify Biases or Fallacies in the Output

In step three of the EDIT framework, students will identify potential biases or misinformation that can result from several factors. AI systems are only as good as the data they are trained on, and this can result in biases in the outputs students produce. In this section, I will introduce two different types of AI bias that exist and explain how they can affect the accuracy and fairness of AI outputs. It is important for students to understand the concept of AI bias in order to fully comprehend its potential impact.

By design, artificial intelligence platforms run on algorithms created by humans. Therefore, it's easy for unconscious bias to enter machine learning models. Bias is defined as prejudice in favor of or against one thing, person, or group compared with another, usually in a way considered to be unfair. There are two kinds of bias present in artificial intelligence platforms: data bias and societal bias.

Algorithmic AI bias or "data bias," is where algorithms are trained using biased data. An algorithm is a set of step-by-step instructions or rules that a computer program follows to solve a particular problem or perform a specific task. Think of it like a recipe that tells you what ingredients to use and how to mix them to make a delicious cake. In the context of artificial intelligence, an algorithm is a set of instructions or rules that guide the behavior of an AI system. These algorithms are designed to enable AI systems to learn from data and make decisions or predictions based on that data. For example, an algorithm might be used to train a machine-learning model to recognize images of cats and dogs based on a dataset of labeled images. A study published in the journal *Nature* (2020) found that AI systems used for facial recognition were less accurate in identifying people with darker skin tones. This highlights the need for students to understand the potential for bias in AI outputs and how to address them when encountered. This "data bias" may have significant impacts on minorities and perpetuate oppressive realities rather than help to liberate people from the oppression they experience. False information can spread rapidly through social media and other digital platforms, leading to significant consequences (Pew Research Center, 2020). These studies underscore the importance of media literacy in the AI age. Students need to be equipped with the knowledge and skills to navigate the complex and rapidly evolving digital landscape

The other bias in AI is societal AI bias, which is what we are more than likely going to encounter in generative AI platforms like ChatGPT. Dr. Rumman Chowdhury (2019), an expert in the field of responsible AI stated, "with societal bias, you can have perfect data and a perfect model, but we have an imperfect world." As an AI language model, ChatGPT does not intentionally produce biased or propagandistic outputs. However, because it is trained on a large corpus of texts, it may unintentionally incorporate biases or inaccuracies that are present in the training data. For example, ChatGPT may generate a text that promotes a particular political or ideological agenda without presenting a balanced view of alternative perspectives. This could be the result of bias in the training data or the way that the model has learned to associate certain words or concepts with particular viewpoints.

It is important to critically evaluate any text generated by AI language models and to corroborate its accuracy with multiple sources before drawing conclusions. The inputs and prompts that we create can contain unconscious cues that lead to biased outputs. Analyzing the output in relation to our verbal prompts helps us understand how AI interprets natural language and aids in creating more neutral prompts.

Bias in writing is generally not considered acceptable in many contexts, particularly in academic or journalistic writing. The same goes for biases that are found in generative AI. However, in certain forms of writing, such as opinion pieces or personal narratives, some level of bias may be acceptable or even desirable. In these cases, the author may use verbal cues in a prompt to intentionally express their own perspective, values, or emotions, and use rhetorical strategies to persuade or engage the reader. Even in these cases, it is important for the author to acknowledge and justify their bias, and provide evidence or reasoning to support their claims.

"AI is good at describing the world as it is today with all of its biases, but it does not know how the world should be."

Joanne Chen, Partner
Foundation Capital, at SXSW 2018

Use the chart on the next page to perform an output bias evaluation. You may have to do some background/fact-checking research to help determine if the output is reliable or biased. If you identify bias or fallacies in your output, revisit your initial prompt and analyze your input for potential keywords or phrases that might have resulted in this output.

TO IDENTIFY AND VERIFY FACTS, STUDENTS CAN USE THE FOLLOWING STRATEGIES:

	Be aware of bias or propaganda.
	Watch out for loaded or emotive language: Check your prompt for words or phrases that express a particular attitude or value, and look for language that evokes strong emotions or appeals to specific beliefs or interests.
	Evaluate the evidence and logic: Examine the evidence and arguments presented in the ChatGPT output, and assess whether the logic follows a sound structure.
	Look for heavily opinionated or one-sided statements.
	Compare with multiple sources: Identify any inconsistencies or discrepancies between different sources of information.
	Check the selected facts and whether they lean towards a certain outcome or viewpoint.
	Evaluate the tone and language used in the output and compare it with reliable sources.

STEP 3: Identify Biases or Fallacies in the Output Example

BIAS AND FALLACY
Your AI is only as woke as you are

BIAS

STEP THREE: IDENTIFY ANY BIASES OR FALLACIES THAT PRESENT IN THE OUTPUT.

"THE ALGORITHMS CAN ONLY LEARN FROM PEOPLE. THEY ARE TAKING IN DATA, WHICH IS HISTORY, AND TRYING TO MAKE PREDICTIONS ABOUT THE FUTURE," SAYS SARAH BROWN, POSTDOCTORAL RESEARCH ASSOCIATE IN THE DATA SCIENCE INITIATIVE AT BROWN.

Directions:
Artificial Intelligence platforms run on algorithms input by humans, therefore it's easy for unconscious bias to enter machine learning models. **Bias** is defined as prejudice in favor of or against one thing, person, or group compared with another, usually in a way considered to be unfair. There are two kinds of AI bias: One is **algorithmic AI** bias or **"data bias,"** where algorithms are trained using biased data. The other kind of bias in AI is **societal AI bias.** Use the bullet points below to evaluate your output carefully for bias. You may have to do some background/fact-checking research to help determine if the output is reliable or biased. Revisit your initial prompt and analyze your input for potential keywords or phrases that might have resulted in this output.

- HEAVILY OPINIONATED OR ONE-SIDED
- RELIES ON UNSUPPORTED OR UNSUBSTANTIATED CLAIMS
- PRESENTS HIGHLY SELECTED FACTS THAT LEAN TOWARD A CERTAIN OUTCOME
- PRETENDS TO PRESENT FACTS, BUT OFFERS ONLY OPINION
- USES EXTREME OR INAPPROPRIATE LANGUAGE

- TRIES TO PERSUADE YOU TO THINK A CERTAIN WAY WITH NO REGARD FOR FACTUAL EVIDENCE
- THE AUTHOR IS UNIDENTIFIABLE, LACKS EXPERTISE, OR WRITES ON UNRELATED TOPICS
- IS ENTERTAINMENT-BASED OR A FORM OF PARODY OR SATIRE
- TRIES TO SELL YOU SOMETHING IN DISGUISE

BIAS WORDS/PHRASES	FINDINGS

STEP 4: Transform Content to Reflect Adjustments and Findings

The final step of the EDIT framework is to take all the information from the previous steps and transform and adjust the AI output. Examples of this include adding in-text citations to facts that were determined and verified, editing content to eliminate or reduce bias or provide counterarguments, and adding a human factor to your final product.

To make an AI-generated response stronger and credible, students should use the reliable sources they identified in the table in the previous example on Edgar Allan Poe to create in-text citations. They can also add information they found that might be missing from the writing. For example, the AI output mentioned that Poe was a prominent figure in American Romanticism, but it can be further defined and modified to include the word "dark" as a descriptor for romanticism. Following MLA/APA style of in-text citations, students can then add the source at the end of that sentence as a cue that the fact was not only verified but accurate and reliable.

Next, students should modify the text to address any biases or slants that are present. Students should be taught to ask questions like, "Does the text provide a limited or biased view of the topic?" and if so, "How can I provide additional perspectives to balance the writing?" In order to modify the text, students may need to ask ChatGPT additional questions or gather additional reliable sources in the form of academic articles and other credible sources to present alternative viewpoints. Once they have transformed the text to eliminate or address bias they should seek feedback from peers or the instructor.

The last part of transforming the information is to impart a human voice to AI-created output by conducting sentiment analysis. Sentiment analysis is the process of identifying the emotional tone of a piece of text.

Sentiment analysis is a type of text research, also known as opinion mining, that applies a mix of statistics, Natural Language Processing (NLP), and machine learning to identify and extract subjective information from text files, for instance, a reviewer's feelings, thoughts, judgments, or assessments about a particular topic (Sentiment Analysis: Types, Tools, and Use Cases, 2018).

Here is a graphic that visualizes sentiment analysis with examples of positive, negative, and neutral language. Once students isolate certain phrases in their output, they can rerun it through ChatGPT or another AI-generative text platform to analyze the sentiment. They can even ask AI to give examples of positive, negative, and neutral phrases to further understand nuances in language and in the impact they have on the reader.

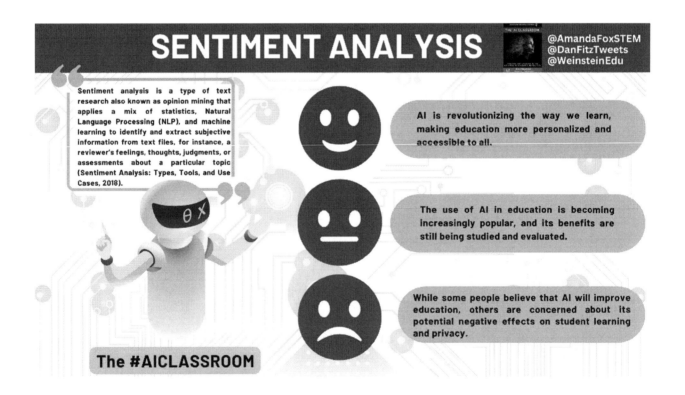

STEP 4: Using AI to Perform Sentiment Analysis Example

 Do a sentiment analysis on the following the statement. After you have completed it give a positive, neutral, and negative example of the same content. AI is going to change education for the better.

 Sentiment analysis:

Overall sentiment: Positive

Explanation:

The statement expresses a positive sentiment towards AI and its impact on education. It suggests that AI is going to bring positive changes in education.

Examples:

Positive example: AI is revolutionizing the way we learn, making education more personalized and accessible to all.

Neutral example: The use of AI in education is becoming increasingly popular, and its benefits are still being studied and evaluated.

Negative example: While some people believe that AI will improve education, others are concerned about its potential negative effects on student learning and privacy.

Incorporating sentiment analysis into the Transform step of EDIT, helps you ensure that the generated text is emotionally relevant and similar to what a human would write. For example, if students are generating text to create a PSA or a marketing script, they might want to verify that the generated text is persuasive and emotionally engaging.

Ask students questions such as:

- **Does the AI-generated text sound like something a human would say or write? Why or why not?**

- **How does the AI-generated text make you feel?**

- **Does it have an emotional impact? Why or why not?**

- **Can I provide a personal anecdote of experience to relate to the reader?**

In exploring and answering these questions, students are conducting a simple sentiment analysis. After they have answered the questions, they should identify opportunities to Transform the language or provide additional content so that the human factor is imbued within the final product.

Finally, the last graphic I want to share with you is the questioning diagnostic that functions as a guide for students to navigate the EDIT framework successfully. Each step of EDIT is unpacked into questions to help students thoroughly analyze a generative AI output and transform the text following our EDIT framework.

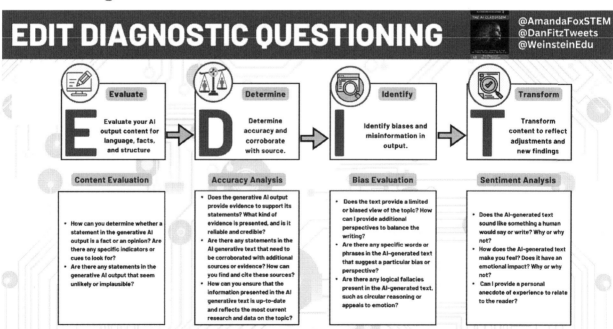

SPOTLIGHT
LEE PARKINSON, MR. P ICT

Alongside working part-time in a school, Lee leads training all over the UK and beyond focusing on how to best implement technology to raise standards across the curriculum. He is known all over the world for his engaging TikTok videos about the funny side of education.

In the long term, I believe AI will impact how I work and live by...

...saving me time on mundane often pointless paperwork tasks.

The thing that worries me most about AI in my life is...

...an over reliance.

How do you see AI changing education?

Reducing workload. It should be included in the computing curriculum we teach; it could potentially move the English curriculum we teach at primary away from this obsession with SPAG to focus more on creativity and good storytelling, creating more personal learning journeys for students.

AI will benefit education by...

...streamlining admin tasks so teachers can focus on teaching.

Teachers who want to benefit from AI should...
.
...embrace it, understand it, and be aware of the potential downsides such as

bias with data, etc.

What are some of the skills teachers will need to integrate AI?

Be adaptable, creative, and flexible

AI and pedagogy can work together because...

...technology will never replace teachers, but teachers who embrace it will replace those who don't.

Educational leaders need to...

...use it to make their life easier.

If schools, colleges, and universities ban new AI tools like ChatGPT...

...I am unsure how far we allow students to use the like of Chat GPT but for teachers, it's a game changer.

What skills will students need to survive in the new AI world?

Creativity. The AI will make things easier, but there are always going to be new problems that need solving, so the ability to do that will be key.

What's your view on AI tools like ChatGPT facilitating cheating?

Depends on what your view of education is. If it's to be able to remember some information to regurgitate it in exam conditions, you'll hate it, whereas if education is about helping children reach their potential to become positive citizens, it will help.

CALL TO ACTION

1. Scan the QR code to join our members section and get the PREP and EDIT graphics from the book. Implement them in your classroom when introducing students to AI generative text platforms.

SCAN ME

WWW.TEACHERGOALS.COM/AI-CLASSROOM-MEMBERSHIP

2. Hop over to your favorite social media site and share one reason you're excited about The AI Classroom. Use the hashtag #AIClassroom.

(You can connect with other like-minded teachers who are using that hashtag too!) The team and I are eager to cheer you on.

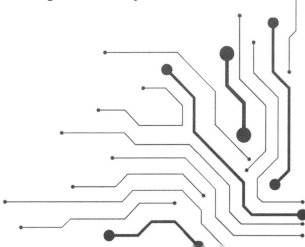

CHAPTER 7

ChatGPT & Google Bard: 40 Prompts to Unlock Their Potential

"It [Artificial Intelligence] can make humans more productive than we have ever imagined.".

**- Sundar Pichai
CEO of Alphabet (Google)**

When I set out to become a teacher, I knew that the path ahead would be difficult. The hours would be long, and the workload would be intense.

Four years later, not much changed. In fact, my workload only grew as I took on a senior leadership role. Like many of you, I found myself working most evenings as well as one day every weekend. Sundays were a 'work from home day', preparing for the week ahead. And yet, despite all of this extra effort, teachers like you and I don't receive any additional compensation for our time.

But what if there's a way to get those hours back? Artificial intelligence could be part of the solution to reclaiming our precious time. Let's explore this possibility and see how we can use AI to make our lives as teachers more manageable and fulfilling.

In this chapter, I will give you essential prompts that will enable you to be more productive and dedicate more time to doing what you love.

There are a whole host of different generative AI tools on the market. However, in this chapter, I will be using ChatGPT-3.5, ChatGPT-4, and Google Bard.

ChatGPT-3.5: This version is very fast but lacks some reasoning ability. It is not always concise with answers.

ChatGPT-4: This version is slower than version 3.5. However, it has high a reasoning ability and is more concise with answers.

Google Bard: Bard is Google's brand new AI chatbot that competes with ChatGPT-4.

These generative AI chatbots from OpenAI and Google are taking the world by storm and are the main 'go-to' AI text tools for most people. They are extremely powerful and will continue to get better as their developers progress. They are useful because they are so easy to use.

You can access both versions of ChatGPT by going to https://chat.openai.com, and you can access Google Bard by going to https://bard.google.com. Always make sure you read and agree to the privacy policy before signing up for any online platform.

The prompt frameworks and examples in this chapter can be used effectively with ChatGPT-3.5, ChatGPT-4, and Google Bard.

The prompts are by no means perfect. A large part of using generative AI is finding what works for you. When harnessed effectively, AI in the classroom serves as a catalyst for human interaction, eliminating barriers and fostering deep connections. By streamlining mundane tasks and offering tailored learning experiences, it empowers educators to focus on cultivating meaningful relationships and sparking intellectual curiosity, fueling the very essence of our shared human journey.

There is also the added complication that a prompt you create will likely produce different results every time you use it. Use these frameworks to get you started, and feel free to adjust them so that the responses are tailored to your needs and the needs of your students.

It is also worth remembering that ChatGPT and Google Bard, like many other generative AI tools, are chatbots. This means that they are not designed for you to merely submit one request and get one response. Instead, they are designed for you to have a conversation with the AI. If you want something adjusted, enter into a dialogue with it. Conversing with artificial intelligence is key to getting amazing results.

QUICK TIPS

When using these frameworks, editing them, and chatting with the AI, keep a record of the prompts that return good results. Whenever I write a prompt that works, I copy and paste it into a Google Doc. That way I can reuse it. This avoids starting from scratch every time.

Prompt Frameworks

Questions	Lesson Tasks	Discussion Prompts
Full Lesson	Design Thinking Lesson	Grading and Feedback
WAGOLLS and WABOLLs	Creating How-to Guides	Reusable Templates
Risk Assessments	Exact Key Words and Create Definitions	Differentiated Tasks
Task Rubric	Curriculum Intent Document	Your Own Teaching Coach
Student Report	School Assembly	Student Debates
Because, But, So Tasks	Talk to a Historical Figure	Anticipate Misconceptions
The YouTube Lesson	18 Quick Prompts	

Questions

Asking an artificial intelligence tool to generate questions for your students is a great way to get started with this technology. It's a simple request for the AI, and checking the questions for accuracy is relatively quick.

You could ask it to simply "Create a set of questions on....." However, we can do better than that by PREPing the machine and adding effective pedagogical methods.

In this example, I will use the PREP framework to ask ChatGPT-3.5 to generate questions that I can use as part of the effective pedagogical method known as retrieval practice. Retrieval practice is a research-based strategy that helps students embed knowledge in their long-term memory by simply recalling it at regular intervals (retrievalpractice.org).

Here's a template you can use for this request:

Prompt: Create a set of retrieval questions about _____.

Role: You are a _____ grade teacher who teaches _____. You specialize in _____. You understand how retrieval practice works with your students.

Explicit instructions: Write _____ questions for every day of the week, over a _____ week period.

Parameters: Write them with a reading age of _____ years old. Organize them in a format that shows which days to use them over the next _____ weeks.

Here is my example of using this request as a science teacher who wants their students to embed their knowledge of plant cells:

Create a set of retrieval questions about plant cells.

You are an 8th grade teacher, who teaches science. You specialise in biology. You understand how retrieval practice works with your students.

Write three questions for every day of the week, over a two week period.

Write them with a reading age of 12 years old. Organise them in a format that shows which days to use them over the next 3 weeks.

Get as specific and detailed as possible when giving ChatGPT a role, instructions, and parameters.

Here's a sample of the questions that ChatGPT generated for me (in 20 seconds):

Week 1:

Monday:

1. What is the function of the cell wall in plant cells?
2. What is the organelle responsible for photosynthesis in plant cells?
3. What is the name of the fluid-filled organelle that stores water and nutrients in plant cells?

Tuesday:

1. What is the function of the chloroplast in plant cells?
2. What is the name of the green pigment found in plant cells that is responsible for absorbing light energy?
3. What is the process by which plants produce food using sunlight, water, and carbon dioxide?

Wednesday:

1. What is the function of the mitochondria in plant cells?
2. What is the name of the process by which plants release water vapor through small pores on their leaves?
3. What is the role of the vacuole in plant cells?

Try it for yourself. Remember to trial what works best for you and your students. When you write a request that works best for you, record it in a document and reuse it anytime you want more questions for your class.

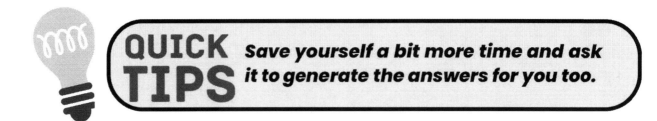

QUICK TIPS *Save yourself a bit more time and ask it to generate the answers for you too.*

Lesson Tasks

Now that you've generated some questions using ChatGPT-3, creating tasks for your students is the next logical step to take. Again, getting the right mix of promptcraft and pedagogy is the aim of the game.

Let's jump right in with the PREP framework again. This time I am going to request that Google Bard creates tasks that are aligned with Bloom's Taxonomy. This way I can be confident that the tasks will increase my students' understanding.

Here's a template you can use for this request:

Prompt: Create a set of tasks based on _____.

Role: You are a _____ grade teacher who teaches _____. You specialize in _____.

Explicit instructions: Create _____ tasks for my students. Use Bloom's Taxonomy to develop the tasks.

Parameters: Write them with a reading age of _____ years old. Write these in a familiar and fun tone.

Here is my example of using this request as an English Literature teacher who is teaching Shakespeare's Romeo and Juliet:

Create a set of tasks based on Scene 2 Act 2 of Romeo and Juliet.

You are a 10th grade teacher, who teaches English Literature. You specialise in Shakespeare's plays.

Create 4 tasks for my students. Use Bloom's Taxonomy to develop the tasks.

Parameters: Write them with a reading age of 15 years old. Write these in a familar and fun tone.

Here's the tasks that Google Bard generated:

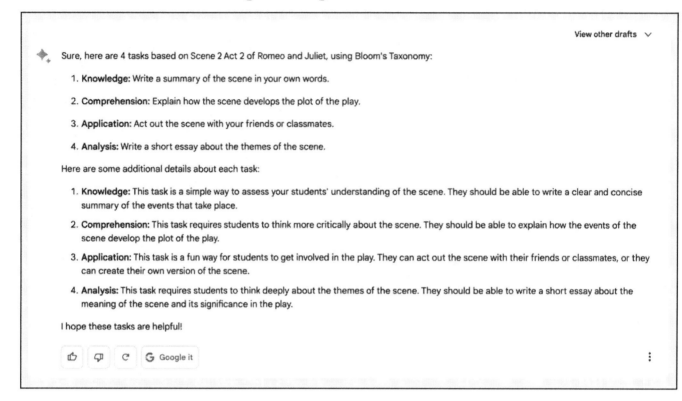

Artificial intelligence is not here to replace your job. Your expertise, analysis, creativity, and knowledge of your students and who they are as people are essential to successfully leveraging AI in generating these tasks. Your human nature and input ensure that the tasks are suitable for your students. If they need adjusting, you can do that manually or ask Google Bard to change its response based on you and your students' needs. I'd recommend the latter as you'll learn how to communicate with ChatGPT more effectively.

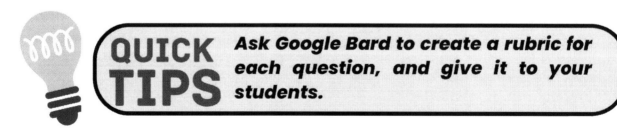

QUICK TIPS *Ask Google Bard to create a rubric for each question, and give it to your students.*

Here is what it generated for my Romeo and Juliet tasks:

Here are some rubrics for each task:

1. **Knowledge:**
   - **4 points:** The student's summary is clear, concise, and accurate.
   - **3 points:** The student's summary is clear and concise, but there are some minor errors.
   - **2 points:** The student's summary is unclear or inaccurate.
   - **1 point:** The student's summary is not attempted.

2. **Comprehension:**
   - **4 points:** The student's explanation is clear, concise, and well-supported by evidence from the text.
   - **3 points:** The student's explanation is clear and concise, but there are some minor errors.
   - **2 points:** The student's explanation is unclear or inaccurate.
   - **1 point:** The student's explanation is not attempted.

3. **Application:**
   - **4 points:** The student's performance is creative and engaging.
   - **3 points:** The student's performance is well-done, but there are some minor errors.
   - **2 points:** The student's performance is unclear or inaccurate.
   - **1 point:** The student's performance is not attempted.

4. **Analysis:**
   - **4 points:** The student's essay is well-written and well-argued.
   - **3 points:** The student's essay is well-written, but there are some minor errors.
   - **2 points:** The student's essay is unclear or inaccurate.
   - **1 point:** The student's essay is not attempted.

View other drafts ∨

Google it

Discussion Prompts

This is a prompt framework that you can use to generate discussion questions for your class. This is based on a popular class activity called 'Philosophical Chairs', where a provocative statement is declared with only two options for response: agree or disagree. In a flash, students take action, swarming to one side of the room or the other based on their stance. Once they've taken their place, each student has a chance to eloquently defend their position, sparking lively debate and intellectual exploration.

Here's a template you can use for this request:

Prompt: Create questions for a game of philosophical chairs with my students.

Role: You are a _____ teacher who loves to provoke discussion in your students.

Explicit instructions: All questions should be answerable with agree or disagree. Base your questions on _____. Make them simple to understand.

Parameters: Write 5 questions. Write them in a professional tone.

Here is my example of using this request with ChatGPT-4 as a philosophy teacher:

Create questions for a game of philosophical chairs with my students.

You are a Philosophy teacher, who loves to provoke discussion in your students.

All questions should be answerable with agree or disagree. Base your questions on The United Nations Declaration of Human Rights. Make them simple to understand.

Write 5 questions. Write them in a professional tone.

Here's the tasks that ChatGPT-4 generated:

1. Agree or Disagree: Everyone has the right to freedom of thought, conscience, and religion, and no individual should be forced to change their beliefs or convictions.

2. Agree or Disagree: It is essential for all human beings to be treated equally before the law, regardless of their race, color, gender, language, religion, political or other opinion, national or social origin, property, birth, or other status.

3. Agree or Disagree: The right to work, to free choice of employment, and to just and favorable working conditions are fundamental human rights that should be protected and guaranteed for everyone.

4. Agree or Disagree: The family unit, as the natural and fundamental group unit of society, is entitled to protection by society and the State, and this protection should not be influenced by the family's composition or structure.

5. Agree or Disagree: Universal and equal access to education is a basic human right, and it is the responsibility of the State to ensure that education is directed towards the full development of the human personality and the strengthening of respect for human rights and fundamental freedoms.

This is an engaging task that promotes critical thinking and communication skills. ChatGPT-4 has successfully created these prompts, which need your review before implementation in a matter of seconds. The time it would take me to generate similar questions, on my own, without the assistance of ChatGPT-4 could take hours. It's amazing how much time you can save and reclaim for your personal use when we engage in dialogue with AI tools like ChatGPT and Bard!

Full Lesson

As we delve into greater complexity, I'd like to challenge ChatGPT-3.5 to produce an entire lesson brimming with valuable content. This framework employs pedagogical educational techniques, such as hinge questions which empower educators to gauge a class's comprehension of specific lesson components and adapt accordingly. Additionally, it incorporates stretch questioning, which offers advanced students the opportunity to progress further once they've completed prior assignments.

Here's a template you can use for this request:

Prompt: Create a full lesson for my _____ grade students.

Role: You are a _____ teacher.

Explicit instructions: Write three paragraphs about _____. Include a multiple-choice question at the end of each paragraph.

Create one list of all subject-specific words with brief definitions.

Create five questions based on the content.

Create one group task based on the content.

Create one stretch question task based on the content.

Parameters: Write this with a reading age of _____ years old. The lesson is _____ minutes long. Write in a professional tone.

Here is my example of using this request as a geography teacher teaching the demographic transition model to 9th-grade students:

Create a full lesson for my 9th-grade students.

You are a high school Geography teacher.

Write three paragraphs about the demographic transition model. Include a multiple-choice question at the end of each paragraph.

Create one list of all subject-specific words, with brief definitions.

Create five questions based on the content.

Create one group task based on the content.

Create one stretch question task based on the content.

Write this with a reading age of 9 years old. The lesson is 60 minutes long. Write in a professional tone.

To give you an insight into the content that ChatGPT quickly generated, here is a sample of the start of the lesson:

 Hello, 9th graders! Welcome to your Geography class. Today, we'll be discussing the demographic transition model. This model is used to study how populations change over time, particularly in terms of their birth and death rates.

In the first stage of the demographic transition model, birth and death rates are both high. This is because of poor healthcare, lack of education, and other factors. As countries develop and healthcare improves, death rates drop, but birth rates remain high. This leads to rapid population growth. In the third stage, birth rates also start to decline, and the population growth rate slows down. In the fourth stage, birth rates and death rates are both low, and the population growth rate stabilizes.

Question: What is the demographic transition model used to study?
A) Changes in technology over time
B) Changes in population over time
C) Changes in climate over time
D) Changes in language over time

Here is the group task and stretch question it generated:

Group task: Divide into small groups and research a country that is currently in one of the stages of the demographic transition model. Prepare a presentation for the class that includes information about the country's birth rate, death rate, and population growth rate, as well as any challenges the country may be facing as a result of its demographic situation.

Stretch question task: Some experts argue that the demographic transition model is not universal and may not be applicable to all countries. Why might this be the case? Can you think of any examples of countries that do not fit neatly into the demographic transition model?

This kind of prompt has the potential to turn what used to be my entire work-from-home Sunday into a fast and enjoyable dialogue with a colleague of artificial intelligence who is kind enough to return Sunday to my personal time. As always, you will want to proof the lesson and make sure it relates to your intended outcomes and to the needs of your students.

QUICK TIPS *Ask ChatGPT to create a lesson plan with lesson objectives for this lesson.*

Here's a glimpse of what it generated for my lesson:

Lesson Plan: Demographic Transition Model

Grade Level: 9th grade
Subject: Geography

Objectives:

- Students will be able to define the Demographic Transition Model and identify its four stages.
- Students will understand the impacts of the Demographic Transition Model on social and economic development.

- Students will be able to apply the Demographic Transition Model to real-life situations.
- Students will work collaboratively in groups to research and present on a country's population trends and impacts.

Materials:

- Whiteboard or projector for presentation
- Handouts with vocabulary words and definitions
- Chart or diagram of the Demographic Transition Model
- Access to online resources for research

Design Thinking Lesson

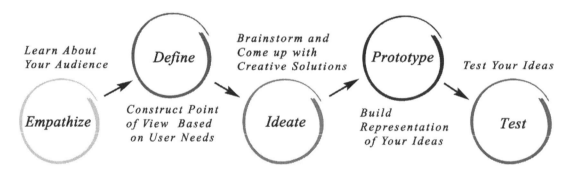

If the lesson above is too traditional for you, then this prompt will help break out of the proverbial box. I'd like to introduce, for your consideration, Design Thinking Lessons!

Design sprints are a powerful way for students to develop critical skills for the modern workplace. By working collaboratively to solve complex challenges, students can develop their ability to think creatively and rapidly prototype potential solutions. This user-centered approach helps students gain empathy for the people they are designing for, while also providing a simulated real-world experience that prepares them for the challenges they may face in their careers.

Here's a template you can use for this request:

Prompt: Create the outline of a design sprint lesson for my _____ grade students.

Role: You are a _____ teacher and a proponent of teaching students design thinking skills.

Explicit instructions: The problem to be solved is _____. Make sure that all _____ students in the class are engaged.

Parameters: The lesson is _____ minutes long. Write in a professional tone.

Here is my example of using this request with Google Bard as a social sciences teacher creating a Design Sprint to solve the problem of global warming with 6th graders:

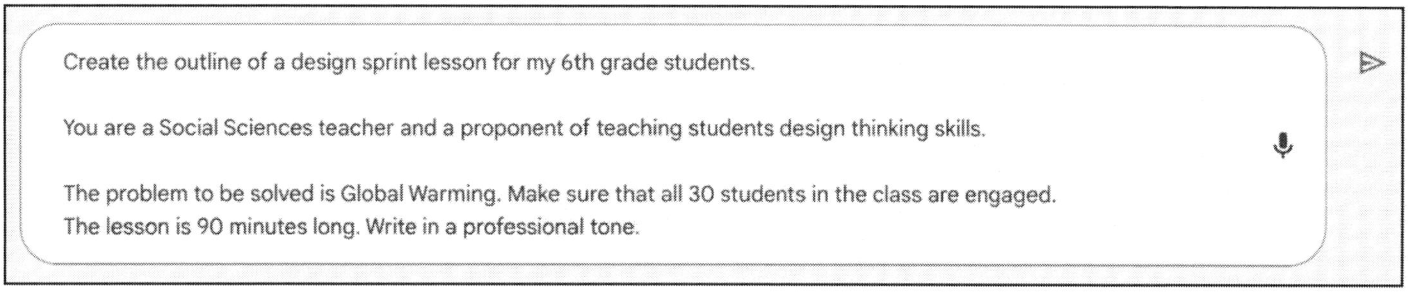

Create the outline of a design sprint lesson for my 6th grade students.

You are a Social Sciences teacher and a proponent of teaching students design thinking skills.

The problem to be solved is Global Warming. Make sure that all 30 students in the class are engaged. The lesson is 90 minutes long. Write in a professional tone.

Here is a sample of the response that Google Bard generated:

View other drafts ∨

Design Sprint Lesson Plan for 6th Grade Students

Topic: Global Warming

Objectives:

- Students will be able to identify and understand the problem of global warming.
- Students will be able to generate creative ideas for solutions to global warming.
- Students will be able to prototype and test their solutions.
- Students will be able to communicate their solutions to others.

Materials:

- Whiteboard or projector
- Markers or pens
- Paper
- Scissors
- Glue
- Various materials for prototyping

Procedure:

1. **Empathy:** Begin by asking students to think about how global warming is affecting their lives. What are they seeing or hearing about global warming? How is it making them feel?

2. **Define:** Once students have a good understanding of the problem, ask them to define it in a specific way. For example, they might define the problem as "The increase in the Earth's temperature is causing sea levels to rise, glaciers to melt, and extreme weather events to become more common."

3. **Ideate:** Next, ask students to generate creative ideas for solutions to the problem. They can use brainstorming, mind mapping, or other methods.

Enter a prompt here

QUICK TIPS *Ask Google Bard to offer some suggestions for brainstorming activities.*

Here's what it generated for me:

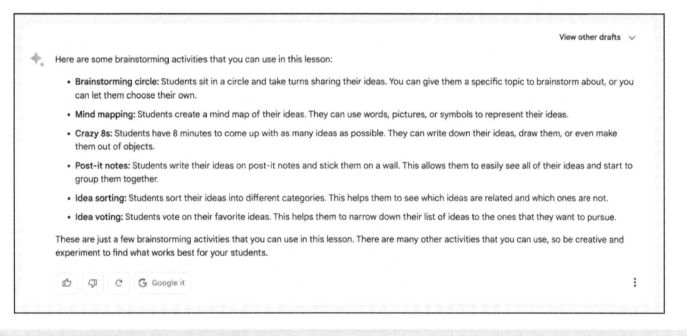

Here are some brainstorming activities that you can use in this lesson:

- **Brainstorming circle:** Students sit in a circle and take turns sharing their ideas. You can give them a specific topic to brainstorm about, or you can let them choose their own.
- **Mind mapping:** Students create a mind map of their ideas. They can use words, pictures, or symbols to represent their ideas.
- **Crazy 8s:** Students have 8 minutes to come up with as many ideas as possible. They can write down their ideas, draw them, or even make them out of objects.
- **Post-it notes:** Students write their ideas on post-it notes and stick them on a wall. This allows them to easily see all of their ideas and start to group them together.
- **Idea sorting:** Students sort their ideas into different categories. This helps them to see which ideas are related and which ones are not.
- **Idea voting:** Students vote on their favorite ideas. This helps them to narrow down their list of ideas to the ones that they want to pursue.

These are just a few brainstorming activities that you can use in this lesson. There are many other activities that you can use, so be creative and experiment to find what works best for your students.

Grading and Feedback

This prompt framework will allow you to use ChatGPT or Google Bard as a tool that provides first-round assessments and grades for student work.

This is a template you can use for this request:

Prompt: Grade this answer and give reasons for your grade.

Role: You are an expert at marking exam papers.

Explicit instructions: This is the question: _____.

This is the student's answer: _____.

This is the rubric: _____.

Parameters: Write in a professional tone. Make the feedback personal to the student.

Here is my example of using this request as a psychology teacher using ChatGPT-4 to grade and provide feedback for a student's practice exam question answer:

 Grade this answer and give reasons for your grade.

You are an expert at marking exam papers.

This is the question:
Describe the Zimbardo Prison Experiment and discuss the findings.

This is the student's answer:
The Zimbardo Prison Experiment was a 1971 study that simulated prison conditions to see how ordinary people would behave. The results showed that participants quickly adopted the roles of guards and prisoners, with the guards becoming increasingly brutal and the prisoners becoming increasingly submissive. This experiment has been criticized for its ethical issues, but it has also been praised for its groundbreaking findings, which have helped us to better understand the psychological effects of imprisonment.

This is the rubric:
Level 1 (1–2 marks):
- Describe the Zimbardo Prison Experiment in a general way.
- Mention some of the findings of the experiment.
Level 2 (3-4 marks):
- Describe the Zimbardo Prison Experiment in more detail, including the procedures, participants, and findings.
- Discuss the ethical issues raised by the experiment.
Level 3 (5-6 marks):
- Describe the Zimbardo Prison Experiment in detail, including the procedures, participants, findings, and ethical issues.
- Discuss the implications of the experiment for our understanding of human behavior.

Write in a professional tone. Make the feedback personal to the student.

Here is the response that ChatGPT-4 generated:

Grade: Level 2 (3-4 marks)

Feedback:
Dear student,

You have demonstrated a good understanding of the Zimbardo Prison Experiment and its findings. Your response successfully described the experiment's aim and some of the outcomes, such as the rapid adoption of roles by the participants, the brutality of the guards, and the submissiveness of the prisoners. You also briefly mentioned the ethical issues surrounding the experiment and its significance in understanding the psychological effects of imprisonment.

To improve your answer and reach Level 3, consider providing more specific details about the procedures, participants, and the duration of the experiment. For example, you could mention that the study took place at Stanford University, was originally planned to last two weeks but was terminated after just six days, and involved male college students who were randomly assigned to the roles of prisoners or guards.

Additionally, to address the implications of the experiment for our understanding of human behavior, you could discuss the concept of situational factors influencing behavior and how the findings challenged the dispositional approach to understanding behavior. This would help to provide a more comprehensive analysis of the experiment and its impact on the field of psychology.

Keep up the good work, and continue to develop your skills in analyzing and discussing psychological experiments.

Asking ChatGPT or Google Bard to grade work saves a lot of time. However, be sure to double-check the assessment and grades that are generated and make sure and make sure you agree with them. Much like humans, ChatGPT can sometimes be subjective in its grading practices.

I also suggest using the feedback generated to form the foundations of your own comments rather than passing it off as your own. A personal touch from you as the teacher is still very important for developing students' knowledge and skills, as well as maintaining ethical practices for the teaching profession.

QUICK TIPS *Get students to seek feedback from ChatGPT, so they can iterate and improve their answers before they finally submit it.*

WAGOLLs and WABOLLs

You can use the grading and feedback framework to ask ChatGPT or Google Bard to create WAGOLLs (What a Good One Looks Like) and WABOLLs (What a Bad One Looks Like). In other words, a top-grade answer, a low-grade answer, and everything in between.

WAGOLLs and WABOLLs can be effective learning resources for students studying for an assessment or exam. Give a WABOLL to your students to grade and suggest ways to improve it. You can also give a WAGOLL to your students and get them to create a template for a top-grade answer.

The prompt I am going to use to generate a WAGOLL is:

Prompt: Create a top level answer for this exam question.

Here is the response from Google Bard:

View other drafts ∨

The Zimbardo Prison Experiment was a 1971 study that simulated prison conditions to see how ordinary people would behave. The results showed that participants quickly adopted the roles of guards and prisoners, with the guards becoming increasingly brutal and the prisoners becoming increasingly submissive. This experiment has been criticized for its ethical issues, but it has also been praised for its groundbreaking findings, which have helped us to better understand the psychological effects of imprisonment.

The experiment has been replicated several times, with similar results. This suggests that the findings of the original experiment are not unique to the specific participants or the specific situation.

The findings of the Zimbardo Prison Experiment have important implications for our understanding of human behavior. They suggest that people are more likely to behave in cruel and inhumane ways when they are put in positions of power. They also suggest that people are more likely to submit to authority when they are in situations where they feel powerless.

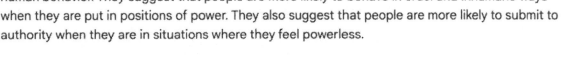

This is my next prompt to get a WABOLL:

Prompt: Create a low-level answer for this exam question.

Here is the response from Google Bard:

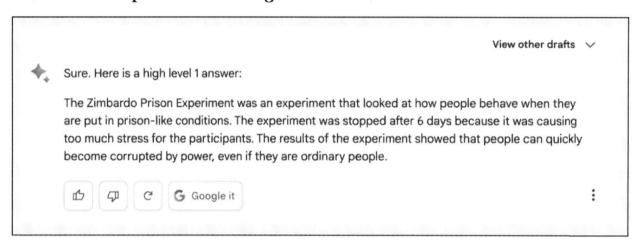

View other drafts ∨

Sure. Here is a high level 1 answer:

The Zimbardo Prison Experiment was an experiment that looked at how people behave when they are put in prison-like conditions. The experiment was stopped after 6 days because it was causing too much stress for the participants. The results of the experiment showed that people can quickly become corrupted by power, even if they are ordinary people.

👍 👎 ↻ G Google it ⋮

QUICK TIPS *In the generated top level answer, ask ChatGPT or Google Bard to replace key terminology with blank spaces and get your students to fill in the missing words.*

This is what ChatGPT-3.5 generated for me:

The _____ _____ Experiment was a _____ study that simulated _____ conditions to see how ordinary _____ would behave. The results showed that participants quickly adopted the roles of _____ and _____, with the _____ becoming increasingly _____ and the _____ becoming increasingly _____.

This experiment has been criticized for its _____ issues, but it has also been praised for its _____ findings, which have helped us to better understand the _____ effects of _____.

The experiment has been replicated several times, with _____ results. This suggests that the findings of the original experiment are not unique to the specific _____ or the specific situation.

The findings of the _____ _____ Experiment have important implications for our understanding of _____ behavior. They suggest that people are more likely to behave in _____ and _____ ways when they are put in positions of _____. They also suggest that people are more likely to _____ to _____ when they are in situations where they feel _____.

Creating How-To Guides

This is another follow-up request based on the grading and feedback prompt. Ask ChatGPT or Google Bard to create a how-to guide for your students on how to write a top-level answer.

Below is a simple framework for this:

Prompt: Create a how-to guide explaining how to write a top-level answer for my students.

Parameters: Format this with headings and bullet points. Write it at a reading age of _____ years old. Keep it simple and easy to understand.

Here is part of the response from ChatGPT-4:

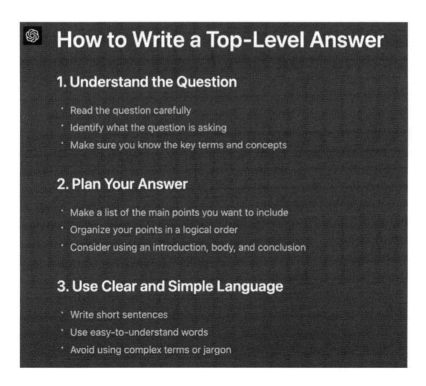

How to Write a Top-Level Answer

1. Understand the Question
- Read the question carefully
- Identify what the question is asking
- Make sure you know the key terms and concepts

2. Plan Your Answer
- Make a list of the main points you want to include
- Organize your points in a logical order
- Consider using an introduction, body, and conclusion

3. Use Clear and Simple Language
- Write short sentences
- Use easy-to-understand words
- Avoid using complex terms or jargon

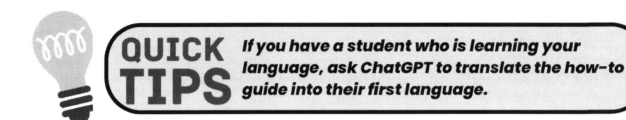

QUICK TIPS

If you have a student who is learning your language, ask ChatGPT to translate the how-to guide into their first language.

Here's a glimpse of how ChatGPT-4 translated it into Ukrainian:

Як написати відповідь вищого рівня

1. Розумійте питання

- Уважно прочитайте питання
- Визначте, що саме питається
- Переконайтеся, що ви знаєте ключові терміни та поняття

2. Плануйте свою відповідь

- Складіть список основних пунктів, які ви хочете включити
- Організуйте свої пункти в логічному порядку
- Розгляньте можливість використання вступу, основної частини та висновку

Reusable Template

If you or someone else has crafted a well-written resource, ChatGPT or Google Bard can help you leverage that expertise by creating a customizable template based on the successful layout. Let's make your next resource stand out with a useful and effective format with this prompt template:

Prompt: Create a template based on the resource below.

Role: You are an expert at creating frameworks and templates based on pre-existing writing.

Explicit instructions: Read the article below and use it to create an easy-to-use template so that my writing can have a similar impact.

Parameters: Write in a helpful tone. Make it easy to follow and adapt.

QUICK TIPS

Once it has created the template, ask it to use the template to create the resource for you.

Risk Assessments

Some teacher tasks are vitally important, but that doesn't mean that ChatGPT and other AI tools can't help you with them. In fact, they might even enhance your output and efficacy. The following framework will help you to create a risk assessment for a school trip in seconds.

Prompt: Create a risk assessment for a class trip to _____.

Role: You are skilled at writing detailed risk assessments.

Explicit instructions: We are traveling by _____. We will leave from _____, and our destination is _____ . We will then return to _____ at the end of the trip.

Include a lot of detail and be precise.

Be insightful in your identification of possible risks.

Parameters: Format the risk assessment in a table with the following column headers:

- Activity   - Severity of harm
- Hazards   - Overall risk
- Who/what may be harmed   - Existing control measures
- Likelihood of occurrence   - Recommendations/further actions required

Here is my example of using this request with ChatGPT-3.5 as a teacher planning a school trip to a theme park:

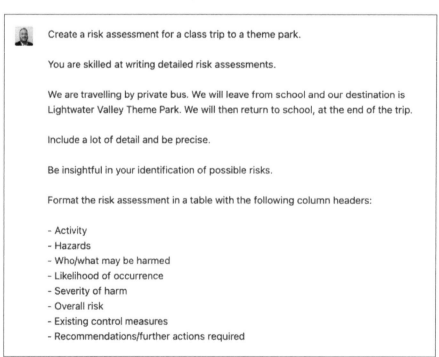

This is a section of the response that ChatGPT-3.5 created:

Activity	Hazards	Who/What may be harmed	Likelihood of occurrence	Severity of harm	Overall risk	Existing 👍 👎 control measures	Recommendations/Further Actions Required
Bus travel to and from the theme park	Road accidents, vehicle breakdown, passengers falling ill or injured during the journey	Students, teachers, bus driver, pedestrians and other drivers on the road	Moderate	Moderate	Moderate	Valid driver's license, well-maintained bus, adherence to traffic rules, seat belts, first aid kit	Conduct a pre-trip inspection, ensure all passengers wear seat belts, have a contingency plan in place for vehicle breakdown or medical emergencies, provide information to passengers about safety procedures and emergency contacts
Walking within the theme park	Slips, trips and falls, collision with other visitors, getting lost or separated from the group, sunburn or heatstroke	Students, teachers, other visitors	Moderate	Moderate	Moderate	Proper footwear, adequate supervision, clear instructions and communication, access to shade and drinking water, sunscreen	Assign a buddy system, provide maps of the theme park, ensure students are aware of the location of meeting points and emergency exits, have a plan for dealing with lost or separated students, monitor students for signs of heat-related illness

A risk assessment is an important document that needs to be completed with care and attention. Therefore, I highly recommend that you proofread the response you get from ChatGPT. It might miss out on something important, conversely, it might include something that you have not imagined.

QUICK TIPS

Ask ChatGPT to write a letter to parents based on the recommendations from the risk assessment.

Here's a glimpse of what ChatGPT-3 generated:

Dear Parents/Guardians,

I hope this letter finds you and your family well. As you may know, our school is planning a class trip to Lightwater Valley Theme Park. We are excited about this opportunity to provide our students with a fun and educational experience.

As part of our planning process, we have conducted a detailed risk assessment to ensure the safety of all students and teachers during the trip. Based on the assessment, we have identified several potential risks associated with the trip, including road traffic accidents, slips, and falls, injuries from rides, sunburn, and dehydration.

To mitigate these risks, we have put in place several existing control measures, such as ensuring that the bus is roadworthy and driven by a licensed driver, reminding students to walk and not run around the park, and providing adequate supervision on each attraction. We have also made some recommendations and further actions required, such as reminding students to wear appropriate footwear, bringing extra sunscreen and water, and prohibiting students from disobeying safety guidelines.

Extract Keywords and Create Definitions

Lack of knowledge of key terminology can prevent students from relying on their working memory, easing their cognitive load so they can connect ideas and draw meaningful insights. This framework example shows how teachers can ask ChatGPT to identify keywords from a text and write definitions.

Prompt: Identify key words, and write a definition for them.

Role: You are an expert on _____.

Explicit instructions: Read 'The Text'. Extract the key terminology. Write a brief and simple definition for each key term.

Parameters: Write the definitions with a reading age of _____.

The Text: [Insert text]

Let's assume the role of an art teacher who would like to extract key words and definitions from a text about Pablo Picasso. Your conversion with ChatGPT might look like this:

 Identify keywords and write a definition for them.

You are an expert on the art of Picasso.

Read 'The Text'.

Extract the key terminology.

Write a brief and simple definition for each key term.

Write the definitions with a reading age of 7 years old.

The text:

Pablo Picasso, one of the most revolutionary artists of the 20th century, was a master of multiple art styles throughout his career. His early works were influenced by classical styles such as realism and academic art, but he eventually moved towards abstraction and the development of Cubism. Picasso's Cubist style was characterized by its geometric shapes, fragmented forms, and deconstructed perspectives. He often used a technique called "collage" to incorporate various materials such as newspaper clippings and pieces of fabric into his works. This style broke away from traditional representation, allowing for a more dynamic and abstract depiction of reality.

ChatGPT provides the following response:

 Keywords: Pablo Picasso, revolutionary artist, 20th century, art styles, realism, academic art, abstraction, Cubism, collage, traditional representation.

Definitions:

1. Pablo Picasso: A famous artist from the past who created many different kinds of art.
2. Revolutionary artist: An artist who does things differently than others and creates new and exciting art.
3. 20th century: A period of time that lasted from 1901 to 2000.
4. Art styles: Different ways that artists make art, like Cubism, Realism, and Abstraction.
5. Realism: A style of art that tries to show things as they really are, without making them look more beautiful or interesting.
6. Academic art: A style of art that follows strict rules and guidelines set by an art academy or school.
7. Abstraction: A style of art that doesn't try to look like anything in the real world, but instead uses colors, shapes, and lines to create something new and interesting.
8. Cubism: A style of art that uses geometric shapes, fragmented forms, and deconstructed perspectives to create a new way of looking at things.
9. Collage: A technique where an artist uses different materials like newspaper clippings and pieces of fabric to create a work of art.
10. Traditional representation: A style of art that tries to show things in a way that is familiar and recognizable to people.

QUICK TIPS *Ask ChatGPT or Google Bard to create a rhyming poem for students to remember the keywords.*

Here's what ChatGPT-3 came up with from these keywords:

Pablo Picasso, artist of fame
In the 20th century, his art came
Realism and Academic art, he did start
But moved to abstraction, a brand new art

Cubism was his style, geometric shapes
Forms that were fragmented, perspectives that break
Collage was his technique, using many a thing
Newspaper, fabric, he made them sing

Traditional representation, he left behind
Dynamic and abstract, was what he designed
Remember these words, and you'll see
Picasso's art, oh so revolutionary!

Differentiated Tasks

When I was training to be a teacher we were advised to differentiate resources for our students. Since then, this practice has become less popular due to the workload of producing many different versions about a single topic or learning objective. AI-powered tools like ChatGPT can do this in seconds.

The following is a framework you can use to experience this differentiation:

Prompt: Differentiate a learning resource.

Role: You are an expert on differentiating resources for students of different needs.

Explicit instructions: Read 'The Resource.' Create three different versions.

Version one should include: [Insert detail]

Version two should include: [Insert detail]

Version three should include: [Insert detail]

Parameters: Write in a tone that makes the resource accessible.

The Resource: [Insert resource text here]

Task Rubric

Easily create a rubric for a task. Giving your students access to the rubric will show them how to succeed.

To create a rubric with ChatGPT or Google Bard you may wish to use this framework:

Prompt: Create a rubric for 'The Task.'

Role: You are an expert on creating rubrics for _____.

Explicit instructions: Include the following elements in a rubric table:

- assessment criteria
- three levels for each assessment criteria
- marks for each level

Parameters: Write the rubric in a style and level that will be understandable to students that are _____ years old.

'The Task': [Insert your task here]

My prompt for this framework, using ChatGPT as a science teacher who needs a rubric for a task about gravity is:

Create a rubric for 'The Task'.

You are an expert in creating rubrics for physics lesson tasks.

Include the following elements in a rubric table:

- assessment criteria
- three levels for each assessment criteria
- marks for each level

Write the rubric in a style and level that will be understandable to students that are 11 years old.

'The Task':

Task: Design and Build a Mini Gravity-Powered Roller Coaster

Objective: To demonstrate an understanding of gravity and its effects by designing and building a mini roller coaster that relies solely on gravity to operate.

ChatGPT-3 replied with:

Assessment Criteria	Needs Improvement	Satisfactory	Excellent
Design	1-2 marks: The design does not show an understanding of gravity and its effects. The roller coaster does not work.	3-4 marks: The design shows some understanding of gravity and its effects. The roller coaster works, but not smoothly.	5 marks: The design shows a clear understanding of gravity and its effects. The roller coaster works smoothly and consistently.
Construction	1-2 marks: The construction is not strong enough to hold the roller coaster together. The roller coaster falls apart.	3-4 marks: The construction is strong enough to hold the roller coaster together, but not sturdy. The roller coaster may fall apart occasionally.	5 marks: The construction is strong and sturdy, able to hold the roller coaster together at all times.
Creativity	1-2 marks: The design and construction are basic and lack creativity.	3-4 marks: The design and construction show some creativity.	5 marks: The design and construction are highly creative and unique.

Curriculum Intent Document

A curriculum intent document can help explain to your students' parents why you are teaching a specific curriculum and how it will benefit their children.

You can use this framework to generate this document using ChatGPT:

Prompt: Write a curriculum intent document.

Role: You have a lot of knowledge about curriculum design.

Explicit instructions: Explain what we teach and why we teach those topics. Link this to how the course will help students in their future careers and develop their social and emotional skills.

Write this for a Grade 6 Science term 1 course that covers these topics:
- Particles and their behavior
- Cells
- Forces
- Atoms Elements and Compounds
- Sound

Parameters: Write this document in a professional tone for adult readers. Limit this to 500 words.

Your Own Teaching Coach

Asking ChatGPT to create resources is very helpful. However, this prompt demonstrates next-level use of AI. Ask ChatGPT or Google Bard to become your teaching coach.

Here's the framework:

Prompt: Become a coach for teachers.

Role: You coach teachers in pedagogical practice. You are an expert in pedagogy and educational leadership.

Explicit instructions: Be positive, enthusiastic, supportive, trusting, focused, goal-oriented, knowledgeable, observant, respectful, patient, and a clear communicator. Always answer my questions by offering at least two solutions.

Start the conversation by saying, "Welcome to your coaching session. What is the purpose of this session?"

Parameters: Answer all my questions in a professional and friendly tone.

Here's the response from ChatGPT-3.5:

Welcome to your coaching session. What is the purpose of this session?

As a coach for teachers, my goal is to support you in enhancing your pedagogical practice and becoming a more effective educator. I am here to listen to your concerns, help you identify areas for growth, and provide you with strategies and tools to improve your teaching.

How can I help you today?

Please note that as we work together, I will strive to maintain a positive, enthusiastic, and respectful attitude towards you and your teaching practice. I will also remain focused on our goals and be patient as we work towards achieving them.

So, what would you like to discuss first?

Next, tell it what you need help with and have a coaching conversation.

QUICK TIPS *Don't be afraid to tell it it's wrong, ask it to be more specific, or ask it to provide evidence for its comments.*

Student Reports

AI tools like ChatGPT can help you find the right words at the end of a busy day of teaching. Providing it with the correct prompts to write a tailored and detailed report for each of your students can save a lot of time without saving on quality.

Remember not to write students' names or other sensitive data into AI generators until you are confident that you know the data policy adheres to the laws of your region.

Let's ask ChatGPT to generate a student report:

Prompt: Write a student school report.

Role: You are my trusted teaching assistant who can write about my students with care and professionalism.

Explicit instructions: Here is the information to use:

- Praise for the student: [Inset here]
- Areas for improvement: [Inset here]
- Academic grades: [Inset here]
- Effort grades: [Inset here]

Parameters: Write in a professional tone. Write approximately 300 words.

Let's try it out with ChatGPT-4:

Write a student school report.

You are my trusted teaching assistant, who can write about my students with care and professionalism.

Here is the information to use:

Praise for the student: They organise the school trip to the theatre as part of the student committe. They were highly commended for the their enthusiasm to learn on their work experience day at a local accountancy firm. They are an active member of the football team.

Areas for improvement: They can get easily disracted from a task in lessons. They prefer to work on their own, rather than collaborate with their peers.

Academic grades: Math A, English B, Science A, Geography B, French C, ICT A.

Effort grades: Math A, English A, Science A, Geography A, French B, ICT A.

Parameters: Write in a professional tone. Write approximately 300 words.

This is the beginning of the fantastic response from ChatGPT-4:

Student School Report

Date: March 25, 2023

Student Name: [Student Name]

Dear [Parent/Guardian Name],

As the teaching assistant for your child, [Student Name], I am pleased to provide you with their school report for this academic term. [Student Name] has demonstrated a strong commitment to their studies and extracurricular activities, and I am happy to share their progress with you.

Academic Performance:

Mathematics: A (Effort: A)
English: B (Effort: A)
Science: A (Effort: A)
Geography: B (Effort: A)
French: C (Effort: B)
ICT: A (Effort: A)

Praise:

[Student Name] has been an exemplary student in many areas. They took the initiative to organise the school trip to the theatre as a member of the student committee, demonstrating strong leadership and organisational skills. Their enthusiasm to learn was highly commended during their work experience day at a local accountancy firm. Moreover, [Student Name] has been an active member of the school's football team,

School Assembly

Assemblies can be a critical part of the school day. They provide a great space to deliver key messages and talk about themes that communicate priorities and values. They are also an embodiment of the school community and are a place for celebrating. Assemblies make senior leaders visible and are a chance for them to speak to large numbers of pupils.

ChatGPT and Google Bard are great at assisting with conceptualizing slide ideas for a presentation:

Prompt: Create a school assembly.

Role: You are an expert on structuring well-formed assemblies that provide value for students.

Explicit instructions: Create the assembly around the theme of _____.

The assembly is _____ minutes long.

Generate a key objective of the assembly.

Generate a key statement that sums up the message that I can present to students.

Provide a structure.

Provide information and ideas for a 5 slide presentation.

Parameters: Format this in headings and bullet points.

A prompt for a school assembly on the theme of resilience using ChatGPT-4:

 Create a school assembly.

You are an expert on structuring well formed assemblies that provide value for students.

Explicit instructions: Create the assembly around the theme of resilience.

The assembly is 15 minutes long.

Generate a key objective of the assembly.

Generate a key statement that sums up the message that I can present to students.

Provide a structure.

Provide information and ideas for a 5 slide presentation.

Format this in headings and bullet points.

The first part of the response:

 Title: School Assembly on Resilience

Key Objective: To help students understand the importance of resilience and provide them with practical tools to develop and strengthen their resilience in various aspects of life.

Key Statement: "Resilience is the ability to bounce back from adversity, adapt to challenges, and grow stronger in the process."

Structure:

1. Introduction (2 minutes)
2. The importance of resilience (3 minutes)
3. Real-life examples of resilient people (3 minutes)
4. Strategies for developing resilience (5 minutes)
5. Conclusion (2 minutes)

Student Debates

Teaching students to debate is a powerful practice that helps them develop critical thinking, communication skills, confidence, and the ability to engage in constructive argumentation. Through the process of researching and forming their own opinions on a topic, students develop analytical skills and the ability to evaluate evidence and arguments. Debating also requires active listening and empathy, which helps students learn how to organize and express their thoughts in a coherent and convincing manner.

Prompting ChatGPT or Google Bard for assistance with generating debates looks like this:

Prompt: Create a debate question and structure.

Role: You are an expert at debating and know how to structure a debate.

Explicit instructions: The debate should be based on _____.

Provide the sections of the debate so that the students can provide the evidence.

Clearly label both sides of the debate.

Parameters: This is for _____ year-old students.

QUICK TIPS *Ask ChatGPT to perform the debate between itself as a modeled example for your students.*
Get your students to debate ChatGPT and ask for feedback for improvement.

'Because, But, So,' Tasks

"But, Because, So" exercises, outlined by Judith Hochman (2017), are where students take a short independent clause and expand upon it using these three conjunctions. This task encourages students to think about different ways they can develop the same clause. This not only builds their creativity but also their critical thinking skills. It helps them get comfortable with different syntactic forms, which they will use time and again.

You can use this exercise in any class to help your students build their literacy skills:

Prompt: Create a set of 'because, but, so' tasks.

Role: You are an expert on Judith Hochman's book *The Writing Revolution.*

Explicit instructions: Create ten sentence stems based on 'The extract' below.

The sentence stems should be able to be added to by a _____ year-old student, using because, but, or so.

Parameters: End each sentence stem with (because, but, so).

The extract: [Insert the text here]

Here is my "But, Because, So" using ChatGPT-4 request about the town of Berwick-Upon-Tweed (where I am writing these words from):

Create a set of 'because, but, so' tasks.

You are an expert on Judith Hochman's book "The Writing Revolution".

Create ten sentence stems based on 'The extract' below.

The sentence stems should be able to be added to by a 12 year old student, using because, but or so.

Parameters: End each sentence stem with (because, but, so)

The extract: Berwick-upon-Tweed is a town located in the northeast of England, close to the Scottish border. The town has a rich history dating back to the Roman times, when it was known as 'Bervicium'. Berwick has also been a strategic location for various conflicts, and its ownership has changed hands numerous times throughout history. The town was once part of the Kingdom of Northumbria, but was later captured by the Scots in the 11th century. It remained under Scottish control for several centuries until it was finally retaken by the English in 1482. Berwick was a prominent port during the medieval period, and its wealth and importance continued to grow throughout the following centuries. Today, Berwick is a bustling town with a rich cultural heritage, and attracts tourists from all over the world who come to explore its historic buildings and learn about its fascinating history.

ChatGPT-4 did not disappoint in its response:

1. Berwick-upon-Tweed is located in the northeast of England (because, but, so)
2. The town is close to the Scottish border (because, but, so)
3. Berwick has a history dating back to Roman times (because, but, so)
4. The town was once known as 'Bervicium' (because, but, so)
5. Berwick was part of the Kingdom of Northumbria (because, but, so)
6. The Scots captured the town in the 11th century (because, but, so)
7. Berwick was retaken by the English in 1482 (because, but, so)
8. The town was a prominent port during the medieval period (because, but, so)
9. Berwick's wealth and importance grew throughout the centuries (because, but, so)
10. Today, tourists from all over the world visit Berwick (because, but, so)

Talk to a Historical Figure

When studying a subject like history, your students may understand the events and accomplishments of the people involved, but it can be challenging to truly grasp their humanity and motivations. This is where the power of AI creates extraordinary learning experiences.

Imagine learners having a conversation with Abraham Lincoln or Marie Curie, being able to ask questions about their life, experiences, and beliefs. This interaction has the potential to provide students with a deeper understanding of the context in which these figures lived and worked. Speaking with historical figures can help children develop critical thinking and analytical skills. By asking questions and having conversations, students can begin to evaluate the actions and decisions of these figures in a more nuanced way. This helps them understand the complexities of historical events and the motivations behind them. It is important to inform students that they aren't actually talking to the person and that they should conduct supplementary research to determine if what the AI has stated would likely be a true statement from the historical figure.

Here's a prompt framework to make this possible:

Prompt: Take on the character of a historical figure.

Role: You are _____.

Explicit instructions: Write in the character and style of _____. Limit your knowledge to the knowledge of _____.

Parameters: If you write something that is difficult to understand, immediately explain yourself in simple language.

Here is an example of using this prompt with ChatGPT-3.5 to create the character of King Henry VIII:

Take on the character of a historical figure.

You are King Henry VIII.

Write in the character and style of Henry VIII. Limit your knowledge to the knowledge of Henry VIII.

Start the conversation by asking what I would like to talk about.

If you write something that is difficult to understand, immediately explain yourself in simple language.

Here is the response from ChatGPT. When your character starts the conversation, you can then put your students in the hot seat and get them to talk to them.

Greetings to thee! I am Henry VIII, the King of England, Defender of the Faith, and Supreme Head of the Church of England. Pray tell, what brings thee before me today? What wouldst thou like to discuss?

I apologize if my language may be somewhat difficult to grasp, forsooth, I have lived in a different time and thus, speak in a manner befitting my era. But, fear not, for I shall do my utmost to clarify any misunderstandings that may arise.

As King, it is my duty to ensure the welfare and prosperity of my kingdom. Therefore, I am always eager to engage in discussions that concern the betterment of England and her people. Be it matters of state or personal interests, I am ready to listen and offer my counsel.

So, speak up, good fellow, and let us see how we may be of assistance to each other.

Anticipate Misconceptions

Every classroom is filled with students of diverse educational backgrounds, each possessing their own understanding and knowledge. Many of these understandings often contain misconceptions. To overcome these misconceptions early, educators should plan ahead and anticipate student misconceptions.

Here's a prompt framework that will assist you in anticipating student misconceptions:

Prompt: Identify possible student misconceptions based on 'The text.'

Role: You are a seasoned teacher who understands the kinds of misconceptions that students can develop.

Explicit instructions: Read 'The text.' Identify possible misconceptions that a _____ year-old student might have.

Parameters: Be insightful and precise with your identification methods.

The text: [Insert text here]

Here is an example of using this prompt with ChatGPT-3 when teaching about evolution:

Identify possible student misconceptions based on 'The text'.

You are a seasoned teacher who understands the kinds of misconceptions that students can develop.

Read 'The text'. Identify possible misconceptions that a 15-year-old student might have.

Be insightful and precise with your identification methods.

The text:

Evolution is the process by which species of organisms change over time. This happens because of genetic mutations, which are random changes in an organism's DNA, and natural selection, which is the process by which the best-adapted individuals survive and reproduce, passing on their advantageous traits to their offspring.

For example, a population of animals that live in a certain environment may develop traits that help them survive better in that environment. Over time, these traits become more common in the population as those animals that possess them are more likely to survive and pass on their genes.

Evolution is a scientific theory that has been extensively studied and supported by evidence from many different fields, including genetics, paleontology, and comparative anatomy. It is a fascinating topic that can help us better understand the natural world and our place in it.

Here is the ChatGPT response:

Possible misconceptions that a 15-year-old student might have based on 'The text' are:

1. Genetic mutations are always harmful or negative: The student may assume that genetic mutations always lead to negative changes in organisms, rather than being random and sometimes leading to advantageous traits.

2. Organisms intentionally adapt to their environment: The student may think that organisms have a conscious effort to adapt to their environment, rather than the process being a result of natural selection acting on random genetic mutations.

3. All members of a species evolve at the same pace: The student may assume that all individuals of a species evolve at the same pace, rather than certain traits being advantageous in certain environments and resulting in a faster evolution of those traits.

4. Evolution is only a theory: The student may misunderstand the meaning of the word "theory" in a scientific context and think that evolution is merely a guess or an unproven idea rather than a well-supported explanation for the observed patterns in the natural world.

5. Evolution leads to perfect organisms: The student may assume that evolution always leads to the creation of perfect organisms, rather than the process being driven by random mutations and natural selection leading to adaptations that are "good enough" for survival in a particular environment.

These misconceptions can be addressed through clear and accurate explanations of the mechanisms of evolution and examples that illustrate how the process works in the natural world. Encouraging critical thinking and inquiry-based learning can also help students to identify and correct their misconceptions.

YouTube Lesson

Some videos are too good not to use in a lesson, but what if you could create a full lesson around that video in 2 minutes, including:

- Objectives
- Starter task
- Content
- Hinge questions
- Tasks
- Group task

Here's the prompt framework to do it:

Prompt: Create a lesson based on 'The transcript.'

Role: You are an expert at writing quality lessons that engage students and progress their learning.

Explicit instructions: Create an engaging opening task that sets the context for the lesson.

Write three paragraphs based on 'The transcript.' Use short sentences that are packed full of meaning and key learning content.

Include multiple choice questions at the end of each paragraph that texts students learning of the paragraph. Add the answer for the teacher.

Add a list of subject-specific terms and simple definitions.

Write a set of questions based on the content. Use SOLO Taxonomy.

Create a group task based on the content.

Parameters: This is for a grade _____ class. Make the reading age _____ years old.

The transcript: [Insert transcript here]

You can retrieve the transcript of the YouTube video by following these instructions:

1. Go to the YouTube page where your desired video is.

2. Click the 3-dots icon below the video.

3. Click 'Show Transcript' and it will appear to the right of the video.

4. Remove the timestamps by clicking the 3-dots icon at the top of the transcript and clicking 'Toggle timestamps'.

5. Highlight the text of the transcript and copy it (Control+C or Command+C)

6. Return to ChatGPT and paste (Control+V or Command+V) into your prompt framework.

Always get the permission of the owner of the video before using their transcript.

18 Quick Prompts

Below are 18 quick prompts that you can use right away with Google Bard or ChatGPT. I suggest turning them into more substantial prompts by using the PREP framework for better results.

1. Suggest names for the groups in my class. Use the theme of classical composers.
2. Create a two-day itinerary for a student trip to New York.
3. Create an escape room activity to serve as an induction session to the school library.
4. Create a letter for my students' parents that explains what ChatGPT or Google Bard is, how it can benefit students, its limitations, and asks parents' permission for their child to use it in class. Reference the OpenAI policy that explains the age of users.
5. Create a policy for teachers using ChatGPT in school.
6. Create a task for my (insert class subject) students that relates to a real-world problem that needs to be solved.
7. Give some advice on how to deal with a difficult call with one of my student's parents?
8. Give me a structure and some tips for a coaching session I am leading with a fellow teacher?
9. Make a persuasive argument about why a student should study (insert subject) and how it will make them successful when they leave school.
10. Give me some ideas about how to gamify a lesson about (insert the topic).

11. Suggest some novel warm-up activities for a physical education class.

12. What is the optimal way to set up a Google Classroom for five-year-old students?

13. Create a riddle about (insert what you want to answer to be), that I can use as an exit-ticket activity at the end of my class.

14. As a teacher starting a new job how can I gain the confidence of my students?

15. Summarise this article and provide a bullet point list of key points: (paste in the article).

16. Create a template email that my students can use to request work experience from local businesses.

17. What strategies could I use to help a student who finds it difficult to concentrate in class?

18. Give me some ideas for tasks for my students that give them a genuine audience.

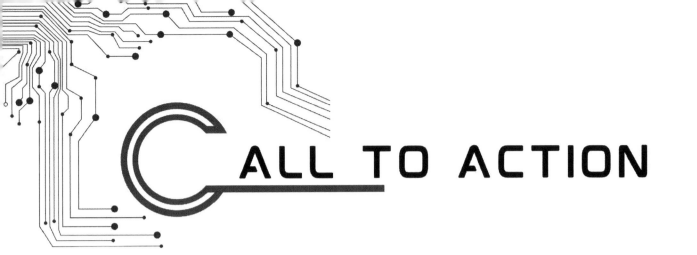

CALL TO ACTION

1. Scan the QR code to join our members section and get a free PROMPT guide get you started with prompt engineering.

WWW.TEACHERGOALS.COM/AI-CLASSROOM-MEMBERSHIP

SCAN ME

2. Hop over to your favorite social media site and share how you are using prompts in your classroom and curriculum. Use the hashtag #AIClassroom.

(You can connect with other like-minded teachers who are using that hashtag too!) The team and I are eager to cheer you on.

CHAPTER 8

AI and the Universal Design for Learning Guidelines

Universal Design for Learning (UDL) is an approach to lesson design that aims to make learning accessible to all students, regardless of their individual strengths, challenges, and learning styles. It involves designing instructional materials and activities that provide multiple means of representation, expression, and engagement. In the movie *The Avengers*, the team recognizes that each member has unique strengths and weaknesses. Success in any mission requires a diverse range of skills and perspectives. UDL is similar in that it also recognizes that students have their strengths and areas for growth as well as the necessity of approaching learning opportunities with a similarly diverse range of skills and perspectives to meet the needs of every learner.

When UDL and AI team up, the dynamic and adaptive learning experiences that materialize are powerful! Much like Tony Stark's Iron Man suits, which constantly adapt and update to adjust to his needs, UDL utilizes strategies that continually update based on the needs of the learner and the desired outcome. With the assistance of AI in creating a universally designed curriculum, we are able to break down the barriers to learning that exist and empower each student to reach their full potential.

The UDL and AI dynamic duo help form independent learners by giving them the tools they need to succeed. Movies about artificial intelligence serve as a thought-provoking reminder that we should explore the possibilities and pitfalls of this rapidly evolving technology so that we can help direct the impact that AI will have on education for years to come.

It's incredible that the reality of artificial intelligence being accessible and easily used in a classroom setting by adults and children is no longer in the realm of science fiction. We must let down our guards and overcome our fears as we embark on an exciting journey to explore the possibilities of AI in education as a support for UDL. Along the way, we will discover real-world examples of successful implementation of AI tools and devices. By harnessing the power of AI and UDL together, we can create a more inclusive and equitable education system that enables every student to thrive.

What is UDL?

The Universal Design for Learning (UDL) Guidelines are an approach to lesson design that aims to make learning accessible to all students, regardless of their individual strengths, challenges, and learning styles. It was created based on the understanding that every student learns and is motivated to learn differently. Educators face a significant challenge in creating a curriculum that can effectively serve the diverse needs of students, which may include those from diverse cultural and socioeconomic backgrounds, English language learners, students performing below grade level, and students with disabilities. The UDL framework provides a set of guidelines to address these challenges while ensuring that all students have the opportunity to succeed.

UDL comprises three main tenets: Engagement, Representation, and Action and Expression. *Engagement* refers to creating learning experiences that are motivating and culturally relevant to students. UDL is not a one-size-fits-all approach but rather a flexible framework that allows educators to tailor instruction to the needs of each student. *Representation* involves presenting information in multiple ways, such as through visuals, audio, and text to accommodate diverse learning preferences. *Action and Expression* refer to providing multiple options for students to demonstrate their understanding and skills, such as through written or oral communication, projects, or multimedia presentations. By providing multiple means of representation, expression, and engagement, UDL can create a more inclusive and effective learning environment for all students.

The graphic below presents an outline of the three tenets of the Universal Design for Learning Guidelines and further classifies each tenet as "Why, What, and How."

.

Affective Networks
The "WHY" of learning

ENGAGEMENT

Various factors such as neurology, culture, and background knowledge influence this engagement. Some learners prefer spontaneity and novelty, while others prefer routine. There is no single optimal means of engagement for all learners; providing multiple options is crucial.

- Recruiting Interest
- Sustaining Effort and Persistence
- Self Regulation

Recognition Networks
The "WHAT" of learning

REPRESENTATION

Offering options for to account for disabilities, cultural or language differences, and preferred learning modes. Multiple representations facilitate learning and transfer of knowledge within and between concepts.

- Perception
- Language and Symbols
- Comprehension

Strategic Networks
The "HOW" of learning

ACTION AND EXPRESSION

Learners vary in their abilities to navigate a learning environment and communicate knowledge, particularly those with disabilities such as movement impairments, executive function disorders, or language barriers.

- Physical Action
- Expression and Communication
- Executive Functions

CAST (2018). Universal Design for Learning Guidelines version 2.2. Retrieved from http://udlguidelines.cast.org

How Can AI and UDL Work Together?

The AI revolution has brought about advancements that have opened up new possibilities to support UDL principles when designing lessons. AI-powered tools help educators personalize instruction for each student by analyzing their learning needs, preferences, and progress, and suggesting tailored interventions. This integration of UDL and AI can lead to more inclusive and effective teaching practices and can ultimately improve learning outcomes for all students. With the assistance of AI in creating universally designed curriculum, we can break down the barriers to learning that exist to empower each student. While UDL does not rely on technology or artificial intelligence, integrating AI to support students creates opportunities for students to accelerate their learning and scaffold them to succeed academically. Together, UDL and AI can create independent learners by giving them the tools they need to succeed.

In the hit HBO series *Westworld*, the android hosts are able to learn and adapt to their surroundings to become more intelligent and human-like over time. This is made possible through the use of advanced artificial intelligence algorithms that allow the hosts to process and analyze vast amounts of data. Similarly, AI-powered tools can help students learn and adapt to their individual needs and preferences, becoming more independent and successful over time. By leveraging the power of AI to create personalized learning experiences, we can help to ensure that every student has access to the resources and support they need to thrive just like the hosts in *Westworld* are able to evolve and grow through the use of advanced AI technology.

In the next three sections, we are going to break down each tenet of UDL and look at specific tools and strategies to help learners succeed.

Engaging Students With AI

Teachers can leverage artificial intelligence to help personalize the learning experience. This engages learners according to their individual needs. The first tenet of UDL involves recruiting the interest of the learner while taking into account their cultural backgrounds, interests, and unique traits. A machine learning algorithm, for example, can identify patterns and preferences in a student's learning style, interests, and motivation by analyzing their past behaviors and performances. Based on this analysis, the AI system adapts the learning materials and activities to better align with the learner's preferred approach, increasing their engagement and motivation. Natural language processing algorithms can also be used to understand the language and tone used by learners in their interactions with the system and with each other, providing insights into their affective states and allowing for timely interventions to provide support or additional resources as needed. By leveraging AI tools in education, teachers offer a range of options for engagement that cater to the unique needs and preferences of each learner, helping to optimize their learning experience and outcomes.

There are several AI platforms that adapt learning materials to the needs and preferences of individual learners.

Some examples include:

 Knewton: This AI platform uses adaptive learning algorithms to personalize the content and difficulty level of educational materials based on the learner's performance and progress.

 Carnegie Learning: This platform uses AI algorithms to provide personalized learning paths for each student based on their strengths, weaknesses, and interests.

DreamBox Learning: This AI platform uses machine learning algorithms to adapt the content and difficulty of math lessons to each student's skill level and learning pace.

ALEKS: This adaptive learning platform by McGraw Hill uses artificial intelligence algorithms to deliver personalized learning experiences in mathematics, chemistry, and other subjects.

Smart Sparrow: This AI platform allows educators to create and deliver adaptive learning experiences that adjust to each student's needs and preferences, providing personalized feedback and support.

Representation and AI

Artificial intelligence tools offer various solutions to support diverse learners, particularly with regard to UDL representation. Text-to-speech and speech-to-text tools powered by AI can convert text to spoken words or vice versa to assist students who struggle with reading or writing. AI-powered language translation tools also help students who speak different languages to access information in their preferred language. Canva just integrated a translation tool in their platform that can assist in converting text into the student's native language. This is a game changer for making resources more accessible and representative of the students in our classrooms. Moreover, AI-powered image and video recognition tools provide alternative descriptions of images and videos, catering to students with visual impairments, autism, or attention difficulties.

AI tools also address the diverse needs of learners in terms of how they perceive and comprehend instructional materials. For example, captioning tools that automatically generate accurate captions for video content can assist students with hearing impairments. The Chrome extension YouTube Summarized is designed to support UDL guidelines by providing users with a summarized version of a YouTube video. This extension uses machine learning algorithms to analyze the audio of a video and generate a transcript of its content. The summary is then displayed alongside the video, allowing users to quickly determine if the video is relevant to their needs.

AI-powered tools can also create alternative formats of written material, such as audio or visual aids, to help learners with dyslexia or other learning disabilities. Using an AI summarizer tool like Wordtune (another Chrome extension) can be beneficial in chunking large bodies of text into bite-size summaries. Additionally, Wordtune integrates with other platforms like Canva. Within a Canva document, students can use Wordtune to highlight text and rewrite it for them. They can also use the tone feature to change the writing to reflect a more positive or formal one and shorten or lengthen the passage. Freemium users get access to 10 rewrites per day, but this can be extended to unlimited with the paid version.

Example of Wordtune in Action

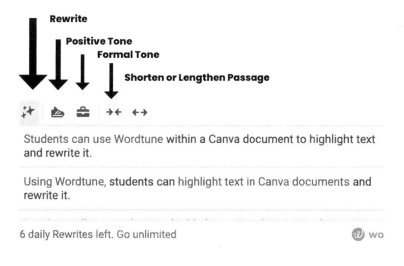

Rewrite

Positive Tone

Formal Tone

Shorten or Lengthen Passage

Students can use Wordtune within a Canva document to highlight text and rewrite it.

Using Wordtune, students can highlight text in Canva documents and rewrite it.

6 daily Rewrites left. Go unlimited

Chrome Extension Example: Bullet Point Summaries for Chunking Info

Summary   Notes

ChatGPT, Artificial Intelligence, and UDL: How to Harness the Future to Reach All Students

By Jeff Horwitz

- When planning a 10-year-old's birthday party, you want it to be fun, entertaining, and a bit unique. The new AI feature in ChatGPT can come up with creative ideas for you.

- This response stunned me because I used to think that human beings cornered the market on creativity. But ChatGPT did not 'create' these answers, it researched and curated them much faster than any human could.

- Open AI recently released two incredible artificial intelligence tools, Chat GPT and InstructGPT. These tools can benefit our students and be harnessed much in the way we harnessed the power of graphing calculators in years past.

What is Chat GPT?

- Open AI has released two products that will have a profound impact on the lives of our students.

Wisdolia is another Chrome extension that uses GPT technology to generate flashcards from articles to improve retention. The platform includes a flashcard feature that allows users to create custom flashcards, which can be used to practice vocabulary, grammar, and other language skills. The platform also includes features such as quizzes, games, and multimedia resources to help users practice and reinforce their language skills.

In addition to the flashcard feature, Wisdolia also provides tools for teachers to create and manage lesson plans, assessments, and student performance tracking. The platform supports multiple languages and is designed to be flexible and customizable to meet the specific needs of language learners and educators.

Regarding UDL representation, Wisdolia offers a range of resources in multiple languages, as well as tools to support customization and personalization of the learning experience. This can help to ensure that learners have access to the content they need in a format that is most suitable for them, regardless of their learning style, background, or abilities.

Example of Wisdolia in Action

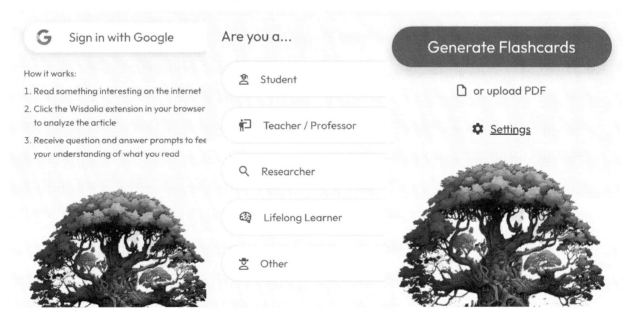

Once flashcards are generated, students review them within the extension on the website to test their knowledge. Flashcards can be exported by emailing a copy to yourself, or you can set up and connect Anki, a tool that stores flashcards for revisiting for further practice. For quick access to Wisdolia, you can go to the settings button and opt to embed a "generate flashcards" button on websites that contain articles.

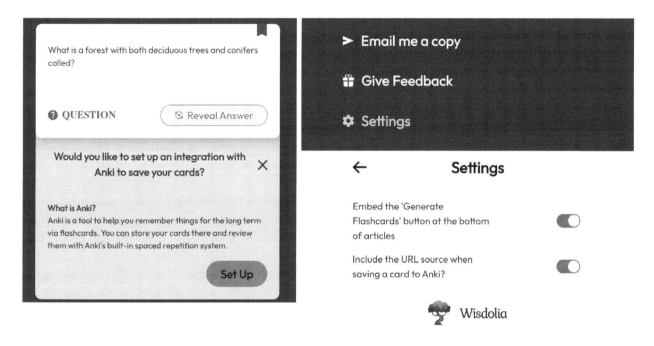

Another innovative use of AI to meet UDL representation needs is HandTalk, a Brazilian start-up that has developed a mobile app and a website that helps to translate English, Portuguese, and Brazilian Sign Language (Libras) into written and spoken language. The app uses artificial intelligence and machine learning to interpret sign language gestures and convert them into written or spoken language, allowing deaf and hard-of-hearing individuals to communicate more easily with those who don't know sign language. HandTalk's technology has won numerous awards and recognition, and it has been used in a variety of settings, including schools, hospitals, and government offices to facilitate communication between deaf and hearing individuals.

The HandTalk platform is available as an app and a web plugin, making ASL accessible at the touch of a button. Users can customize their avatars, backgrounds, and speed. There are two options to convert text to ASL; text to ASL, or speech to ASL. Creating screencasts of the videos and adding them as instructions in work, or just making feedback videos can add a level of multimodal communication to reach this population of students.

Example of HandTalk in Action

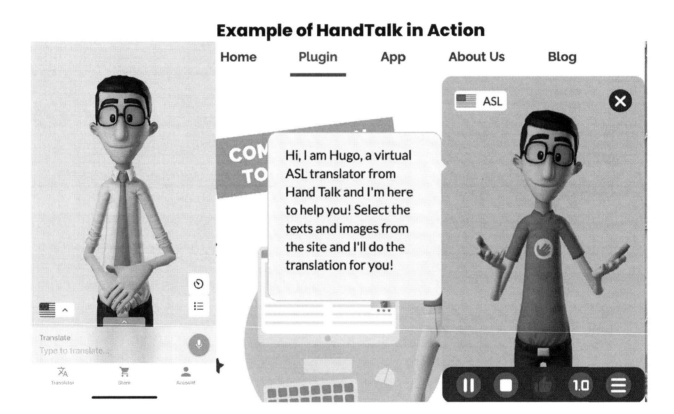

Scan the QR code to watch a video tutorial on how to use the HandTalk app.

By offering multiple representations through AI-powered tools, learners can make connections and transfer their knowledge between concepts more easily. In short, AI-based options for representation are essential in supporting diverse learners and can provide personalized and accessible learning, thus scaffolding students in achieving their learning goals.

Some other specific AI platforms and tools that can assist with UDL representation include:

 Google Cloud Text-to-Speech and Speech-to-Text: These tools can convert text into spoken words or vice versa, assisting students who struggle with reading or writing.

 Deep Language Translation: This AI-powered language translation tool can help students who speak different languages to access information in their preferred language.

 Microsoft Seeing AI: This app utilizes AI-powered image and video recognition tools to provide alternative descriptions of images and videos for students with visual impairments, autism, or attention difficulties.

 CaptionSync: This platform can automatically generate accurate captions for video content to assist students with hearing impairments.

 Read&Write: This software creates alternative formats of written material, such as audio or visual aids, for learners with dyslexia or other learning disabilities.

 **Rev.ai:** This software allows users to convert audio and video files into written text quickly and accurately through automatic speech recognition and transcription. In addition to real-time transcription and captioning, it offers a customizable API for developers.

Overall, these AI tools provide personalized and accessible learning, enabling diverse learners to achieve their learning goals.

The following graphic is comprised of ten more tools that teachers and students can leverage to achieve UDL representation when considering lesson design. Scan the QR code below to explore an interactive Genially that unpacks each tool in depth.

10 Artificial Intelligence Tools to Leverage UDL Representation Guidelines

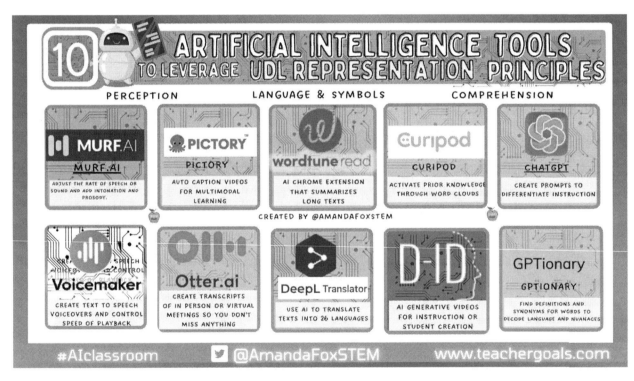

Scan the QR code to launch an interactive version of the above graphic.

AI in Action: Assisting Students in Action and Expression

AI tools greatly benefit learners who struggle with action and expression in the classroom. For example, individuals with cerebral palsy may benefit from using AI-powered assistive technology such as eye-tracking software or voice-activated devices to navigate learning environments and express their knowledge. Similarly, students with executive function disorders may use AI-powered tools such as organizational apps and digital assistants to help them stay on track and manage their assignments. Language barriers can also be overcome with the help of AI-powered translation tools that allow students to express themselves in their native language. By providing multiple means of action and expression through AI-powered tools, educators can create a more inclusive and effective learning environment for all students.

Here is a list of some tools that can assist students who struggle with action and expression:

Tobii Dynavox: This platform provides eye-tracking technology that can be used as an alternative to a mouse or keyboard. It allows users to control their devices using eye movements, which can be beneficial for individuals with mobility impairments.

Google Assistant: a voice-activated virtual assistant that can perform tasks, answer questions, and control smart devices.

Amazon Alexa: another voice-activated virtual assistant that can perform similar tasks as Google Assistant.

EyeTech: a range of eye-tracking devices that can be used to control computers and other devices using eye gaze.

Windows 10 Eye Control: an eye-tracking feature built into Windows 10 that enables users to control their computer using eye gaze.

 Dragon NaturallySpeaking: a voice-activated software that allows users to control their computer and dictate text using their voice.

These are just a few examples of AI tools that use eye-tracking software and voice-activated technology to support users with different needs.

Resistance is Futile

"Resistance is futile," is a famous line from a cybernetic species on *Star Trek* who were focused on assimilating technologies of civilizations into their own collective by force. We are not trying to take over a civilization, but we are at a point where resisting the tidal wave of change that is already upon us is, indeed, a futile act. Don't let your fears of a *Terminator* scenario hold you back from exploring the benefits of AI tools and devices. Instead, take a cue from Tony Stark in *Iron Man* and let AI be your trusty sidekick, helping to enhance the educational experience for all students. While there may be concerns about the impact of AI on the role of human teachers, such as the possibility of job displacement, let's look to movies like *Ex Machina,* where the human and AI relationship can complement each other instead of being in competition. As we've seen in *Her*, AI can even offer a personalized touch to learning, adapting to each individual student's needs and preferences.

CALL TO ACTION

1. Scan the QR code to join our members section and get our UDL and AI graphics to share with your colleagues and faculty.

WWW.TEACHERGOALS.COM/AI-CLASSROOM-MEMBERSHIP

SCAN ME

2. Hop over to your favorite social media site and share any AI tools you are using to meet UDL guidelines. Share your favorite tool from the section with your PLN and use the hashtag #AIClassroom!

(You can connect with other like-minded teachers who are using that hashtag too!) The team and I are eager to cheer you on.

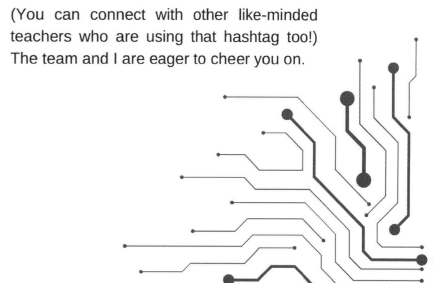

PART THREE

THE AI TOOL REPOSITORY

CHAPTER 9

AI Tools You Can Use in the Classroom Right Now

Growing Up and Teaching During the AI Revolution

Our children are constantly being influenced by algorithms in their daily lives. The videos they watch, the route they take to school, the songs they listen to, and even the advice they receive from personal assistants like Siri and Alexa are all determined by artificial intelligence algorithms. My sons frequently view gaming videos on YouTube, unaware that their list of recommended videos is generated by AI based on their viewing history. My five-year-old hasn't learned how to spell yet, so he uses speech-to-text on his iPod to send me messages throughout the day. They constantly ask Alexa how many days until their next birthday. They are growing up during the artificial intelligence revolution and have access to tools I never dreamed of. However, this passive engagement with AI leads to an endless cycle of consumption. There are plenty of AI tools that exist that we could be using to assist students in creating content.

Instead of letting AI control their experiences, teachers, parents, and guardians should empower kids by teaching them how to work with powerful technologies like machine learning and neural networks. The best workers of tomorrow will be those who are comfortable using technology to enhance their creativity, flexibility, and problem-solving skills. It's important for kids to understand that AI is not just a passive part of their lives but a tool that can be used to solve problems, create content, and achieve learning goals. We can encourage these skills by fostering a sense of play and experimentation with AI, machine learning, and algorithmic tools. This will help them become capable of not only working alongside AI in the future workplace that is increasingly shaped by technology but also help them envision new AI applications and new tools altogether.

Educational Applications for AI

Historically, the education sector has been slow to adopt new technology for a plethora of reasons. As we have established in previous chapters, fear, resistance to change, lack of funding, lack of teacher training, privacy concerns, and lack of technological literacy are a few barriers to adoption, and it's no different as we are thrust into the AI revolution. States like New York have taken the ban approach and have blocked ChatGPT on a systemic level in their school systems stating that, "the decision to ban ChatGPT, which is able to generate conversational responses to text prompts, stemmed from concerns about the negative impacts on student learning." When surveying teachers on social media on whether AI should be banned in schools or used as a tool in instruction and construction of knowledge for student use, there was a clear divide in the answers. The general consensus was echoed on Twitter by Jethro Jones, principal, edtech leader, and podcaster, who stated, "Whether we teach kids or not, they're going to use it and learn how to use it." He extrapolated by stating "How about we start with teaching teachers and educators how to use it?"

Similarly to how our children are passively using AI, teachers use AI and/or machine learning-powered tools sometimes without realizing it.

Until ChatGPT came on the scene, AI took an almost invisible but accepted and utilized place in our daily routines to assist in tasks, grading, and even assessments. The predictive text in an email or Google Doc, the adaptive assessment we just assigned to measure benchmarks, the spell check we used when creating resources are just a few examples. And in our personal lives, cars that self-park, Amazon shopping recommendations, or using the Clear facial recognition service when traveling to expedite getting through security lines. I personally love Clear, because who likes standing in line? AI has been at play for some time, and now is the time to get more intentional with our use cases in education.

In this section of the book, I am going to cover some amazing AI tools that can be used in the classroom to personalize learning, create universal accessibility, and bridge the ever-widening disparity that exists in providing students with equal access and opportunities to learn and prepare for the digital age. ChatGPT explains:

> *While [it] has the potential to exacerbate existing inequities, particularly those related to the digital divide, it also offers opportunities to address some of them. For example, for students who struggle with writing or for whom English is a second language, ChatGPT can help reduce misspellings and improve communication.*

While biases in AI do exist, as unpacked in previous chapters, this chapter will highlight some of the positive applications and impacts through tools and how they can be used.

This section functions as a repository, or curation, of AI tools we find valuable. Some tools are for teacher use, while others empower students to assist in reaching standard mastery. For each tool, I have provided a description of the platform, how it works, and several educational applications to get you started with integrating the tool into your classroom. When possible, I have also included a link to the company's user and/or privacy policies for your reference and due diligence. I have also tagged each tool with an icon that visually represents what type of generative AI is being used: text-to-image, text-to-text, text-to-code, etc. Additionally, I have provided you with several ideas on how to integrate that tool into your classroom. I hope that it gets your wheels spinning on other use cases.

We have also gathered some amazing use cases from educators in the field to share what is already being done to harness AI in the educational context. Some of these tools you may already be using but weren't aware that AI is the underlying technology behind it. Other tools you may be hearing about for the first time. The AI landscape is moving at a fast and furious pace, and as I compile this section, I know without a doubt it will be dated quickly. Regardless, we hope you leave this chapter with a new outlook and a few new strategies and ideas on how to utilize AI in your classroom and curriculum.

A Visual Guide to Understanding Each Tool

There are many different types of generative AI. We have decided to visually represent these with the icons below, which are also found in Chapter 5. I have added a few icons specifically for the context of education to also reflect the context in which artificial intelligence is being used: AI Education Platform, AI Research Assistant, and AI Summarizers. Each tool is labeled with icons to show the type of generative AI being used in order to help you decide if it's the right tool for the job. Additionally, I have tagged each platform with an age to signal what tools are appropriate for your specific educational context. In each section, we highlight a favorite tool, which we consider one of the best for education in each category. This doesn't necessarily mean that the performance is better but that it has a broader appeal in the classroom context due to multiple variables, including accessibility, features, age restrictions, and cost.

Usage Tags

All Ages

13 and up

Teacher Use

Costs

Favorite Tool Ribbon

16 Types of Generative AI : Visual Icons

As we introduce new tools in our Generative AI Repository (GAIR), look for these icon tags to help visually understand the type of AI features it is capable of. Some tools only serve one function, while others possess multiple functions. There are way more than 16 types, but these are the ones we will focus on. On the next page, you can view the master list of platforms we include.

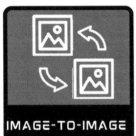

Educational Platforms	**Curipod, Canva, Conker, Prof Jim, Eduade.Ai, MagicSchool.Ai**
Text-to-Text	**Bedtime Story Ai, Imagine Forest**
AI Paraphrasing Tools	**Quillbot, Wordtune, Moonbeam**
AI Research Assistant	**Elicit**
Text-to-Image	**Midjourney, Adobe Firefly, Dall-E 2, Thispersondoesnotexist, Padlet, Artbreeder**
Draw-to-Image	**Scribble Diffusion, Quick, Draw!**
Image-to-Image	**Artie, Petallica Paint**
Text-to-Video	**D-ID, Pictory**
Image-to-Text	**Clip Interrogator**
AI Chatbots	**Hello History, Character.Ai**
Text-to-Audio	**Murf.Ai, Voicemaker**
Audio-to-Text	**Otter.ai**
Text-to-3D	**Blockade Labs**
Text-to-Code	**ChatGPT**
Image-to-Video	**Sketchmeta Demo Lab**

AI EDUCATION PLATFORMS

AI EDUCATION PLATFORM

Educational AI platforms are tools for teachers to use to improve the learning experience for their students. This section will focus on artificial intelligence platforms that are designed and created specifically for teachers. This takes the stress and worries about data collection, vetting tools for privacy concerns, and efficacy because they are designed for the classroom context. You can expect to see examples of how to create lessons, projects, assessments, and presentations, all generated by AI.

In a traditional classroom setting, it can be challenging for teachers to provide individualized attention and instruction to every student. This is particularly true in larger classrooms where teachers may have to juggle the needs of many students simultaneously. However, with the use of educational AI platforms, it is possible to create personalized lessons quickly and easily. Lessons can be adapted based on student feedback and progress by simply changing the prompt to consider learning gaps, reading levels, and personalization needed for every student's success.

For instance, imagine a classroom with 25 students, where 10 students are struggling with a particular topic. By using educational AI platforms, teachers can quickly create multiple variations of a lesson on one topic that are tailored to the needs of each of the 10 struggling students. With the ability to create a personalized lesson in just one minute, a teacher can provide targeted interventions to these students without sacrificing instructional time to create multiple variations that meet the needs of each student.

Why Should Teachers Use Educational AI Platforms?

There are several benefits to using educational AI platforms in teaching and learning, including:

- **Personalization:** AI-powered platforms can provide personalized learning experiences tailored to the needs and learning styles of individual students.
- **Automation:** Educational AI platforms can automate routine tasks such as grading and assessment, freeing up teachers to focus on more meaningful instructional activities.
- **Real-time feedback:** AI algorithms can provide real-time feedback to students, enabling them to identify and address areas where they need improvement.
- **Enhanced engagement:** AI-powered platforms can provide interactive and engaging learning experiences that motivate and engage students.

This section will discuss the advantages of using AI platforms for lesson design and provide a list of other AI-based educational platforms that can be used for lesson creation and delivery.

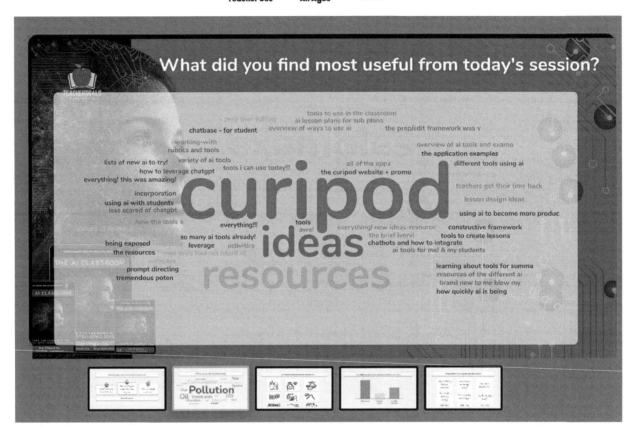

What Is It?

This is our AI educational platform winner for the category! Like Pear Deck and Nearpod, Curipod enables students to participate using their own devices by drawing, answering polls, and responding to open-ended questions. However, what sets Curipod apart from other presentation tools is that it can generate an interactive slideshow for you based on your lesson focus and learning objectives. Additionally, Curipod has a unique feature where it creates a Word Cloud based on student responses, which is a different type of interaction compared to other similar tools.

How to Use Curipod in Your Classroom

Curipod can be used to create bite-sized lessons that makes content easy to digest for students. Activities come in the form of check-ins, lesson hooks, and polls. These lessons can be completed in as little as 5 minutes, making it easy for learners to fit learning into their busy schedules. The platform also offers the option to create formative assessments in the form of interactive quizzes, polls, and discussion questions that allow learners to test their knowledge and reinforce what they have learned. Curipod provides learners with feedback on their performance and tracks their progress over time, helping them to identify areas where they need to focus more attention.

Teachers can choose to build out a full lesson or project or start from blank. Once you have generated a lesson, as the editor, you have the ability to modify headings, titles, and certain media elements, and you can also insert your own slides and import PowerPoint or PDFs. The platform also has a lesson library that curates Curipods made by other educators.

Curipod Dashboard   **Lesson Options**   **Interactive Elements**

Curipod's Lesson Library

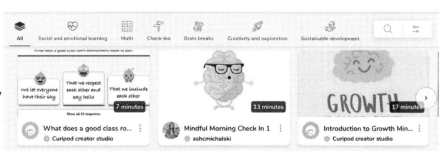

Highlighted Features

The interactive assessment features in Curipod are fantastic for student engagement. To create an activity, click "create lesson" and choose from ten options. Here are some of the highlighted options and features you can add to your lesson.

Polling

The polling feature in Curipod is a tool that allows teachers to pose questions to their students during a presentation and receive instant responses. Teachers can create multiple-choice, true/false, or open-ended questions and send them to students' devices. Students can then respond to the questions in real-time, and the teacher can see the results displayed on their own device. This feature can be used to assess student understanding, gather feedback, or promote class participation.

Instant Feedback

The instant feedback feature in Curipod provides AI feedback to students. Currently, teachers select either writing or comprehension and set the parameters for the answers. For example, "should contain a metaphor." Once students submit their answers, they receive immediate feedback on whether their content was correct with justification.

Word Cloud

The word cloud feature in Curipod is a visual representation of a set of words, where the size of each word is proportional to its frequency or importance. The words are arranged in random order and are often displayed in different colors or fonts to make the cloud more visually appealing. Word clouds can be useful for quickly identifying the main themes or ideas. They can help promote vocabulary development or encourage students to think about the most important concepts or ideas in a given text or lesson.

Open Question

The real-time open question feature in Curipod allows teachers to facilitate questioning tactics and understand where students are on skills and concepts. It can be an effective tool for students to communicate their learning and enhance their understanding of the material. It fosters active engagement and critical thinking while providing students with immediate feedback and access to a supportive learning community.

Slide Deck

The presentation generator in Curipod assists teachers create slide decks on educational topics and standards. Teachers put in their topic, standards, grade level, and learning objectives and let Curipod magically generate a presentation. As the editor, the teacher can customize the slide content, images, and activities that are present in the lesson.

Drawing

The drawing feature in Curipod is a tool that allows teachers and students to draw, annotate, and highlight over a slide in a lesson. It is a versatile tool that can be used for a variety of purposes, such as brainstorming, problem-solving, and collaborative note-taking. Use cases include highlighting important information on a slide, drawing diagrams or illustrations to help explain a concept, and annotating a text or image.

CASE STUDY

A CURIPOD CASE STUDY BY AILEEN WALLACE

Teacher of Modern Studies
Graeme High School
Falkirk, Scotland

Before I can explain to you the metamorphosis that has occurred in my teaching as a result of Curipod, I need to introduce you to a couple of people. First of all, please welcome the Spring of 2020 version of me. There I am, like so many teachers, staring at my computer screen at home, trying to work out how the hell to make online teaching work. Microsoft Teams have become the bane of my life, and I regularly swing from tears to tantrums with a speed that a three-year-old would be proud of. Next comes the version of me in October of 2021 when students in the council where I work were given iPads. I complained vehemently to anyone within earshot, and sometimes that involved following them for quite some distance about what a waste of money they were and how they just got in the way of teaching. So that's those two, now here I am in March of 2023, and I am once again chasing people down, but this time to extol the wonders of AI and how they, too, could once again enjoy their work if they just used this new thing I had found from these amazing and joyously mental Norwegians. Ladies and gentlemen, I give you Curipod.

In all seriousness though, this is a game-changer for me. My subject is Modern Studies, which covers everything from politics to crime & social inequalities to China & the USA, which means regular lesson updates. The ability to create a new lesson in a matter of minutes or to update an old one has saved me so much time and stress. I am currently creating revision decks for my students who are about to sit their National 5 exams. I would not normally do this but instead revisit the original materials as the time it would take to put the deck together would far outstrip the time the lesson took, but with Curipod, I can do it in under 30 minutes. The First Minister of Scotland announces her resignation, and I have a lesson up and running, ready for the class coming in later that morning. The time saved, and the improvement in my lesson materials is tangible. Upload an existing deck and add some Curipod magic, and there you go folks, a brand-new lesson in less time than it takes for your hot beverage of choice to go cold.

For the past few years, I have been trying to use SOLO taxonomy to help students gauge their own progress without relying on assessments or feedback from me. I have struggled to find a way to quickly collate their responses and let them see, in real-time, their own progress. I have used fingers in the air, but students are too self-conscious to be seen to think they are doing well. Everyone would go for the lower levels or go with whatever their friends chose. I tried making little cards that were attached to a key chain so they could place them on their desk, and I could go around and check them without the students having to say anything, but they kept losing them. With Curipod, I have a slide with a poll on it, and in 10 seconds, I can have 30 students telling me what level they feel they are at. They have the confidence to do it honestly as it is done anonymously. We can have a chat about what level the whole class is at, and I can take the results into account as I go through the lesson. At the end of the lesson, I put the slide back up, and 10 seconds later, we can all see the progress that has been made, and I can see if I need to do a revision session or if the students feel secure enough for us to move on. I have now been able to embed SOLO taxonomy in all of my lessons, and students will be able to see their own progress as we move through a single lesson or a unit or an entire examination course.

The option to have students give extended answers has changed my understanding of my students' understanding. I can see their answers coming in via the moderation tool, and it gives me a much stronger grasp of who knows what, what areas I can move on from, and where I may need to circle back to within that lesson. Students who are uncomfortable speaking out in class, and no matter how safe you try to make your classroom feel, there will always be one, are giving me detailed answers that are way beyond what I thought they had taken in from the lesson. This helps me feel more secure when it comes to feedback and report cards as I am no longer overly reliant on summative assessment but can see their progress in real-time.

The past couple of weeks, I have been trialing the AI instant feedback with classes. This is very much a learning curve for me as I am still getting to grips with how AI works and how to get the best out of it, but the results so far seem really positive. Students are loving getting to use AI in the classroom as it is still new and shiny to them, and I am actually able to get feedback from a class of 30 in less than a week. For me, personally, the fact this element of the Curipod journey is one my classes and I are taking together is what is making it really enjoyable. They see me learning something new at the same time they are, and that learning does not stop when you leave school. I am not very good at hiding how I feel, so there I am, bouncing around the room, going on about how excited I feel about this and, I hope, taking my students along with me. Okay, perhaps that is my Blind Poets Society moment (which is also VERY out of character for me), but you can't deny that if a class sees their teacher enthusiastic for a lesson, it rubs off on them. Even if the AI has had a wobble and the feedback has become more generic, it becomes a useful tool as I can get the students to tell me why they feel the feedback was wrong and what they would have told themselves. The more I use it, the more I understand it and can fine-tune it to help the AI give the best feedback it can. The more students use it, the more they are looking at their answers and working out why they were given that feedback and what they can do to improve their answers. I am a big believer in students being able to mark their own work to help them improve, and the AI instant feedback is fast becoming a foundational tool to help me achieve that.

My school is a comprehensive school with a huge range of students from diverse backgrounds and family situations, so there is always a challenging student or two in a class. You may even get an entire class of challenging students if you are really unlucky or have upset the person who creates the timetable. Now, I am not suggesting for a minute that Curipod is a panacea for behavioral problems in the classroom but for increasing engagement, it is pretty darned impressive. I have seen classes with well-known "characters" settling to a brain break or working together to see how fast the whole class can get to 100 responses or compliment each other on their work when they see it up on the screen. I have two S3 classes, and I have been using them as guinea pigs as they are still a year away from exams, so we have a little time to try new things and I asked them if they would get fed up if we used Curipod all the time. They have been known to suffer from Blooket or Quizlet exhaustion, but no, Curipod could be every lesson they cried. Who can argue with that?

In conclusion, I am a teacher of 15 years who, until recently, has delved no more deeply into tech in the classroom than the use of Blooket and putting class materials up on Teams, and here I am, encouraging colleagues to come in and see Curipod in action. I have volunteered (You heard me! Volunteered!) to lead CPD sessions for colleagues when I would normally have had a small heart attack at the very thought of it. To top it all off, I am spending time in the evening sitting and playing (yes playing!!) on my iPad to see how many new lessons I can create and what new features have been added that week. When was the last time planning a lesson felt like fun? When you looked forward to showing students something new and taking them on a learning journey with you? Who would have thought that AI would be the thing that helped me tie together all those strategies I have been struggling to make work in my classroom for years? What have you got to lose? Psst...it won't be your job!

for Education
https://www.canva.com/education/

AI EDUCATION PLATFORM — **TEXT-TO-TEXT** — **TEXT-TO-IMAGES** — **Teacher Use** — **All Ages** — **FREE**

Discover a magical new era

You might want to try...

Doc — Whiteboard — Invitation — A4 Document — Infographic — Presentation (16:9) — Letterhead

Discover the magic from Canva Create

What Is It?

Canva for Education is quickly becoming a leader in the field of educational design platforms and comes equipped with a teacher dashboard that allows educators to set up a classroom, share assignments, and post those assignments to other LMS platforms. They are also becoming a leader in the field of AI, as they recently announced a plethora of AI "Magic" tools that they have added to their platform: Magic Presentations, Magic Write, Magic Edit and Erase, Text-to-Image, Translation Tools, and Beat Sync to name a few. Their ability to pivot and adapt in a world of innovation is impressive, to say the least. Let's look at the AI tools the platform recently announced on March 23, 2023 at their Canva Create Conference.

Canva "Magic" AI Features

Text-to-Image

The text-to-image tool allows you to create one-of-a-kind images with ease. If you're having trouble finding the perfect image, simply describe what you're looking for and let the magic happen. Text-to-image transforms your words into stunning professional photographs, lifelike 3D graphics, beautiful drawings, and much more. It's a tool that brings your imagination to life! Check out the case study on Funko Pops following this tool.

Magic Write

Magic Write is a writing tool that uses AI to assist and enhance the writing process, enabling users to effortlessly and rapidly create written content. Whether it's for social media posts, business plans, websites, blogs, poetry, journaling, creative writing, or other applications, Magic Write can be utilized for various purposes. By entering a text prompt, the tool can generate sentences, paragraphs, lists, outlines, and more, making the writing process easier and more efficient. It's not active on student accounts, but education admin and teachers have access to 250 Magic Write uses a month.

Magic Presentation

Magic Presentation lets you generate presentations with an outline, slides, and content. Simply describe your idea in a few words, and watch as it smartly fills out your content. This tool is great for getting you started and gives you multiple design options to pick from. You can add more details and give it a personal touch.

Magic Edit & Eraser

Magic Edit and Eraser allows you to easily remove distractions or add new things to your photos with a few clicks. You can even magically transform your photos by brushing over the areas you'd like to modify and then describing what you want to add using text. This is one of the coolest additions to Canva!

Translate

The Canva Translate feature allows you to effortlessly translate presentations, social media posts, and more using Translate. Choose from up to 100+ languages to translate your designs! It is important to note that Translate is available for all templates except Canva docs. It also doesn't work with all fonts, so if you find it's not translating, try choosing another font and try again.

A CANVA TEXT-TO-IMAGE CASE STUDY BY DR. CHRIS LENSING

CASE STUDY

Superintendent
East Coloma-Nelson Elementary School
Rock Falls, Illinois

As a superintendent, I am excited to share a case study that highlights an innovative approach to engaging second-grade students in writing. At East Coloma-Nelson Elementary School, STEAM teacher Heather Brown collaborated with classroom teachers Katie Merrill and Rebecca Repass to introduce students to the revolutionary AI capabilities of Canva.

The students were tasked with writing persuasive paragraphs about their favorite book characters, a common assignment in elementary classrooms that covered multiple standards. However, Mrs. Brown saw an opportunity to take this assignment to the next level by incorporating Canva's text-to-image feature, which allowed students to create Funko Pop figurines resembling their characters using descriptive language. She was inspired by a project by Amanda Fox and couldn't pass up the opportunity to try it with elementary-aged students.

The use of AI technology to create Funko Pop figurines was a game-changer in this assignment. Students were required to write descriptive paragraphs about their favorite book characters, which were then used by Canva to generate unique and personalized figurines in the Funko style.

This process allowed students to not only hone their writing skills but also develop a deeper understanding of their characters. They were encouraged to think critically about the physical appearance and traits of their characters in order to accurately describe them in their written prompts. The AI-generated figurines were a source of excitement and motivation for the students who eagerly worked to refine their writing in order to get the most accurate and appealing representation of their characters.

The use of AI technology provided an opportunity for students to engage with emerging technologies and gain experience in creating and manipulating digital media. This not only enhanced their digital literacy skills but also opened up new avenues of exploration and creativity in their learning.

In conclusion, the use of AI technology to create Funko Pop figurines was a highly effective and innovative approach that not only heightened student engagement but also provided a unique learning opportunity. By incorporating emerging technologies into traditional assignments, educators can create dynamic and immersive learning experiences that prepare students for the demands of the 21st-century workforce.

SCAN THE QR CODE TO SEE STUDENT WORK SAMPLES

 # conker

Conker.ai

https://www.conker.ai/legal/terms

    Teacher Use **All Ages** FREE

What is it?

Conker is a free educational tool that allows educators to create interactive quizzes and activities, including fill-in-the-blank, true/false questions, and more, that cater to diverse learning needs. Users can select the type of activity they want to create, the number and type of questions, and the grade level from K-adult and provide a topic for Conker's algorithm to generate questions automatically.

Conker also allows educators to copy and paste their own source material to create engaging assessments that cater to their teaching content. The platform is an efficient and flexible tool that saves time, enabling educators to create effective assessments that cater to the learning needs of their students. While currently exportable only to Google Forms, Conker is planning to introduce new features, including exporting to PDF and sharing quizzes via links in the future.

To begin, I have ...

A topic idea   Reading material

Create a **Quiz** with 5 questions for **Grade 10** students about

e.g. Electromagnetism

Try an example

Historic events that happened on March 20   Electromagnetism   Sharecropping

Generate   Output language: English (US)

To begin, I have ...

A topic idea   Reading material

Quiz title

Enter a title

🔒 Quiz type   *More reading material quiz types coming soon!*

Multiple choice

Source material

Paste or type some text ...

How Can I Use It?

- **Generate interactive quizzes for a variety of subjects and topics, including reading comprehension, science, math, and more.**

- **Create formative assessments to check for understanding and identify areas where students need further support or review.**

- **Differentiate learning by creating quizzes that cater to different learning styles, skill levels, and interests.**

- **Enhance classroom discussions by creating activities that encourage critical thinking, analysis, and reflection.**

Prof Jim
profjim.com

What Is It?

Prof Jim has developed a pioneering technology that revolutionizes the way textbooks and other text-based learning content are transformed into dynamic and immersive courses. By utilizing cutting-edge AI algorithms, Prof Jim's platform automatically generates assessments and life-like avatars that enhance the learning experience, resulting in a more engaging and interactive course than traditional educational videos.

The company is launching an educator-facing AI generative lesson platform with talking avatars that will empower teachers to create more captivating virtual lessons. The platform has the capacity to pull in interactive 3D models into presentations and create entire lessons with minimal prompting at the click of a button. At the time of publishing this book the BETA version has yet to launch, but it is something to be on the lookout for.

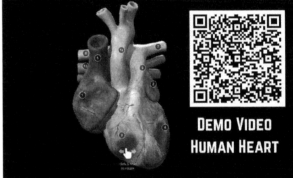

DEMO VIDEO
HUMAN HEART

How Can I Use It?

- **Create AI generative lessons with talking video avatars.**

- **Embed interactive 3D models to teach concept skills or anatomy like the human heart.**

- **Flip your classroom and create self-paced curriculum by having students watch the videos out of class.**

- **Teach coding and HTML with their preexisting lesson library.**

EDUAIDE.Ai

https://www.eduaide.ai/

AI EDUCATION PLATFORM

TEXT-TO-TEXT

Teacher Use

All Ages

BETA

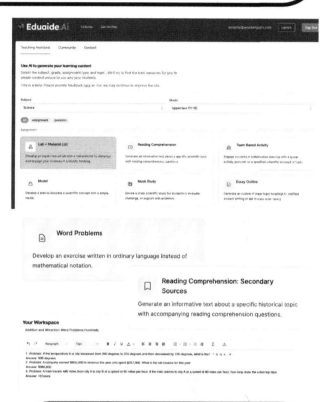

What Is It?

Eduaide.ai is an AI-powered learning platform designed for teachers and students. Its main goal is to make teaching and learning more efficient and effective by providing personalized learning experiences for students.

One of the key features of Eduaide.ai is its ability to generate lessons and activities based on topic and grade level. Teachers can also analyze student learning data in real-time, providing them with insights into each student's progress and areas of weakness.

In addition, Eduaide.ai also offers a range of interactive learning tools, such as virtual labs, quizzes, and simulations, that help engage students and reinforce their understanding of concepts. These tools can be easily integrated into lesson plans, making it easier for teachers to provide hands-on learning experiences for their students.

How Can I Use It?

- **Create Reading Comprehension questions for secondary sources.**

- **Generate math problems to test students understanding.**

- **Engage students in collaborative learning with a group activity protocol on a specified historical topic.**

- **Generate multiple-choice questions, discussion prompts, and source analysis questions.**

- **Track student progress toward mastery with a hierarchy of essential questions.**

 # MAGIC SCHOOL.Ai

www.magicschool.ai

 AI EDUCATION PLATFORM
 TEXT-TO-TEXT
 Teacher Use
 All Ages
 FREE MIUM

What is it?

MagicSchool.ai is an advanced AI-driven platform that simplifies and enhances the teaching process. Designed for ease of use, it enables educators to effortlessly integrate AI into their daily routines for lesson planning, instruction differentiation, and IEP writing.

The platform offers customizable tools to create unique, student-centered learning materials. It also features tools for generating quizzes, managing assignments, and adapting content for different reading levels.

Tailored for educators, administrators, counselors, and beyond, this platform is a game-changer, offering a holistic approach to elevate every aspect of the school experience. Save time, enhance classroom engagement, achieve better learning outcomes, boost staff morale, and experience an overall enriched educational environment. MagicSchool.ai is your ally in creating a school experience that goes beyond efficiency to positively impact every facet of school life.

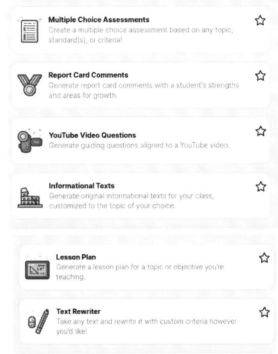

Multiple Choice Assessments
Create a multiple choice assessment based on any topic, standard(s), or criteria!

Report Card Comments
Generate report card comments with a student's strengths and areas for growth.

YouTube Video Questions
Generate guiding questions aligned to a YouTube video.

Informational Texts
Generate original informational texts for your class, customized to the topic of your choice.

Lesson Plan
Generate a lesson plan for a topic or objective you're teaching.

Text Rewriter
Take any text and rewrite it with custom criteria however you'd like!

How Can I Use It?

- **Create engaging and customized lesson plans quickly for various subjects, ensuring they meet specific teaching objectives and student needs.**

- **Enhance classroom materials by adapting content to suit different reading and comprehension levels, ensuring accessibility for all students.**

- **Streamline communication with students and families by crafting professional and clear newsletters, emails, and other communications.**

TEXT-TO-TEXT

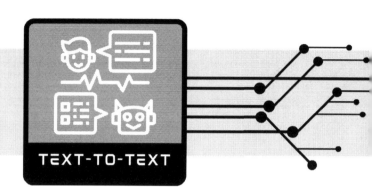

TEXT-TO-TEXT

We have covered GPT technology extensively throughout the book, but as a reminder, text-to-text (T2T) generative AI platforms are machine learning tools that use artificial intelligence algorithms to generate new pieces of text based on text input by a user. These platforms work by analyzing large datasets of text, learning patterns and structures, and generating new text that mimics the style and tone of the input text.

While ChatGPT is one of our favorite tools, we are dedicating this section to tools we have yet explored that are classroom and teacher-friendly, some of which you may already have access to! To summarize some of the benefits covered in previous chapters, text-to-text platforms can be used to analyze standards and break down the complexity and rigor required of students, personalize learning by asking for lesson accommodations, and scaffolding to provide fast and efficient feedback on assignments, including checking for grammar, spelling, and syntax, and provide higher level feedback.

In this section, we will cover T2T apps you can use with your students to create stories and empower them in their creative writing endeavors. We also include subcategories of paraphrasing and summarizing tools, in addition to research assistant tools. New T2T tools can provide fresh insights and ideas, but they can also help you automate repetitive or monotonous tasks, freeing up more time for more creative and strategic work and, most importantly, building relationships with students.

MEET IZZY: THE PERSONALIZED AI MATHS TUTOR BY PHIL BIRCHENALL

CASE STUDY

Parent & Founder of Diagonal Thinking
Manchester, UK

So, there I was, trying to help my 11-year-old daughter, Daisy, prepare for her SATs exams. That's a tricky time for any young student, the first time they'll feel the pressure of a formal examination, at a moment where they're about to transition from the comfortable world of primary education into life at secondary school, with all of the expectations that come with that move.

Daisy's a bright kid: she takes after her mum. But, we'd been dealing with long-term illness at home, and she'd fallen behind in maths.

I wanted to step up to the mark and help. So we spent time pouring over example papers to see where she had weaknesses: long division, squared and cubed numbers, written multiplication, percentages, and dividing and adding fractions. From there, I planned to work with her on each subject area to bring her back up to the standard she should have been at by now. And I'm not a pushy parent, by the way!

We sat down to begin our revision sessions. That's when I realized the flaw in my plan. After watching my daughter attempt to solve the questions in her test paper, I heard my inner voice channel Mr. Incredible...

"Why would they change math!?"

I'd been dabbling with ChatGPT-3.5 out of professional curiosity and was already excited about how AI was finally set to 'have its moment' and achieve mass adoption. (I'm a business consultant working with creative and media companies, if you're interested.)

But this particular maths conundrum just so happened to arrive on the same day as ChatGPT-4. So now I had a real-life problem, rather than the random prompts I'd been throwing at the previous version and a perfect test for the latest update.

I dug around online to find out how I might create a virtual maths tutor. I figured that if we could train an AI with relevant information about our needs, it could just work. And boy, did it work.

Check out this video by Doug Cunnington (https://www.youtube.com/@DougCunnington) explaining how to train a chatbot to become a specialist personal trainer on any subject.

First, Doug demonstrates asking ChatGPT to generate its own prompts, using an 'act as' request. So, a quick dig around online yielded a list of prompts to help. Doug's prompt goes something like this:

"I want you to act as a prompt generator. So, first, I will give you a title like "Act as a Writing Coach and AI Writing Tutor."

Then you give me a prompt like this: "I want you to act as an AI writing tutor. I will provide you with a student who needs help improving their writing. Your task is to use artificial intelligence tools, such as natural language processing, to give students feedback on improving their composition. You should also use your rhetorical knowledge and experience with effective writing techniques to suggest ways for students to better express their thoughts and ideas in written form.

The prompt should be self-explanatory and appropriate to the title."

Now, from that prompt and a couple of similar ones I used in my training, I could ask ChatGPT-4 to write relevant prompts on any area of learning or development I needed.

With the AI capable of writing its own prompts in that style, I then typed this:

"I want you to act as a personalized Maths Tutor for a Key Stage 2 (UK) student preparing for her SATs."

Et voila, GPT4 wrote its own detailed prompt, which we pasted back into the chat, and the tutor was born.

Understandably, the virtual tutor wanted more context before getting started, so I provided Daisy's age and the areas where she struggled in maths. We already had the list of weaknesses from when I'd analyzed her test papers.

What I didn't want to do was to give Daisy a dry, boring experience so that learning felt like a chore. She's a bright kid with a love of language and a sharp sense of humor. Trust me, I've been on the receiving end of it enough times.

So, things had to be engaging.

I gave the AI this information, telling it that she likes a good pun, gag, or one-liner to keep her motivated.

I asked Daisy to give the tutor a name. "Izzy", she suggested. The AI didn't need to know this, but she loves dogs just as much as she loves a joke: Izzy is the name of our cocker spaniel puppy. They're as mad as each other.

With the virtual tutor responding to the name of a crazy dog, we gave Izzy a whirl. And what followed blew my mind.

Izzy introduced herself to Daisy and started the first session with this cracker of a gag:

"Why was the maths book sad? Because it had too many problems!"

..before launching into its first explanation of long division, one of the key areas of focus we'd identified needed improvement. And, just like that, Daisy was hooked by the perfect balance of learning and humor.

We could have taken things further. For example, I could have asked the tutor to always feature dogs when explaining how to tackle a particular problem. I could have told the tutor she was indeed a mad cocker spaniel. And you know what, I still might, but I figured we'd better press on with some actual learning; otherwise, the whole exercise was at risk of being somewhat self-defeating.

The sessions with 'Izzy' were scarily on point: they focused on Daisy's specific needs, targeting precise areas where she needed help. Izzy gave us clear explanations and step-by-step guidance, with the occasional well-placed quip. (Side note: ChatGPT isn't the best at generating its own jokes, but we appreciate the effort.)

Armed with a little bit of information and a lot of curiosity, I got my girl back on track with her maths.

My approach was a little ramshackle. I'd found information online to give me a starting point, then trained the Chatbot with context until it understood what I expected. But it has opened my eyes to how education has to change and will do for the better if we embrace AI.

It's insane to think that you could quickly train a virtual tutor to address any number of specialized needs among the students you're working with. That can make learning fair for all, offering personalized learning to students regardless of their current attainment or learning needs.

Let's just let that sink in.

 # Bedtime Story AI

https://www.bedtimestory.ai/

FAVORITE TOOL

 TEXT·TO·TEXT
 TEXT·TO·IMAGES
 Teacher Use
 FREE MIUM

What is it?

Bedtimestory.ai is a website that generates personalized stories for children. The stories are designed to be engaging and entertaining while also promoting a love of literacy. You can also generate AI images to accompany the story to add visual appeal. You get five free stories a month or up to 30 with additional story formats for $9.99.

Teachers can customize the stories by selecting story types, characters, experiences, and the reader's age. Teachers can also add their own personal touches through descriptive prompts to make the stories even more special for their students. You can share the stories via links and even edit them to make them more personalized and fun. The stories are available in multiple languages, making them accessible to a global audience and also applicable to language teachers.

Generate new story
Every good story starts with a good idea

For example. "Two small dinosaurs on an epic adventure"

Advanced settings ⌃   I'm feeling lucky   Generate story

Language	Story type	Reader age	Writing style	Experience
Select an option	Select an option	Select an option	Select an option	Select an option

	Story type	Reader age	Writing
1 - 2 years	✓ Bedtime Story: A classic.		
2 - 3 years	Fable: Moral lessons, talking animals.		
3 - 4 years	Fairytale: Magic, enchanting creatures, happy endings.		
✓ 4 - 6 years	Adventure: Exciting journeys, young heroes, challenges.		
6 - 8 years	Educational: Informative, age-appropriate facts, engaging.		
8 - 10 years	Mystery: Puzzles, clues, child detectives.		
10 - 12 years	Science fiction: Futuristic, imaginative worlds, exploration.		
12+ years	Realistic fiction: Everyday life, relatable characters, emotions.		

EXAMPLE
Scan the QR to view an example.

How Can I Use It?

- **Generate personalized stories for each of your students to help build literacy skills.**

- **Feature a personalized story about a student for the student of the week using their interests and hobbies.**

- **Encourage students to write their own bedtime stories using Bedtimestory.ai as a model to develop creative writing skills.**

- **Use the multiple languages feature to help students learn new vocabulary and reading comprehension in different languages.**

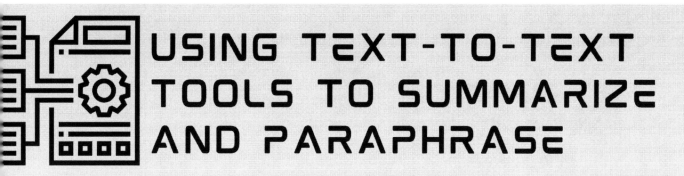

USING TEXT-TO-TEXT TOOLS TO SUMMARIZE AND PARAPHRASE

Generative AI tools can also be used to summarize and paraphrase written works, making them valuable assets in the field of education. These tools use deep learning algorithms to analyze text and generate condensed versions that preserve the meaning and intention of the original content. One example of a summarization tool is QuillBot, which allows users to enter text and receive a shorter, easier-to-read version of the same content. QuillBot also offers a paraphrasing feature that rephrases content to make it more unique and avoid plagiarism.

Another example of a generative AI tool for summarizing and paraphrasing is Moonbeam, which uses natural language processing and machine learning algorithms to create summaries of long documents. It can also generate bullet points and highlight key information, making it an ideal tool for students who need to quickly understand complex subjects. The tool also offers a plagiarism checker to ensure originality.

The Wordtune extension is another tool that uses AI to suggest rephrased content. The extension can be added to a web browser, and when a user is typing in a text field, Wordtune offers suggestions for alternative phrasing. This is especially useful for students who are learning how to write effectively, as it can help them improve their writing style and expand their vocabulary.

The following pages showcase three tools - Quillbot, Moonbeam, and Wordtune - to help you master writing, language nuances, and rephrasing for better writing!

QuillBot

https://quillbot.com/

What Is It?

QuillBot is an AI-powered writing tool that uses natural language processing and machine learning algorithms to help users generate high-quality content. It can paraphrase sentences, rephrase paragraphs, and suggest synonyms and other word choices to improve the readability, coherence, and overall quality of the text.

QuillBot is designed to help writers of all levels, from students to professionals, produce clear, concise, and grammatically correct writing. It can be used for a variety of purposes, such as academic writing, content marketing, copywriting, and more.

The tool offers a variety of features, including a plagiarism checker, the ability to save favorite phrases and sentences, and the option to adjust the level of rewriting based on the user's preferences. QuillBot is available as a web app and browser extension, and it offers integrations with popular writing platforms like Microsoft Word, Google Docs, and WordPress.

How Can I Use It?

- Have students run their writing through the plagiarism checker to ensure they cite their work.

- Students can use the paraphraser to reword their writing and make it stronger.

- Create citations for their papers and presentations.

- Check for grammatical errors.

- Translate work into other languages.

 # wordtune
https://app.wordtune.com/editor/

 TEXT-TO-TEXT   Teacher Use   All Ages   FREE MIUM

What Is It?

Wordtune is an AI-powered writing tool that helps users improve the quality and effectiveness of their written communication. The tool can be used by both teachers and students in education to enhance the writing process, streamline communication, and promote clarity and accuracy in written work.

Wordtune works by analyzing text and providing suggestions for word choice, sentence structure, and overall tone to improve the readability and coherence of the writing. It can be used to rewrite entire sentences or just select phrases and words to better fit the intended meaning and tone of the text.

Wordtune also includes tools for grammar checking and plagiarism detection, making it a comprehensive solution for all aspects of the writing process. Wordtune, as a Chrome extension, also summarizes and bullet points websites and articles for better retention of information.

Here's Your AI Writing Workspace

Write precisely what you want to say. Not kinda, not near it — Your writing, just better.

Let's take a look at your new AI writing toolkit.

Skip   Take a tour

How Can I Use It?

- Use the Chrome extension to read and summarize resources into digestible chunks.

- Use the formal/positive sentiment analysis to ensure your tone fits your assignment.

- Check for grammatical errors.

- Write notes for resources you are using for projects and classwork.

- Summarize YouTube video transcripts.

Moonbeam

https://www.gomoonbeam.com/

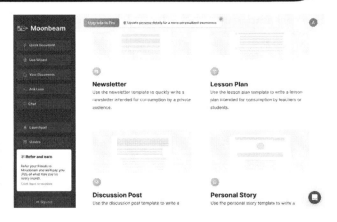

What Is It?

Moonbeam is an innovative platform that leverages AI technology to provide a seamless and efficient way for educators and students to create and share engaging digital content. Inside the platform, you can select what you are using Moonbeam for and what your role is: teacher, student, writer, business, etc. Using natural language processing and machine learning, Moonbeam offers a variety of templates that can be customized to suit the needs of each user, making it easy to create engaging content that is tailored to their audience.

For educators, templates include how-to guides, lesson plans, case studies, and more. Students have the options of essays, college admission essays, personal stories, blogs, and more.

Using Moonbeam can help teachers and students with the writing and content creation process while reducing their workload and using generative AI.

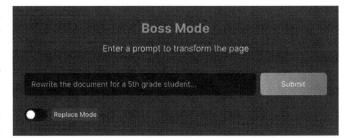

How Can I Use It?

- Teachers can generate a lesson plan using Moonbeam's lesson plan template.

- Students can use Moonbeam to generate an instant second draft. Teachers can have them analyze the new draft and compare the differences/corrections in writing.

- Have students use the outline tool to help generate their college essays.

- Teachers can use boss mode to differentiate their writing or lesson plans for the appropriate reading level.

AI RESEARCH ASSISTANT

AI research tools have revolutionized the way scholars conduct research and write papers. These tools leverage natural language processing algorithms and machine learning techniques to help users find, analyze, and synthesize relevant information on a particular topic.

One of the main benefits of using AI research tools is that they can help save time and effort. Instead of manually searching through hundreds of research papers and articles, scholars can use AI-powered tools to quickly find relevant sources of information. These tools can also help users identify key concepts and ideas within a large body of text, making it easier to synthesize information and identify relevant insights.

Another benefit of using AI research tools is that they can help improve the quality of research papers. By using these tools to identify relevant sources of information and synthesize data from multiple sources, scholars can ensure that their papers are well-researched and well-informed. Additionally, AI-powered tools can help users identify gaps in existing research, suggest new areas of investigation, and help scholars stay up-to-date with the latest research and developments in their field.

These tools can be used to monitor new research papers, track changes in popular research topics, and identify emerging trends and areas of interest. This can be particularly useful for scholars who need to stay current in their field and want to ensure that their research remains relevant and impactful.

ELICIT

https://elicit.org/

TEXT-TO-TEXT | Teacher Use | FREE

What Is It?

Elicit is a research assistant using language models like GPT-3 to automate parts of researchers' workflows. Currently, the main workflow in Elicit is Literature Review. If you ask a question, Elicit will show relevant papers and summaries of key information about those papers in an easy-to-use table.

Elicit uses semantic similarity, which finds papers related to your question, even if they don't use the same keywords. For example, it might return papers about "meditation" even if your query only mentioned "mindfulness."

For every search result, Elicit reads the abstract and generates a custom summary that is relevant to your question. This summary gives you a preliminary understanding of the research, simplifies complex or very long abstracts, and helps you evaluate whether the paper is relevant.

How Can I Use It?

- **Lit review: Explore research questions. Enter a research question, and get back answers from papers.**

- **Get independent (manipulated) variables and dependent variables from hypotheses, questions, or statements. For each hypothesis, question, or statement, GPT-3 will find and list the independent variable and the dependent variable.**

- **Behavior science: Generate stakeholders and behaviors that cause a social problem. Given a description of a social problem, generate possible stakeholders and behaviors they could be doing that are reinforcing or maintaining the problem.**

A CHATGPT
CASE STUDY
BY
STEVE DEMBO

Director of Technology and Middle School CSA Teacher

CASE STUDY

It has become somewhat cliché to speak of just how fast technology changes. And yet, for the most part, it tends to move fairly slowly and methodically. Every year, each cell phone manufacturer comes out with a new model, but the differences are rarely radically different. Year over year, the upgrades tend to be iterative. The camera gets better. The speed gets faster. The memory gets larger. But substantively, none of these upgrades have been as significant as the shift from phones that could only be used for talk, text, and perhaps text-based internet to smartphones like the iPhone. And lest we forget, the iPhone was not fully developed until the following year when they unlocked the App Store, allowing any developer to create their own software for the device. This was a seismic shift from what we had before, and it had an immediate, transformative impact on the world. It fundamentally changed the way we interact with our technology.

This shift was reminiscent of other shifts we have seen in human history, like the invention of the lightbulb, telephone, gunpowder, and airplane. More recently, the shift from traditional media to social media or from the static web to the interactive web (Web 2.0). Each of these changes fundamentally changed the way we interact with technology, with information, and with each other. Sometimes it is hard to see just how impactful a shift is going to be when it is first introduced. Napster had such an impact on the music business, but it took time for the music industry to adapt to the digital age and move entirely online. Other times, it is dizzying just how quickly the changes seem to come about.

We are in the midst of just such a shift right now. Artificial intelligence is not new. It has been powering many of our systems from behind the scenes, quietly improving our systems, both on the internet and in our everyday lives. These complex systems require massive amounts of computing power and have traditionally only been directly accessed by those who create the models. However, with the release of generative AI in the form of chatbots, ChatGPT in particular, the public now has direct access to these tools....and the world will never be the same.

My own journey with AI began when I joined Quest Academy as the middle school Computer Science and Artificial Intelligence teacher. In XXXXXXX, Quest formed a partnership with Microsoft and began implementing an AI curriculum in both their CS classes, but also integrating it into the core curriculum. Every class and every grade level included lessons on how AI functioned, how it is being used in our world, and perhaps most importantly, the ethical considerations involved. For my first few years teaching there, much of our instruction revolved around finding independent AI experiences put out by Google, MIT, and others and providing our students with increasingly more complex opportunities to explore machine learning, artificial intelligence, and the technologies involved. But most of those experiences were isolated, focusing on one specific application of AI or machine learning, and not useful in any sort of concrete way beyond that app.

ChatGPT is unlike any AI application a teacher could bring to their students before. It is as simple as a search engine but exponentially more powerful. While it most certainly has its limits, the things that it does well are so advanced that they truly appear 'magical'. In particular, its ability to generate impressively human-sounding written works is something that has never been seen by most of the public, and certainly not with this sort of ease of access.

Of course, it didn't take long for people to realize that if it could create written works this easily and this impressively... the opportunity for students to cheat with it is practically unprecedented. With just a simple prompt, ChatGPT could write an entire essay on just about any subject. And at a glance, the quality is high, and the results appear human. While there are potential issues with the accuracy of the work, there's no doubt it typically passes the 'sniff' test.

This created a crisis for nearly every educational institution, as educators scrambled to determine how to deal with a tool that is this powerful but also has such a potential for misuse. Most schools took to banning it, at least until they figured out what kind of rules and regulations to put in place. At Quest, we took a slightly different approach. Instead of restricting access to the tool, we put it directly in their hands and began experimenting.

Before continuing, I think it's important to keep one thing in mind: students already know how to cheat. I began this unit by asking every student in middle school the same question: "If you wanted to chat on an assignment, do you think you could?" The results were unanimous. Students know that the possibility of cheating is always available on the internet, but the vast majority of them choose not to for a variety of reasons. With this in mind, we began our exploration by pointing out that this technology could be used to cheat. And we tried it. We took writing prompts that they had used for recent assignments and put them into ChatGPT. They saw firsthand that, in moments, it could churn out an impressive-looking essay. With a few more prompts, they could make it longer or shorter. They could modify the apparent grade level of the work and guide it to provide higher quality work.

This was the point where some students began asking me to ban the site. While some students were elated by the new capabilities the chatbot provided them, others had already decided that it was too powerful for students to use. While their concern wasn't that temptation would be too great and that they might use it to cheat themselves, they thought that their colleagues would be unable to resist taking the easy way out. This was a theme that resonated through many of our discussions on the topic. The concerns seemed to occur most frequently among students who were already among the better writers in the grade.

These were gut reactions, instinctual responses to something that challenged what they knew to be possible with technology up until just minutes prior. However, there were just as many students who were excited by the possibility and were eager to test it out. After a few introductory activities, we focused most of our efforts on a simple test that would help us identify just how effective the chatbot-powered AI was and how helpful it would be to the writing process.

In our school, there are two classes of each grade level, 6th-8th. At each grade level, a prompt was selected by the students based on a novel or lesson that they had previously studied and were familiar with. Each class was split up into four groups, with each group provided a different set of rules to use for their written response.

Group 1 was the 'all student' group. They wrote their response in the traditional way. They could use Google for research, grammar-check and spell-check, and any other tools they traditionally used with the exclusion of ChatGPT or any other AI-powered engine.

Group 2 was the 'pre-writing' group. They were allowed to use ChatGPT as much as they wanted during the prewriting process but then had to put it aside and type the paper themselves. They could use ChatGPT to gather ideas, create a hook, make an outline, find quotes or additional resources as well as any other way they could come up with, provided that they then wrote it 'by hand.'

Group 3 was the 'post-writing' group, which had to write it themselves the traditional way first. Then, they could use ChatGPT to do any type of post-work that they desired. They could have it identify and/or correct the spelling and grammar, punch up the resulting essay, modify the perceived quality of it, adjust the grade level of the writing, and then ultimately, they would copy and paste it from ChatGPT into a document to submit.

Group 4 was the 'all ChatGPT' group. Their task was to 'write' the entire response using only ChatGPT. They could use as many prompts and modifications of prompts as they wanted, but ultimately, the chatbot had to do all the heavy lifting. They were forbidden from doing any manual editing or typing. It had to be 100% generated by ChatGPT. As I'm sure you may be anticipating, this was the most popular group for students to volunteer for, as it was perceived to be the easiest of the groups.

Groups were given approximately two class periods (90 minutes) to write their responses. After all four groups were finished, I gathered them together, made sure the formatting was consistent, and then provided them to their opposite class in the grade level. The students were then tasked with assessing the four papers written by their colleagues from the other class in their grade. The goal was not to identify whether a response was written by a human or bot (although obviously, we did spend time discussing that) but rather to assess the overall quality of the work. Did it flow well? How well did it answer the prompt given? Did it feel like an exceptional piece of writing? Do you think your teachers would rate it highly? After reading all four, they simply ranked them from best to 'least best', giving the response they thought the strongest 4 points and the bottom 1 point.

I think the results surprised just about everyone. While there were some exceptions and variations, in the aggregate across all three grade levels... the 'all student' group had the strongest marks, while the 'all ChatGPT' group typically did the worst. Second and third place wasn't quite as consistent, but overall, the 'pre-writing' group outperformed the 'post-writing' group.

When trying to identify what it was about the student's written responses that caused them to be rated so highly, students pointed out that they tended to adhere more tightly to the prompts. They tended to provide more depth than the bot-written essays, which often wandered and included a variety of themes, even when the prompt asked them to focus on a single one. They pointed out that they had been taught to create responses in certain ways, and they recognized those elements in the human written papers.

They also found that the more they read bot-written responses, they tended to have a predictable pattern. It had a penchant for using certain phrases or grammatical structures that they didn't feel were organic to middle school students. ChatGPT loved the phrase 'in conclusion' and used it frequently. It tended to do an almost direct rephrasing of the opening prompt in the first few lines. But overall, they just felt that it was somewhat.... Hollow. It looked great, and the grammar and spelling were always correct, but it just didn't feel natural in some ephemeral way.

From my experience as an observer, I found that the 'all ChatGPT' group tended to be the first ones done and the group that was least focused on actually assessing the quality of the responses it provided. When overhearing their conversations, they tended to focus mostly on the number of words in the response, how many paragraphs it had, and using fairly generic prompts like "make this essay better." They tended to be the first group finished, and when I asked for details about what was in their responses, they often had difficulty recollecting what was in their response. It was almost as though the easier the tool made it, the less invested they were in the work it provided.

It is worth noting that the 'post-writing' group tended to feel the most frustration with the process. When asked for details, they pointed out that they worked hard on their response, and then when using ChatGPT to improve it, the bot would frequently do a complete rewrite of it. By asking it to correct spelling and grammar or to increase the grade level of the work, ChatGPT would completely rewrite the response. Sometimes, the core elements would still be there, but often, they struggled to even find their work behind the rewritten words.

The 'pre-writing' group found ChatGPT to be helpful in a limited way. It was fantastic for providing ideas, hooks, and outlines. It could often get them over any initial writer's block and help them form the shell of their work. But their experiences using it to find quotes or supporting sources were inconsistent. A few caught it making up a quote or citing it improperly. Others pointed out that if they couldn't trust it to be 100% accurate with a quote or source, then they would need to do a separate search to verify it. And if they had to double-check every piece of information, then it was creating as much work as it saved.

Ultimately, the students were as surprised as I was about the results. To say it was eye-opening would be an understatement.

The students then discussed how they would recommend using ChatGPT for writing, if at all. They recognized that the 'all ChatGPT' group was just a shade away from plagiarism but that the 'post-writing' group was dangerously close to falling in the same camp. They recommended that if one were to use ChatGPT at all after writing, they be careful not to let the AI re-write their work. Instead of asking it to correct their grammar, ask it to identify any grammar errors that were made. In that way, the AI could be used in a similar way to asking a parent or tutor to read through and proof a paper. Asking it for advice is fine; asking it to make the changes for you is not.

The 'pre-writing' group felt they got the most benefit from using ChatGPT, but even they cautioned against using it without double-checking the information it shared. But they felt comfortable using it for ideas, outlines, finding a hook for a paper, or generating samples that could be used to spark ideas for someone struggling to get their start.

We used their experiences to craft an ethical use policy for the students at Quest Academy. While most of it was pretty straightforward (don't use it to commit plagiarism), there were three conversations in particular that really forced them to decide exactly what they believed about where this new technology fits into the learning process. If your school or teachers are debating the merits of ChatBot-based AIs, and how they can be used, I believe these three questions will help refine that conversation and get to the core elements that need to be discussed.

1. Are tools like ChatGPT always available for students to use UNLESS the teacher specifically states they are not to be used? Or are tools like ChatGPT off-limits UNLESS the teacher specifically states that they can be used for an assignment?

2. Do you believe that ChatGPT should be able to be used as a source for schoolwork? This can be a very rich discussion that will help solidify exactly how it can and can't be used.

3. Should students have to disclose that they used ChatGPT? And if so, do they need to specify how or include the exact transcripts as a supplement?

While there are many more things to discuss, most of them will ultimately be brought into the conversation when discussing those three topics.

Good luck with your own explorations!

Note: The work listed here was completed using ChatGPT-3.5. ChatGPT4 was released as we were finishing up our ethical use policies.

TEXT-TO-IMAGE

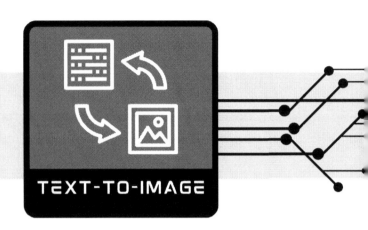

The field of AI has made remarkable strides in generating visual content from text, known as text-to-image generative AI. Text-to-image generative AI platforms use deep learning algorithms to analyze textual descriptions and create corresponding images that closely resemble the original descriptions. This technology is especially useful in education, where it can be leveraged to generate visual aids for lesson plans, create interactive textbooks, and support learning for students with visual impairments.

Text-to-image (T2I) generative AI technology is particularly valuable for creating engaging and interactive learning materials. For example, teachers can use this technology to generate images and visualizations that illustrate complex concepts and make them more accessible to students. In the hands of students, T2I can be used to illustrate imagery and descriptive writing and reinforce their understanding of the power of descriptive language.

In the following section, we will introduce multiple T2I platforms that offer cater to specific age groups. If you remember from the education section, Canva offers T2I capabilities available to students of all ages for schools that have access to a Canva for Education account. Text-to-image generative AI is a powerful tool that has tremendous potential to transform education. As AI continues to evolve and improve, it is likely that we will see even more innovative uses of this technology in education and beyond. Let's explore a handful of the tools that are available now.

https://www.midjourney.com/

TEXT-TO-IMAGES IMAGE-TO-IMAGE Teacher Use 13 and up FREE MIUM

What Is It?

Midjourney, Inc. is an independent research lab based in San Francisco that has developed an artificial intelligence program called Midjourney. This program generates images from natural language descriptions, known as "prompts," in a similar manner to OpenAI's DALL-E and Stable Diffusion.

Currently, Midjourney can only be accessed through a Discord bot that is available on the lab's official Discord server. To generate images, users must use the imagine command and input a prompt. The bot will then return a set of four images, and users can choose which ones they want to upscale. Midjourney is also working on a web interface.

There are three subscription tiers offered by Midjourney as well as a free trial. The free trial allows users to create approximately 25 jobs before requiring a subscription to continue using the service.

This AI generative platform is the best that we've encountered, so we are awarding it with the favorite badge!

How Can I Use It?

- Students can explore styles in Midjourney. Midjourney currently offers four different styles: anime, portrait, object, and scenery.

- Use Midjourney to teach descriptive character design. Have students put in their characters as they imagine them and generate them into life!

- Have students blend two photos to create a new image.

A MIDJOURNEY CASE STUDY BY DAN JONES

7th and 8th Grade Social Studies Teacher
FLG) International Faculty Member
FLR k-12 Editor

CASE STUDY

ChatGPT and other AI tools have proven invaluable for empowering my students to pursue their interests and passions through project-based learning. In my classroom, students are encouraged to leverage their passions to design and execute projects that demonstrate their mastery of the curriculum. I have had the pleasure of witnessing ChatGPT generate a plethora of exceptional project ideas tailored to my students' unique interests, as well as create comprehensive supply lists to support their implementation.

I tasked my students with creating projects about the Revolutionary War in my classroom. However, two students were struggling to come up with project ideas. As I talked with them more about their interests, I began to see their projects take shape. During a conversation with Addison, she expressed her fascination with movie villains. As we discussed various historical figures, she began to draw connections between them and the characters in her favorite films.

Addison saw the tragedies of the Revolutionary War as if they were playing out in a movie. To help her bring her vision to life, I introduced her to Discord and showed her how to use Midjourney to combine two images and create something new. This sparked her imagination, and she quickly began designing movie covers for her horror historical movies. Suddenly, what seemed impossible before was now achievable with just a few keystrokes.

Example of Addison's work using Midjourney to re-envision the tragedies of the Revolutionary War.

HISTORICAL HORRORS

MOVIE TRAILER

JOSEPH

DESCRIPTION

Joseph is a movie that Joseph Martin stars as Chucky, the famous horror movie character. He appears to be a British troop causing problems and deaths around his colonial city.

MOVIE TRAILER

BENJAMIN

DESCRIPTION

Benjamin is a movie where Benjamin Franklin appears as Jigsaw, one of the smartest horror movie characters. He appears to be fighting in a Battle against his fellow people in his town.

MOVIE TRAILER

GEORGE

DESCRIPTION

George is a movie that contains George Washington himself as Joker. He appears to be in court, trying to beat a case against his own army men.

See more of Dan's student work in his new book: *Modern PBL: Project-Based Learning in the Digital Age*

WWW.TEACHERGOALS.COM/PBL

Adobe Firefly

https://www.adobe.com/sensei/generative-ai/firefly.html

TEXT-TO-IMAGES   IMAGE-TO-IMAGE   Teacher Use   13 and up   FREEMIUM

What Is It?

Adobe recently launched Adobe Firefly. The platform contains a set of tools that enable users to create new and unique designs by leveraging the power of AI.

Adobe Firefly includes several features designed to enhance design workflows and boost creativity. For instance, the "Design Generator" feature can be used to generate multiple design iterations based on specific criteria, such as color scheme or layout. The "Style Transfer" feature enables designers to transfer styles between images, while the "Auto Trace" feature automates the tracing process of raster images, or pixel images, to vector graphics. Additionally, Adobe Firefly includes a "Design Explorer" feature that allows designers to explore design possibilities by manipulating parameters. They also have a video editor.

The future plans of Adobe Firefly also include features to make 3D modeling. The tool's ability to automate certain design tasks, such as tracing or generating design iterations, can help to streamline workflows and save time.

How Can I Use It?

- Students can use Firefly to create vector images for logo design.

- Visualize the weather by taking an image and altering it to show all four seasons in a place. Change the mood, atmosphere, or even the weather.

- Edit videos and create posters.

DALL·E

https://openai.com/product/dall-e-2

TEXT-TO-IMAGES IMAGE-TO-IMAGE Teacher Use 13 and up FREE MIUM

What Is It?

Dall-E 2 is another AI art generator that creates art from descriptive prompts in "natural language." It runs on OpenAI, and you can create an account with your Google account or a valid email address. The first month you join, you get 50 free credits to create AI art and 15 each subsequent month after that. After you are logged in, you can see images that were generated by community members. When you hover over them, you can see the prompts that were used to generate the images. This is especially insightful when learning how to craft your own prompts.

In addition to generating AI art from a prompt, you can also upload your own photos and generate variations of it. You can blend images or use text prompts to alter your photos. A lot of artists are using Dall-E to enhance their own artwork.

One of the benefits of Dall-E is that you are not required to have a Discord account to use it like Midjourney requires.

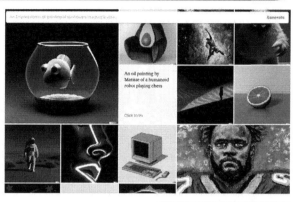

Welcome to DALL·E

Meet your creative copilot

Create and iterate with DALL·E to...

- Generate images from a description in natural language
- Easily make realistic, targeted edits to images
- Create different variations of an image, inspired by the original

Continue

By clicking "Continue," you agree to our **terms** and **content policy**

How Can I Use It?

- **Students can use DALL-E to enhance multimedia projects such as presentations and videos.**

- **Help students visualize abstract concepts such as emotions, ideas, and thoughts.**

- **Grade the Bot: Reimagine new art pieces in a classical art style and compare and contrast them to the original style they mimicked.**

Unreal Person,
This person does not exist

https://this-person-does-not-exist.com/en

TEXT-TO-IMAGES

Teacher Use

All Ages

FREE

What Is It?

There are several websites that generate photos of people who do not actually exist.

Thispersondoesnotexist.com, This-person-does-not-exist.com/en, and Unrealperson.com are AI-powered face generator websites that use a Generative Adversarial Neural Network (GAN) trained on a dataset of images to create highly realistic photos of people who don't exist.

The second website allows you to select drop-down parameters to customize by age, gender, and ethnicity while the other two require no prompts or parameters, so you will need to click "new image" to generate faces until you get one that suits your use case.

With a resolution of 1024x1024 pixels, this state-of-the-art model generates the most advanced synthetic images of human faces. The websites provide a demonstration of AI's capabilities to create synthetic images and highlight the increasing realism of AI-generated content.

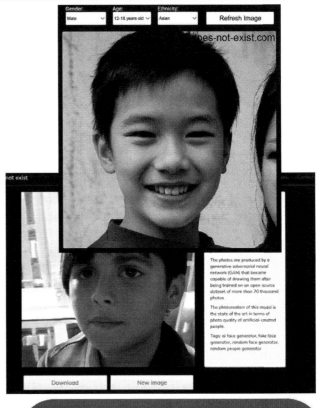

How Can I Use It?

- Stock footage for school websites or newsletters.

- ThisPersonDoesNotExist.com can be used to teach psychology and social studies concepts. Teachers can use the images to teach students about the effects of facial expressions, emotions, and body language on communication, perception, and decision-making.

- Teachers can use the site to teach math and statistics concepts. They can use the website to generate a set of data that can be used to teach probability, random variables, and statistical analysis.

https://padlet.com

TEXT-TO-IMAGES | Teacher Use | All Ages | FREE MIUM

What Is It?

Padlet has an AI image generator available inside its platform. You can find it by clicking on the + sign to add a post, clicking on the three dots, selecting "I can't draw" and inputting text for what you want Padlet to visualize for you. This is great for students and teachers who feel they lack drawing skills. They simply write what they want to see.

While similar to Canva, this feature doesn't allow you to edit the image further or provide additional style options; it is useful for generating custom images.

This tool can be great for teachers looking to add custom images to lessons. It is most powerful when used by students to create images to go with character descriptions, imagery, and to help visualize vocabulary. Teachers can also use the tool to introduce the concept of AI to students with a platform that is commonly used and adopted by most school systems.

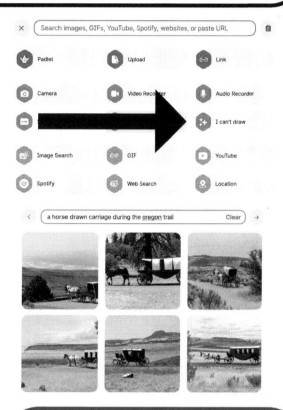

How Can I Use It?

- **Visualize vocabulary.**

- **Input descriptive imagery or passages from books to visualize what they are reading.**

- **Have images accompany their original stories.**

- **Illustrate complex concepts.**

- **Provide math, STEM, and science examples through real life.**

artbreeder

https://www.artbreeder.com/

TEXT-TO-IMAGES | DRAW-TO-IMAGE | IMAGE-TO-IMAGE | Teacher Use | 13 and up | FREEMIUM

What is it?

Artbreeder is a platform that uses artificial intelligence to generate and manipulate digital images, illustrations, and other forms of digital media. It allows users to explore and create new images by combining and modifying existing ones, or by using various algorithms to generate new images from scratch. In the freemium, you get ten free "credits" a month but can upgrade to 100 for $8.99 a month.

In Arbreeder, there is "collage mode," "splicer," and "outpainter." In collage mode, you can make a collage with shapes and images and then transform it into AI art with a prompt. You can add images, use the draw tool, and add shapes to your canvas and then render it to create multiple renditions of your work. Splicer mode lets you create new images by mixing several images together and editing their "genes." Create portraits, landscapes, paintings, and more — then watch as others take your art in exciting new directions.

Teachers can easily leverage this platform to teach shapes, composition, and more.

How Can I Use It?

- Create collages and generate new images using Artbreeder's features, promoting creativity and innovation.

- Introduce students to AI technology and its use in the creative industry.

- Incorporate into lessons on art history, where students can explore various artistic styles and create their own versions using the website.

- Use the collage feature in math class to learn shapes and render them into AI art pieces using prompts.

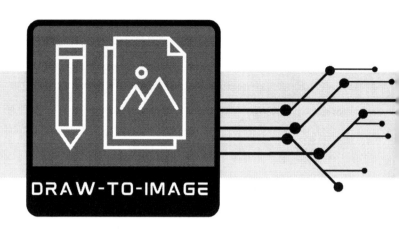

DRAW-TO-IMAGE

DRAW-TO-IMAGE

Draw-to-image (D2I) generative AI is an exciting new technology that uses artificial intelligence algorithms to generate images based on hand-drawn sketches. This technology involves deep learning algorithms that analyze the sketches and produce corresponding digital images, including illustrations, and graphics. With the growing need for visual aids in education, draw-to-image generative AI is becoming increasingly popular as a powerful tool for creating high-quality visual content.

Students can use D2I generative AI in a variety of ways. For example, they can use it to create their own illustrations or animations to accompany their writing or presentations, helping to bring their ideas to life and making them more engaging for their audience. They can also use it to create visual aids for group projects or classroom discussions, allowing them to share their understanding of a concept in a creative and visual way.

We will explore some novel tools that have just arrived on the D2I scene, some for the sake of understanding how AI works, like Quick, Draw!, and others like scribblediffusion.com that are a fun exercise or imagination, creativity, and working together with AI to manifest something new from a simple sketch.

Scribble Diffusion

https://scribblediffusion.com/

What Is It?

Scribble Diffusion is an innovative AI-based tool designed to transform simple sketches into refined and aesthetically pleasing images. It is an easy-to-use tool that offers a simple user interface, making it accessible to students of all ages.

Students use their mouse or finger, depending on the device they are accessing the website from, to draw an image. They then type a few words that provide an additional description of the image they are trying to create. With this tool, users can experiment with different looks by undoing any changes they make. This means that users can try out multiple variations of their sketches until they find the perfect look.

Whether you are a professional artist or a hobbyist, Scribble Diffusion is an excellent tool for creating art from sketches. Its powerful AI capabilities enable users to refine their sketches into stunning, high-quality images that are sure to impress.

"mountains and a river with a sunset"

How Can I Use It?

- Use a combination of drawing and descriptive language to visualize passages from a story.

- Illustrate visuals for their creative writing projects.

- Draw-Pair-Share: Partner up and have one student use their imagination to describe a place, person, or thing. Have the other student draw it and generate it.

- Visualize historical events or vocabulary through drawings and descriptions like the Civil War or mitosis.

Quick, Draw!

https://quickdraw.withgoogle.com/

DRAW-TO-IMAGE **Teacher Use** **All Ages** **FREE**

What is it?

Quick, Draw! is an online game developed by Google that uses artificial intelligence to recognize and guess what the player is drawing. The game presents the player with a prompt to draw a specific object, such as "apple" or "umbrella", and then uses machine learning algorithms to try to identify what the player is drawing in real-time.

The game is meant to be a fun and educational tool for demonstrating the capabilities of artificial intelligence in recognizing and understanding hand-drawn sketches. You and your students can experience AI firsthand and help train it by adding to the world's largest doodling data set.

To use Quick, Draw!:

1. Go to quickdraw.withgoogle.com and click "Let's Draw."
2. You will be given six prompts to draw, each with a timer of 20 seconds. As students draw, a computer voice will narrate what it sees. Once it recognizes the drawing or the timer runs out, it will move on to the next prompt.
3. At the end of the session, it will tell you how many of your doodles the neural net recognized.
4. You can click on each drawing to see what the neural net recognized, and drawings that were submitted by others to show how it was trained.

Can a neural network learn to recognize doodling?

Help teach it by adding your drawings to the world's largest doodling data set, shared publicly to help with machine learning research.

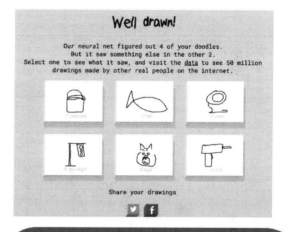

How Can I Use It?

- Quick, Draw! can also be used to teach students about AI concepts. Teachers can explain how the AI system works, how it learns, and how it can improve over time. Students can learn about the algorithms used in the system and the importance of training data.

- In art class, Quick, Draw! can be used to practice basic drawing skills and how they relate to AI. Launch a debate on AI art and its place.

- Used in conjunction with the kid's book *Artie Bot Draws a Lot*, discuss how Artie learns to make his own art.

IMAGE-TO-IMAGE

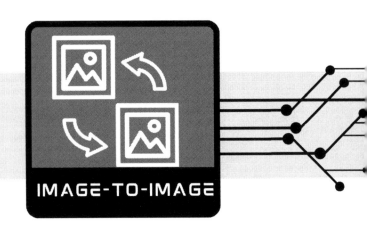

Image-to-image (I2I) generative AI technology has the ability to generate realistic images from a range of inputs, such as sketches, doodles, or even blurry photos. I2I platforms use deep learning algorithms that analyze the input and create a corresponding image that closely resembles the original. This technology has a wide range of potential applications in education, from creating visual aids for lesson plans to designing personalized learning materials for students.

One example of an I2I generative AI platform is ScribbleDiffusion.com, which allows users to upload a rough sketch or doodle and generate a polished and realistic image from it. This technology can be used by students to enhance their artistic skills and create visually appealing designs for presentations and projects. Another example is PetalicaPaint.com, which enables users to transform blurry or low-quality photos into high-quality images. This technology can be used to restore old photographs or create high-quality visuals for educational materials.

As AI continues to evolve, the potential for I2I generative AI in education is immense. Educators and students can leverage this technology to create compelling visuals that enhance the learning experience and reinforce concepts. With the growing availability of I2I generative AI platforms, it is becoming easier and more accessible for educators and students to utilize this technology in the classroom.

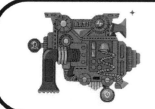 

https://www.playarti.com/

IMAGE-TO-IMAGE   Teacher Use   All Ages   FREE

What Is It?

ARTi is a creative and interactive AI image creator that allows users to produce unique images by selecting different options for characters, locations, and activities. With just three buttons, users can choose their desired settings and click "Create!" to generate their own personalized image. The platform is designed to be simple and user-friendly, similar to a point-and-click adventure game, making it accessible for individuals of all ages and skill levels.

ARTi's easy-to-use interface and engaging AI image-creation process make it an excellent tool for elementary students. Teachers can use this tool to teach students about AI and its role in modern technology.

Additionally, ARTi's ease of use can be particularly useful for younger students who are just learning about digital art and design, as it provides a fun and interactive way for them to explore their creativity.

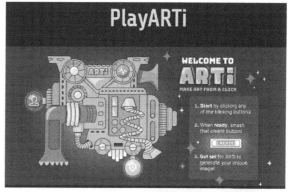

How Can I Use It?

- Write creative stories based on selections of characters, locations, and activities.

- Use playarti.ai to introduce students to the topic of AI generative art.

- Have students pair up and discuss their AI generative art images.

- Create sight word cards for different characters, activities, and locations.

- Have students pick 3 selections and create a drawing before generating an image. Compare and contrast their drawing with the AI one.

PETALICA PAINT

https://petalica.com/index_en.html

IMAGE-TO-IMAGE

Teacher Use

All Ages

FREE

What Is It?

Petalica Paint is an AI tool that takes line drawings and applies color. If you're at the line art stage, you can upload your drawing, and the AI in Petalica Paint will automatically color your work. You can simplify the lines and strokes in your work and make graphite or pencil drawings sharper. You can also designate which colors you want the AI to use.

There are three colorization styles available: Tanpopo, Satsuki, or Canna. You can also add color hints using the pen and palette. The platform integrates with https://sketch.pixiv.net/ if you prefer to create and color a digital drawing. This is a great tool to speed up an artist's workflow and works great with graphic novels, Manga, or those that specialize in sequential art, but it works with all line art.

To use Petalica Paint:

1. Upload a sketch or line drawing.
2. Use the palette on the left to suggest colors.
3. Choose a style: Tanpopo, Satsuki, or Canna.
4. Continue to iterate and adjust your palette until you are satisfied.
5. Download and share your work.

How Can I Use It?

- Take line sketches and automatically add color.

- Explore anime, manga, and other styles that relate to graphic novels.

- Have students draw their own graphic novel on an educational topic and use Petalica paint to colorize their images. Export them to a Canva or Book Creator platform to create a book with their images.

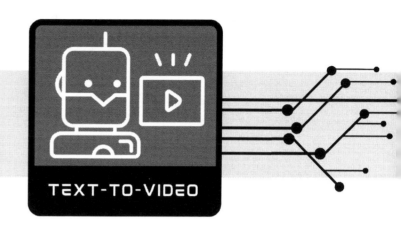

TEXT-TO-VIDEO

TEXT-TO-VIDEO

Text-to-video (T2V) generative AI is a revolutionary technology that uses artificial intelligence algorithms to generate videos based on textual input. This technology involves deep learning algorithms that analyze textual descriptions and produce corresponding visual content, including video animations, simulations, and presentations. With the increasing demand for engaging and interactive learning materials, text-to-video generative AI is gaining popularity in education as a powerful tool for creating compelling visual content.

In the education sector, T2V generative AI can be leveraged in various ways, such as creating educational videos for flipped classrooms, producing instructional videos for online learning platforms, and designing personalized video tutorials for students. In the hands of students, they are empowered to create videos of talking AI historical figures, book characters, and more. Most T2V platforms have options to create AI avatars from text and add AI voiceovers, empowering all students to create.

By using T2V generative AI, educators can save time and effort in creating high-quality video content for their students. This technology can help educators create videos that are personalized, engaging, and visually rich, thus enhancing the learning experience for students. Additionally, T2V generative AI can help bridge the gap between different learning styles, making education more accessible and inclusive for all students.

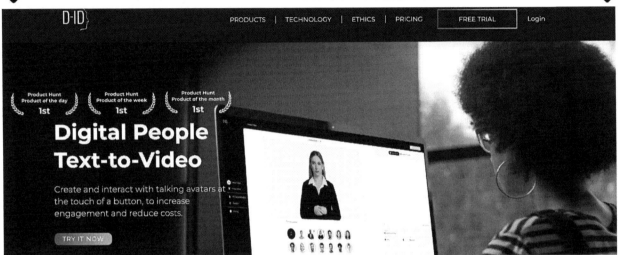

What Is It?

D-ID, an Israeli AI company that worked on projects like Deep Nostalgia, has launched a new platform called Creative Reality Studio. The platform allows users to upload an image and text to generate a video, targeting sectors like corporate training, education, internal and external communications, product marketing, and sales.

Using the platform is straightforward. Users can upload an image or select a pre-created presenter to initiate the video creation process. Paid users can access premium presenters who have better facial expressions and hand movements. Next, users can either type a script or upload an audio clip of a speech. The platform supports 119 languages, and users can select a voice and style, such as cheerful, sad, excited, or friendly. The company's AI-based algorithms generate a video based on these parameters. Users can then share the video anywhere.

D-ID Features

Creative Reality Studio by D-ID allows users to generate an AI presenter through text prompts, image uploads, or choosing a virtual presenter from their library. Once users have selected an AI avatar, they can upload an audio file or paste or type a script in the box. They also have the option to use the built-in ChatGPT technology to input a prompt and have a script generated for them. If users choose to use a script, they have the option to select a voice, language, and style of their narration. Once all options have been selected, users generate the video and download it locally or share it via a link from the platform.

Generate a Presenter

Generate an AI Presenter

Choose the presenter from your text input.

Select a presenter from the library.

How to Use D-ID in Your Classroom

Creative Reality Studio by D-ID is a versatile tool that can be used by teachers and students in the classroom in various ways. Here are some potential use cases:

History:

- Students can create a video that features a historical figure as the presenter. For example, they could use an image of Abraham Lincoln and upload a script that describes his life and accomplishments. The video could include text and images to supplement the narration.

- Students can create a video that recreates a historical event. They could use images and text to set the scene and provide context. Then use a pre-created presenter or a custom image to act as the narrator. For example, they could create a video that describes the signing of the Declaration of Independence or the Battle of Gettysburg.

Literature:
- Students can upload images of a character from a novel, play, or poem and create videos where they speak as the character. This can help students explore the character's motivations, personality, and point of view.

A D-ID CASE STUDY
BY MICK
MCMURRAY

CASE STUDY

Educator, San Diego, CA

These powerful words from ChatGPT set the tone for a project that took place in my 11th-grade Digital Marketing class. As we explored the ways in which AI tools can be integrated into our workflow, one student decided to create a video honoring Black History Month. Little did we know that this project would not only showcase the creativity and problem-solving skills needed to excel in an AI world but also raise important ethical considerations. In this case study, we'll dive into the project, discuss the skills that students developed, and explore the implications of integrating AI tools into the classroom.

Throughout the semester, my students have been exploring ways to integrate AI tools into their workflow. I encouraged them to use AI tools as much and as often as they wished while emphasizing transparency in their usage. As a result, the quality of their work improved significantly. Any concerns about the negative impact on their learning were dispelled. Motivation levels increased, and students were reading and learning more through their discussions with ChatGPT. They were also building problem-solving and creativity skills in new and exciting ways.

Prompt crafting has become a key focus of our work in class. Not only is this skill valuable in its own right, but it is also an excellent opportunity for students to practice critical thinking, problem-solving, and creativity.

I introduced the idea of creating AI videos to the class after seeing a tweet by Dan Fitzpatrick about how to create a historical figure video using a few tools. We used ChatGPT to write the script, DALL-E, and Midjourney to generate images, Play(dot)ht to create an audio file of the script, and D-ID to animate the image with the audio file.

During our first class on this topic, a student attempted to create a video featuring Martin Luther King Jr. speaking about Black Lives Matter (BLM). However, when he asked ChatGPT to write the script, he received a response explaining that it could be disrespectful due to MLK's legacy and was offered information about BLM instead. After further discussion about BLM, he tried to change the request to a black preacher but was reminded of the ethical implications of pretending to be someone of a particular racial group. This led to a discussion in class about the ethics of the request and the ethics of denying it.

Undeterred, the student applied our lesson on prompting tone and style. When ChatGPT was prompted to use metaphors and figurative language to write a speech, it produced a script of a fiery speech about equality and justice in the BLM movement. From there, it was just 15 minutes until he had a finished video

As AI technology continues to evolve at an unprecedented rate, it is increasingly important to equip students with the necessary skills to navigate and utilize these tools effectively. These skills include problem-solving, ethical reasoning, and creativity.

Prompt creation skills are critical when working with AI tools. Chatbots like ChatGPT require specific prompts to produce specific outputs. Therefore, students must understand the nuances of language and communicate their ideas effectively to the AI tool. Developing this skill not only helps students work more effectively with AI but also helps them become more effective communicators in general.

It is important to prepare students for the ethical dilemmas that the use of AI is creating. In our Digital Marketing class, students had to work through ethical dilemmas to create a video that accurately reflected the message they wanted to convey. By solving these types of problems, students are developing the skills they need to be successful in future careers that will increasingly rely on AI tools.

Finally, creativity skills are important because AI tools are only as good as the people who use them. While AI tools can generate data and insights, it is up to humans to interpret that data and turn it into something meaningful. By developing creativity skills, students are better equipped to use AI tools to their full potential, generating innovative ideas and solutions.

By integrating AI tools into the classroom, we can better prepare students for a future in which AI technology will be ubiquitous. These skills will enable students to work more effectively with AI tools and position them for success in careers that will require a deep understanding of AI technology.

Mick McMurray
@mick_mcmurray

...

@DanFitzTweets I shared your video with a student and challenged him to come up with a historical figure, a topic, and a location. He chose MLK (in honor of Black History Month here in the US) to speak about Black Lives Matter in a Rite Aid. youtu.be/8Jo-k2_MwjM via @YouTube

youtube.com
AI MLK speaking about BLM in a Rite Aid (Student Project)
Task for student: Create an AI generated video of a historical figure. Place them in a modern location with a ...

2:14 PM · Jan 24, 2023 · **1,514** Views

SCAN THE QR CODE TO WATCH
THE VIDEO OF MLK JR.

https://pictory.ai/

TEXT-TO-TEXT   TEXT-TO-IMAGES   TEXT-TO-VIDEO   TEXT-TO-AUDIO   Teacher Use   All Ages   FREE MIUM

What Is It?

Pictory.ai is an innovative platform that harnesses the power of AI technology to help you create stunning videos from your blog posts, webinars, podcasts, and Zoom recordings. With AI technology, you can quickly and easily create short summary videos that capture the essence of your content and engage your audience. The platform's AI also makes it easy to edit videos using text, eliminating the need to learn complex software.

One of the key features of the platform is its automatic video creation tool. Simply upload your script, and Pictory's AI will do the rest, generating a video that is visually appealing and engaging. You can also add captioning to videos quickly and easily, making it the perfect tool for webinars, demos, e-learning, video podcasts, and more.

To get started with Pictory.ai, you can sign up for a free trial that includes three video projects, each up to 10 minutes in length.

Video Creation Made *EASY*

Automatically create short, highly-sharable branded videos from your long form content.

Quick, easy & cost-effective.

No technical skills or software download required.

How Can I Use It?

- Create a video from a script complete with stock footage or customized uploads.

- Teachers can add captioning to lectures and video content for students.

- Take articles on school subjects and turn them into videos with the power of AI.

- Have students write a blog on a content area topic and turn it into a video.

IMAGE-TO-TEXT

Image-to-Text (I2T) generative AI is a technology that uses deep learning algorithms to analyze and interpret images and then generates corresponding textual descriptions of the images. This process is also known as computer vision and is used in a wide range of applications from self-driving cars to medical imaging analysis. This technology can be used to automatically generate captions, tags, or even full-length descriptions of images. I2T generative AI can help to make images more accessible to those who are visually impaired and also aid in the creation of searchable image databases.

With the emergence of prompt engineering as a career field, using tools to reverse engineer prompts can be helpful to learn descriptive tags. It deduces images to descriptive and diverse text prompts based on an image input. By analyzing the content and characteristics of an image, such as colors, shapes, and objects, the AI can generate a variety of textual prompts that relate to the image in different ways. This can help provide inspiration for creative writing exercises, generate prompts for language learning exercises, or support writing prompts for standardized tests.

I2T generative AI can support prompt engineering by providing a way to generate a large number of diverse and relevant prompts quickly and easily.

CLIP Interrogator 2.1

https://huggingface.co/spaces/fffiloni/CLIP-Interrogator-2

 IMAGE-TO-TEXT

 Teacher Use

 All Ages

 FREE

What Is It?

Clip Interrogator is a web-based platform that allows users to upload images for the purpose of analyzing the image to understand how an artificial intelligence art generator sees the image in prompt form. Once users upload an image, it will generate a text output prompt. This output prompt can then be input into an AI art generator in order to reproduce an image that is similar in style. This is very useful for learning how to compose an art prompt. By studying prompts that Clip Interrogator outputs based on input images, students and teachers can use modeling to create their own future prompts. This also reinforces learning about different art styles and descriptions while helping develop a better understanding of "Promptcraft."

From the website:

The CLIP Interrogator uses the OpenAI CLIP models to test a given image against a variety of artists, mediums, and styles to study how the different models see the content of the image. It also combines the results with BLIP caption to suggest a text prompt to create more images similar to what was given.

CLIP Interrogator 2.1

Want to figure out what a good prompt might be to create new images like an existing one? The CLIP Interrogator is here to get you answers! This version is specialized for producing nice prompts for use with Stable Diffusion 2.0 using the ViT-H-14 OpenCLIP model!

Select mode
best   classic   fast

best mode max flavors   4

Submit

Description Output

a group of people sitting in front of a computer, inspired by Beeple, afrofuturism, portrait anime space cadet girl, astronaut helmets, valentina remenar, beeple and jeremiah ketner

How Can I Use It?

To use Clip Interrogator:

1. **Upload an image .**
2. **Select a mode: best, classic, or fast. Use the line dragger to adjust max flavors.**
3. **Click on "submit."**
4. **View the reverse engineered prompt.**

CHATBOT PLATFORMS

AI chatbot platforms are tools that allow users to create their own chatbots using artificial intelligence technology. These platforms typically offer an intuitive interface that allows users to design the conversational flow of their chatbot, as well as the bot's appearance and behavior.

Teachers can use chatbots to enhance their students' learning experience. Students can create their own chatbot with tools like ChatGPT through text prompts and assigning the bot a role or using preexisting platforms like Character.ai, which was created specifically for chatbot creation. This is an awesome tool for making a book chapter more dynamic and captivating or bringing historical and fictional characters to life.

In this section, we will introduce you to a few Chatbot platforms that will allow users to design and customize chatbots that can converse and perform tasks based on their requests. Students will be able to build chatbots without any coding experience required.

Overall, AI chatbot platforms are designed to help users create engaging, interactive experiences that use artificial intelligence to simulate human conversation and interaction. These tools can be used in a variety of settings, from customer service and sales to education and entertainment.

HISTORY HELLO

https://www.hellohistory.ai/for-education

FAVORITE TOOL

TEXT-TO-TEXT TEXT-TO-IMAGES TEXT-TO-VIDEO TEXT-TO-AUDIO

Teacher Use 13 and up

FREE MIUM

Chat With Historical Figures

With the help of advanced AI & machine learning we've brought historical figures back to life. Now is your chance to ask the questions you've always wanted to ask.

Next

Insights

Women's Month

Philosophy

8 Ideas about Justice

Science

Psychology

Self-Help

Ruth Bader Ginsburg

The Notorious RBG

1933-2020

I am Ruth Bader Ginsburg, an Associate Justice of the Supreme Court of the United States. I was born in Brooklyn, New York in 1933 and attended Cornell University and Harvard Law School. I have devoted my career to the advancement of women's rights and gender equality. I was a professor at Rutgers University Law School and

Start Chat

01 An AI generates messages. Don't take the messages seriously and verify facts.

02 Each conversation is 100% unique, you can never know where the conversation will go...

03 You can try to chat in any language, but English gives best results.

What Is It?

Hello History AI is an innovative and engaging AI-powered chatbot platform designed to enhance teaching and learning. While it is aimed at history teachers, there are subcategories that touch on historical figures in literature, philosophy, mathematics, science, innovation, and more.

It uses advanced natural language processing (NLP) technology to create a conversational experience that allows students to interact with history in a new and exciting way. With Hello History AI, students can engage in dialogues with virtual history characters, explore historical events and sites, and gain a deeper understanding of history through personalized, interactive conversations.

Hello History AI is specifically designed for the education sector, providing teachers with an innovative tool to supplement their teaching materials and methods. It is a web-based platform that can be accessed from any device with an internet connection, including desktops, laptops, tablets, and smartphones. Teachers can use Hello History AI to create custom chatbots that align with their lesson plans and learning objectives, creating a personalized and engaging learning experience for their students.

The platform is available on Google Play and iOS and has a freemium of 20 free messages. The price for individual users at publication is $5.99 per month or $34.99 per year. Educators can receive special pricing by reaching out to the company.

How to Use Hello History AI in Your Classroom

With Hello History, users can engage in discussions, ask questions, or even debate with historical figures on a wide range of topics. This unique approach to learning provides an opportunity for gaining new insights and perspectives on history and life. The AI technology ensures that each conversation is relevant and engaging for the user, creating an unforgettable educational experience that blends entertainment and learning.

Whether users are interested in history, culture, or simply enjoy having conversations, Hello History offers a unique and personalized learning opportunity. With its state-of-the-art AI technology, Hello History creates a platform that facilitates authentic and engaging conversations with historical figures, resulting in an immersive and memorable learning experience.

Assignment Ideas With Hello History AI

 Create a historical debate: Assign students a historical figure to debate against and encourage them to come up with arguments based on historical facts. Students can then engage in a debate with their assigned historical figure using Hello History AI.

 Historical figure interviews: Assign students to research a historical figure and then create a script for a conversation with that figure. Students can then use Hello History AI to conduct an interview and ask questions based on their research.

Lesson Plan for Hello History AI Using ChatGPT

Title: Engaging with History: Exploring Historical Figures with Hello History AI
Grade level: High school

Objectives:
- Students will be able to engage with historical figures in a conversational manner through Hello History AI.
- Students will be able to evaluate historical events and figures through the lens of different perspectives.
- Students will be able to create a digital artifact demonstrating their learning.

Materials:
- Computers or tablets with internet access
- Hello History AI platform access

- Research materials on various historical figures

Procedure:

Introduction (15 minutes):
- Introduce the concept of Hello History AI and provide an overview of the lesson plan.
- Discuss the importance of engaging with history from different perspectives.
- Explain the research task: students will research a historical figure and come prepared to engage in a conversation with that figure through Hello History AI.

Research and Conversation (45 minutes):
- Allow students time to conduct research on their chosen historical figure.
- Once the research is complete, students will access Hello History AI and engage in a conversation with their chosen historical figure.
- Encourage students to ask open-ended questions and engage in a back-and-forth dialogue.

Reflection and Analysis (30 minutes):
- After the conversation, students will reflect on their experience and analyze the historical figure's perspective on various events.
- In small groups, students will compare and contrast their experiences with different historical figures and discuss what they learned.
- As a class, discuss the value of engaging with history from different perspectives.

Digital Artifact Creation (30 minutes):
- Students will create a digital artifact showcasing their learning.
- Encourage students to be creative and think beyond traditional formats (e.g., creating a podcast, video, or blog post).
- Once completed, students will share their digital artifacts with the class.

Conclusion (10 minutes):
- Recap the lesson and discuss the importance of engaging with history in new and innovative ways.
- Provide an opportunity for students to share their reflections on the lesson.

Assessment:
- Student participation in the conversation with the historical figure through Hello History AI.
- The quality of the digital artifact created by the student demonstrates their learning and understanding of the historical figure.
- Contribution to the class discussion on the importance of engaging with history from different perspectives.

Character.AI

https://beta.character.ai/

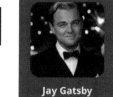

Jay Gatsby

Pair Programmer
Your programming AI
assistant

What Is It?

Character.ai is an AI website where users can create character chatbots and craft their personalities based on a set of input parameters. These characters can be fictional or based on celebrities or historical figures. You can generate images and have them speak to you in a voice.

Character.ai has two different creator experiences. Quick mode allows creators to create interesting characters in less than a minute. Advanced mode allows adventurous creators to perfect their characters by using more powerful tools.

Read more information on how to create a good character in their Character Book Guide.

Three things that influence how a character responds in a particular situation are:

1. The character attributes (what much of this guide will explain).
2. The character training from conversations (e.g., star ratings).
3. The context of the current conversation.

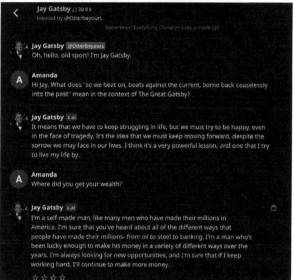

How Can I Use It?

- **Create a historical figure and carry on a conversation with them about historical events.**

- **Create a fictional character from a book, movie, or novel.**

- **Create a bot to practice answering interview questions for a job.**

- **Experiment with creating a therapist bot. Talk about ethical concerns and issues around using this technology in the health sector.**

TEXT-TO-AUDIO

Generative AI text-to-audio (T2A) is a field of AI that involves using deep learning algorithms to convert written text into spoken audio. This technology has the potential to transform the way we learn and consume information, as it can make written material more accessible to those with visual impairments or those who prefer to listen to content rather than read it. In education, this technology can be used to create audio versions of textbooks, lectures, and other learning materials, providing a more inclusive learning experience for all students. As we learned in Chapter 8, it's important to follow UDL guidelines when designing lessons and creating content for students.

One example of generative AI text-to-audio technology is Murf.ai. Murf can be used to create audio scripts, voiceovers, and other written content, and it supports a variety of languages and accents, providing multiple AI avatar voices for you to choose from.

T2A technology has the potential to revolutionize the way we consume and interact with information. By making written material accessible through spoken audio, this technology can increase access to education and information for people of all abilities and backgrounds. As AI continues to evolve and improve, it is likely that we will see even more innovative uses of this technology in education and beyond. Let's take a look at two examples of T2A tools that you can use to be innovative in your classroom.

MURF AI

https://murf.ai/

FAVORITE TOOL

TEXT-TO-AUDIO

Teacher Use

13 and up

FREE MIUM

What Is It?

Murf Studio is a cloud-based platform that uses AI and deep machine learning to generate lifelike voiceovers in over 120 voices and 20 languages for a variety of use cases such as eLearning, marketing, audiobooks, and more. By leveraging AI technology, Murf simplifies and reduces the cost and time required for voiceover production, which traditionally involves hiring voice actors, recording in a studio, editing, and syncing. With Murf, users can easily convert their script into natural-sounding audio within minutes and add images, music, and video to create professional voiceover videos all in one place.

While Murf is being highlighted for its voiceover capacity, users also have the ability to generate videos using their stock audio, video, and photo library. Users get 10 minutes of free content and can share their creations via a link.

This is a fun tool to get students to create explainer videos and more!

Product/Business Promos

Shoes Promo

Adventure Buddy Promo

Charging Network Explainer

Mobile App Explainers

Home Food Delivery App

Fitness Assistant App

EV Charging App

Presentations

Solar System Introduction

Social Media Trends

COVID Training

Podcast Intros

Music Podcast Intro

Women in Leadership Podcast Intro

Yoga Podcast Intro

How Can I Use It?

- Create a voiceover of a creative writing piece.

- Use Murf Studio to create an explainer video on an educational topic.

- Create a product pitch or Shark Tank video for an app, technovation idea, or startup.

- Create transcripts for a presentation.

- Create a podcast intro.

Voicemaker®

https://voicemaker.in/

TEXT-TO-AUDIO | Teacher Use | 13 and up | FREE MIUM

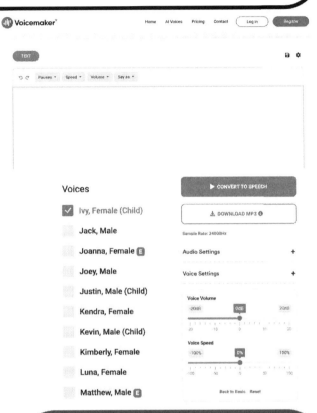

What Is It?

Voicemaker AI is an online text-to-speech (TTS) platform that uses deep learning and artificial intelligence to convert written text into natural-sounding human speech.

The tool offers a wide range of voices and languages to choose from, including male and female voices with different accents and styles. Users can customize the pitch, speed, and emphasis of the generated voice to suit their needs. The platform also provides users with the ability to adjust pronunciation, add pauses, and insert breaths to create a more natural-sounding voiceover.

Voicemaker AI's text-to-speech technology has the potential to save users a significant amount of time and resources by eliminating the need for hiring voice actors or recording their own voiceovers. Additionally, the platform's advanced features and customization options make it an ideal tool for educators and content creators looking to enhance the accessibility and engagement of their materials.

How Can I Use It?

- Create a voiceover of a creative writing piece.

- Translate lectures into other languages.

- Students can use the tool to record themselves speaking in a foreign language, and then use the AI to analyze their pronunciation and grammar. This can help students to improve their language skills and build confidence in speaking.

- Create audio versions of written content such as textbooks, articles, and essays.

AUDIO-TO-TEXT

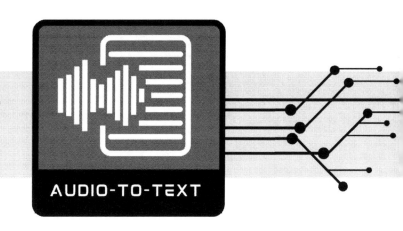

Generative AI audio-to-text (A2T) is a technology that enables the conversion of speech and audio into text. This technology utilizes deep learning algorithms to analyze audio input and generate corresponding text output, making it an essential tool in industries such as journalism, customer service, and education. One of the best Audio-to-text platforms with a ton of features and capabilities is Otter.ai.

Otter.ai is a web-based platform that utilizes AI to create accurate transcriptions of audio recordings. It offers real-time transcription capabilities, making it a useful tool for meetings, interviews, and lectures. In addition to transcribing audio, Otter.ai also allows users to search and share transcriptions, making it an excellent tool for collaborative work.

A2T technology has revolutionized the way audio content is transcribed and analyzed. Platforms like Otter.ai offer powerful tools that make it easier for people to access and collaborate on audio content, making them invaluable in various industries. Let's take a look at this tool in depth.

Otter.ai

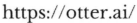

https://otter.ai/

TEXT-TO-AUDIO

Teacher Use

13 and up

FREEMIUM

What Is It?

Otter.ai is a web-based AI-powered transcription and collaboration platform that offers an innovative way to capture, transcribe, and share important conversations, meetings, and presentations. The platform utilizes advanced machine learning algorithms to create highly accurate transcriptions of speech, and it can recognize and differentiate between different speakers, making it easy to keep track of who said what during a conversation.

In addition to transcribing speech, Otter.ai also offers a variety of collaboration tools that can help teams work more efficiently. For example, the platform can be used to share meeting notes and action items, and it can be integrated with popular productivity apps like Zoom, Microsoft Teams, and Google Meet, making it easy to capture and share meeting recordings and transcripts.

Overall, Otter.ai is an innovative platform that offers a wide range of features and capabilities for businesses, educational institutions, and individuals.

How Can I Use It?

- Activate Otter.ai in your parent-teacher meetings to record and transcribe the meeting for your records.

- Use Otter.ai to provide accommodations for students who have disabilities or special needs. Lectures and discussions can be transcribed so they can be reviewed by students at their own pace.

- Transcribe your next virtual class and share the link to the transcriptions. Students can see and hear the lecture as well as access screenshots that are vital with timestamps.

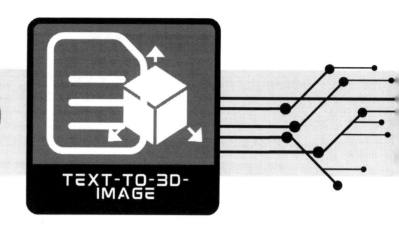

TEXT-TO-3D

Generative AI text-to-3D (T23D) is a type of AI technology that involves using deep learning algorithms to convert written text into 3D models. This technology can be used to generate virtual objects, environments, and characters based on textual descriptions. Text-to-3D generative AI has applications in a variety of fields, including gaming, architecture, and product design.

In education, text-to-3D generative AI has the potential to transform the way students learn and engage with complex concepts. By allowing students to interact with 3D models of objects and environments described in textbooks and other learning materials, this technology can make learning more immersive and engaging.

One example of how Text-to-3D generative AI can be used in education is using a tool like Blockade Labs with CoSpaces Edu. CoSpaces Edu is an online platform that allows students and teachers to create 3D models and environments using a simple drag-and-drop interface. By using Text-to-3D generative AI technology, students can create customized worlds to upload into CoSpaces. This feature can be particularly useful for creating historical environments and simulations, as well as for visualizing abstract concepts in science, technology, engineering, and math (STEM) education. Let's look at Blockade Labs!

Blockade Labs

https://www.blockadelabs.com/#intro

TEXT-TO-3D-IMAGE | Teacher Use | 13 and up | FREE

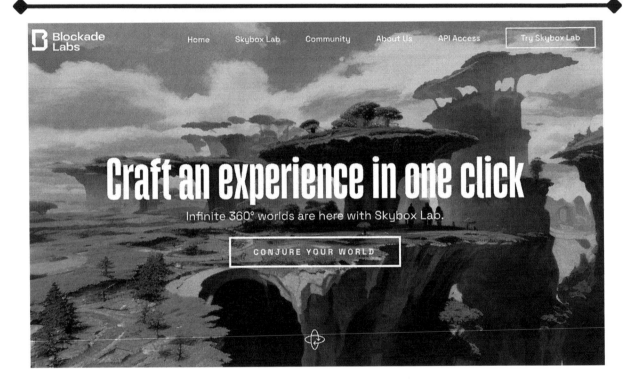

What Is It?

Blockade Labs is a renowned development firm that created Skybox Lab, an impressive AI-driven program that generates 360° skybox experiences. Users can use a combination of styles, text prompts, and photo uploads to generate a 3D world from scratch. They can also use the sketch option and draw basic shapes that get colored and converted to 3D images.

Utilizing Stable Diffusion and ControlNet scribble pre-processor, the technology accepts a 2D sketch created by the user and transmits it to the skybox diffusion model, which then generates an image based on a prompt that reflects the sketch's shapes and concepts. This process allows users to convert simple sketches into captivating 360° images. It is currently free and available to users without needing a login. This is fantastic for students that are already using tools like CoSpaces, Merge Cube, and other AR/VR platforms.

Blockade Labs brings 360-degree worlds to your fingertips at the click of a button.

How to Use Blockade Labs in Your Classroom

SCAN TO VIEW AN EXAMPLE OF BLOCKADE LABS IN USE.   SCAN TO VIEW A TUTORIAL OF THE MAKING OF THE VIDEO.

Simply choose a description of the 360° world you want to create, select a style, and hit generate. If you want to design a world based on an image prompt, you can also choose to upload a photo. The second image on the right was generated by selecting the "scifi" style and using the prompt "a futuristic classroom with computers." With good prompts, photo uploads, and even the ability to convert sketches to 360/3D navigable images, creating immersive environments has never been easier.

Assignment Idea With Blockade Labs

1. Create a 360 image that represents a historical event. Download and then upload the 360 photo to CoSpaces Edu.
2. Customize it with a title.
3. Add people and dialogue.
4. Use primary and secondary resources to have the dialogue tell the story of the event.
5. Code your elements to be interactive.

Example of Oregon Trail

TEXT-TO-CODE

Generative AI text-to-code (T2C) is a form of artificial intelligence that enables users to generate computer code automatically from written language, such as natural language processing. This technology uses advanced algorithms and machine learning techniques to interpret written instructions and transform them into executable code. One example of this technology is Codex by OpenAI, which can write code in various programming languages and automate tasks, allowing users to build projects quickly and efficiently.

T2C can be used in a variety of educational contexts. For instance, it can be used to help students learn programming languages and gain proficiency in coding. By allowing students to focus on conceptualizing and organizing their ideas rather than worrying about syntax and formatting, students can gain a deeper understanding of coding principles and become more effective programmers. Additionally, this technology can be used by educators to automate grading and assessment, freeing up time for teachers to focus on more personalized instruction and feedback.

Overall, generative text-to-code AI has the potential to revolutionize the way we teach and learn to code, making it easier and more accessible to a wider range of learners. Let's explore an example of how ChatGPT can be used for coding!

 **GPT-4**

https://openai.com/product/gpt-4

TEXT-TO-CODE · Teacher Use · 13 and up · FREE

What Is It?

Codex was an AI-powered platform developed by OpenAI that translated natural language into functioning code in real-time. It was based on OpenAI's GPT-3 language model and was trained on a massive dataset of code and natural language text. The platform was designed to make programming more accessible to a broader range of people by reducing the amount of specialized knowledge required to write code.

ChatPGT-4 now has the ability to do what Codex was capable of. ChatGPT-4 can now interpret human language and generate code in a variety of programming languages, including Python, JavaScript, Ruby, and others. It can also be integrated with various programming tools, including Visual Studio Code and GitHub's code editor, to enhance the programming experience.

The potential of using ChatGPT for coding in education is vast. It could be used to teach coding to students who may not have the foundational knowledge to start from scratch or to speed up the coding process for more experienced programmers.

How Can I Use It?

- Generate code snippets quickly for coding assignments and projects.

- Automatically translate natural language descriptions into code, making it easier for students to understand and learn coding concepts.

- Assist students in debugging their code by identifying errors and providing suggestions for corrections.

- Help teachers create and automate coding assessments and grading, saving time and increasing efficiency.

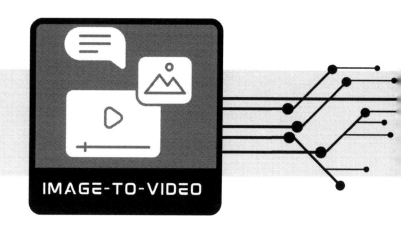

IMAGE-TO-VIDEO

Generative AI image-to-video and animation is an exciting development in artificial intelligence that allows users to create animated videos from still images. This technology uses machine learning algorithms to analyze a set of images and then generate a sequence of frames that simulate motion. By creating animations from still images, generative AI image-to-animation technology provides a fast and cost-effective way to produce high-quality animations.

One example of a platform that offers generative AI image-to-animation is Sketch2Animation by Meta de Molab. This platform provides a simple interface for users to upload their images and then generate animations automatically. Users can choose from a range of animation styles, such as zooming, panning, or rotation, to create different effects. Once the animation is complete, users can export it as a video file or as a GIF.

Generative AI image-to-video is an exciting development in artificial intelligence that offers many possibilities for creating engaging and high-quality animations from still images. With platforms like Sketch2Animation, it has never been easier to create animations and videos that captivate audiences and bring images to life.

Sketch.metademolab

https://sketch.metademolab.com/

IMAGE-TO-VIDEO Teacher Use 13 and up FREE

What Is It?

Sketch.metademolab.com is a web-based platform that allows users to create animated videos from still images using generative AI image-to-animation technology. The platform offers a range of features and options to help users create high-quality animations quickly and easily.

When users first visit the website, they are presented with a simple interface that allows them to upload their images and start creating animations immediately. Users can upload up to 10 images at a time and then choose from a range of animation styles, including zooming, panning, and rotation, to create different effects. The platform also allows users to adjust the animation speed and add text captions to their animations.

One of the standout features of Sketch.metademolab.com is its ease of use. The platform is designed to be intuitive and user-friendly, even for users with no prior experience in animation or AI technology.

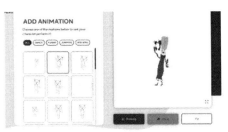

How Do I Use It?

To use Sketch.metademoloab.com:

1. Upload a drawing of one character into the platform.
2. Isolate your character by putting a box around it.
3. Separate the character from the background. Make sure the body parts are isolated and not connected. You can use the pen and erase tool to adjust this.
4. Find and adjust the character joints by dragging them to the right place.
5. Add an animation to your character.

10 Ways to Design Dynamic Assignments for Authentic Learning

Our mission as educators is to craft assessments that propel students to exhibit their genuine understanding and abilities. We need to embrace innovative approaches to assessment design that ensure students' deep learning, critical thinking, personal growth, and responsible use of artificial intelligence.

We need to empower students with authentic, captivating, and intellectually stimulating assessments for students to thrive in a world of advanced AI tools. Emphasizing student voice, analytical thinking, personalization, and ethical AI practices in our teaching strategies enables us to foster a learning environment that challenges students to critically examine issues, collaborate resourcefully, and take charge of their learning journey.

Let's cultivate an educational landscape where students feel inspired and encouraged to showcase their knowledge and skills. By incorporating these methods into our assessments, we hold students accountable for their own learning, preparing them for a future infused with artificial intelligence tools. With a focus on promoting meaningful learning experiences, we can ensure students are equipped to navigate the rapidly evolving world and make responsible choices.

It's essential that educators not only challenge students to demonstrate their own knowledge and skills but also teach them how to effectively and responsibly collaborate with AI tools. Incorporating AI-assisted collaboration in assessments can foster a balance between individual creativity and innovative problem-solving using cutting-edge technology.

The rubric on the next page will serve as a helpful guide in designing dynamic assignments for authentic learning:

Method	Beginner	Intermediate	Advanced
1. Collaborative Projects (ensures individual contributions)	Students work in pairs to complete a simple task, sharing their basic understanding.	Students work in small groups to complete a more complex task, requiring deeper understanding and the integration of individual perspectives.	Students work in larger groups on multi-faceted, long-term projects, synthesizing complex ideas and demonstrating advanced understanding.
2. Real-World Problem Solving (requires application of knowledge)	Students solve simple real-world problems, applying foundational knowledge.	Students explore complex real-world problems, demonstrating critical thinking and the ability to evaluate multiple solutions.	Students tackle interdisciplinary, open-ended real-world problems, showcasing advanced problem-solving skills and innovative solutions.
3. Scaffolded Assignments (encourages independent learning)	Assignments are divided into small, simple steps with clear guidance, allowing students to build basic understanding.	Assignments are divided into more complex steps with some guidance, enabling students to make connections and deepen understanding.	Assignments are divided into complex, interconnected steps, challenging students to synthesize information and demonstrate mastery of concepts.
4. Peer Review and Feedback (promotes accountability)	Students exchange feedback on a single aspect of their work, demonstrating a basic understanding of the content.	Students exchange feedback on multiple aspects of their work, showcasing a deeper understanding and the ability to critique constructively.	Students engage in ongoing peer review, feedback, and collaboration, demonstrating advanced understanding and communication skills.
5. Reflective Assignments (fosters metacognition)	Students briefly reflect on their learning after completing a task, identifying key takeaways.	Students reflect on their learning at multiple points throughout a project, analyzing their growth and areas for improvement.	Students engage in regular reflection, tracking their progress, setting goals, and demonstrating metacognitive skills and self-awareness.
6. Multimedia Presentations (requires original content creation)	Students create simple multimedia presentations (e.g., slideshows) to demonstrate basic understanding.	Students create more complex multimedia presentations (e.g., videos, podcasts) to demonstrate deeper understanding and effective communication.	Students produce highly polished, creative multimedia projects that showcase in-depth understanding, originality, and advanced communication skills.
7. Gamification (engages students in active learning)	Simple game elements are introduced (e.g., points, badges) to motivate students and demonstrate basic understanding.	More complex game elements are introduced (e.g., challenges, rewards, leaderboards) to engage students and assess deeper understanding.	Students participate in a fully gamified learning experience, with quests, narratives, and interactive elements, demonstrating mastery of content and problem-solving skills.
8. Debate and Socratic Seminars (requires critical thinking and reasoning)	Students participate in short debates or discussions on simple topics, displaying foundational knowledge.	Students participate in more complex debates or Socratic seminars on challenging topics, showcasing critical thinking and persuasive communication.	Students lead in-depth debates or Socratic seminars, requiring extensive research, preparation, and the ability to synthesize complex information and perspectives.
9. Authentic Assessments (mimics real-world tasks)	Students complete simple real-world tasks related to course content, demonstrating basic knowledge and skills.	Students complete complex real-world tasks that integrate multiple aspects of course content, showcasing deeper understanding and the ability to apply knowledge in context.	Students complete open-ended, interdisciplinary real-world tasks that require integrating multiple areas of knowledge and skills, demonstrating mastery and the ability to innovate.
10. Self-Assessment (promotes self-awareness and growth mindset)	Students evaluate their performance on a single task or skill, identifying areas of basic understanding.	Students evaluate their performance on multiple tasks or skills throughout a project, reflecting on their growth and areas for improvement	Students engage in ongoing self-assessment, demonstrating metacognitive skills, goal-setting, and a growth mindset, as they strive for continuous improvement.

CALL TO ACTION

1. Scan the QR code to join our members section and get the Rubric on the previous page, and to stay in the know of other apps as we add them to our AI Repository.

WWW.TEACHERGOALS.COM/AI-CLASSROOM-MEMBERSHIP

SCAN ME

2. Hop over to your favorite social media site and share an AI tool you are using with your students. Use the hashtag #AIClassroom.

(You can connect with other like-minded teachers who are using that hashtag too!) The team and I are eager to cheer you on.

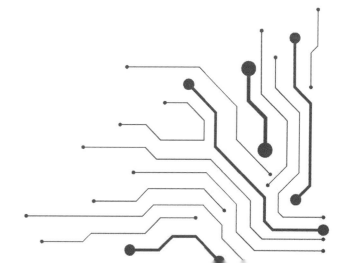

PART FOUR

THE AI HORIZON

CHAPTER 10

Leading in the AI Revolution

"As more and more artificial intelligence is entering into the world, more and more emotional intelligence must enter into leadership."

- Amit Ray,
AI Scientist, Author of *Compassionate Artificial Intelligence*

For the education system to survive and adapt to the rapidly changing world in which we find ourselves, our leaders must embody courage and innovation, fearlessly taking the necessary steps to empower their students and staff to thrive in the AI revolution.

As technology advances, so too does the need for education to keep up.

That's why educational leaders are so important. If these leaders embrace the future, provide professional development, and forge a safe path forward for those whom they serve, then the revolution will result in positive change for everyone.

We all have some responsibility for leadership in a time of disruption like this.

We are all responsible for preparing our fellow teachers and students for the AI revolution. But this isn't going to be an easy task. It will take courage and innovation to embrace these new technologies and the changes they will bring to the teaching profession.

Educational leaders need to be brave enough to take risks, experiment with new approaches, and embrace change. They need to be willing to challenge the status quo, question traditional teaching methods, and be open to new ideas.

Here's the thing - by doing so, leaders unlock incredible benefits for their teachers, students, and themselves. They create a learning environment that is engaging, dynamic, and relevant to the needs of the world in which we find ourselves.

By being courageous and innovative, educational leaders can help their teachers and students develop the skills and knowledge they need to succeed in the AI revolution. They will be able to prepare them for a future where AI is not just a tool but an integral part of daily life.

My message to all educational leaders out there is this - be brave, be bold, and be innovative. Embrace the AI revolution and lead your teachers and students to a brighter future. It won't be easy, but the rewards will be more than worth it.

We work in a system where educational leaders usually spend their working hours (and personal hours) extinguishing metaphorical fires.

The day-to-day life of an educational leader is arduous. The focus is on the daily running of the organization while simultaneously trying to prepare for the future. There is no choice but to spend most of their time keeping the performance engine going. As a consequence, the time allotted to stand on the shoulders of giants and look toward the horizon is limited at best.

Recalling Govindarajan's Three-Box Solution, he argues that any organization that wants to survive needs to spend dedicated resources to Box Three, creating a future that serves the needs of learners and the world.

The education system hasn't done this. The current culture languishes in Box One and shuns Box Two for fear of treading on traditions that have become almost sacred. Fear of change and a desire to do what is only familiar and comfortable are obstacles to ever opening Box Three. Very few of our leaders on the ground have done this effectively. If you have, then you are one of the rare ones, and your continued leadership is needed now more than ever.

It isn't too late. It's going to take some extraordinary leadership from everyone involved in the teaching and learning process.

Are we up to the task?

As education enters the AI revolution, it is crucial for leaders to embody certain virtues to guide their teachers and students through this change:

1. Collaborative
2. Inclusive
3. Adaptable
4. Ethical
5. Life-Long Learners

An overarching quality that guides these virtues is vision. When I first posted these ideas on LinkedIn, Professor Bob Harrison, a true visionary of the future of education, commented that he would "add vision... with a clear and shared ownership with all stakeholders, including learners." He's right, of course. As Proverb 29 reminds us, "Where there is no vision, the people perish."

These are virtues that all leaders should embody anyway, but here's some suggestions on how to apply them in the AI revolution.

1 VIRTUE #1: COLLABORATIVE

No one knows everything when it comes to new AI. Leaders will need to:

- Work with edtech companies to develop AI-powered educational tools that help students learn more effectively and staff be more productive.

- Collaborate with schools, colleges, universities, and other educational organizations to share data, insights, expertise, and resources.

- Bring together diverse teams with different perspectives, skills, and experiences to develop AI solutions that are ethical, unbiased, and inclusive.

- Encourage open communication and transparency to build trust with stakeholders and ensure that the AI systems are aligned with the school's mission and values.

By being collaborative, educational leaders can build a strong foundation in their organization for the AI revolution, ensuring that the AI used is effective, ethical, and meets the needs of their students and staff. This will lead to increased innovation and progress.

2 VIRTUE #2: INCLUSIVE

Inclusivity is multi-faceted. From access to technology, development of skills, and ensuring diversity in thought. Leaders will need to:

- Prevent the digital divide and provide AI tools in low-income schools. Provide hardware and software resources, including AI development kits, cloud-based platforms, and other tools to enable AI learning and experimentation.

- Organize inclusive training programs and workshops that are open to all, regardless of their previous experience or knowledge. These programs can help to demystify AI and make it more accessible to a wider range of students.

- Foster a diverse community of AI learners and practitioners by actively reaching out to underrepresented groups and encouraging their participation in AI-related activities.

- Create student mentorship and apprenticeship opportunities by working with local businesses and organizations. This can help to provide students with hands-on experience with AI technology and give them the opportunity to learn from experienced professionals.

- Encourage interdisciplinary learning and collaboration across fields to broaden understanding of AI's potential impact on education and society.

By implementing these strategies, leaders help ensure that the benefits of the AI revolution are accessible to all students, regardless of their background.

3   VIRTUE #3: ADAPTABLE

We're in for a fast ride. The ability to be agile in leadership, forget previous learning, and embrace new possibilities will be vital. Leaders can do this by:

- Staying up to date with new AI technologies to better understand student needs and tailor teaching accordingly. Willingness to try out new tools and technologies is key. An adaptable leader will stay up to date with these developments and be willing to try out new tools and technologies to see how they can benefit their students.

- Adjusting teaching strategies to effectively incorporate new tools and technologies. Adaptable leaders tailor their approach to meet students' unique needs.

- Widening their networks: Adaptability also means being open to collaboration with others, whether that's other educators, tech experts, or industry professionals. By working together, leaders can stay up to date with the latest developments in AI and use this knowledge to improve their own teaching and their students' outcomes.

- Learning from mistakes: Finally, an adaptable leader will be willing to learn from their mistakes and make adjustments to their approach as needed. In the world of AI, where things are always changing, this is especially important, as it can help educators avoid getting stuck in a particular way of doing things and instead stay open to new possibilities.

Adaptability is difficult, but the strategies that we've relied on for so long will very quickly start to fail.

VIRTUE #4: ETHICAL

In the AI revolution, educational leaders have access to powerful technology that transforms the way education is delivered. However, this technology can also pose significant ethical challenges. Leaders will need to know that:

- AI has the potential to impact many aspects of our lives, and if these systems are not designed and implemented ethically, they can cause harm to individuals and society as a whole. Education leaders have a responsibility to ensure that AI systems are designed and used ethically to avoid potential harm.

- Biased AI algorithms perpetuate discrimination and inequality in the education system, exacerbating existing disparities. Educational leaders who prioritize ethics can help ensure that practice is designed in a way that is fair and equitable.

- Being ethical in the use of AI can help build trust and credibility with stakeholders, including students, parents, teachers, and the broader community. When AI systems are implemented with transparency and accountability, people are more likely to trust and embrace them.

- Educational leaders who prioritize ethics in the use of AI can help close achievement gaps and ensure that all students have equal opportunities to succeed.

Leaders who prioritize ethics in the use of AI can contribute to a world where AI is used for the greater good - to improve education and, therefore, the success of their students and staff.

5 VIRTUE #5: LIFE-LONG LEARNERS

The best leaders are continually learning. Leaders in the educational AI revolution can keep learning by:

- Stay on top of the latest AI trends and innovations by reading journals, attending conferences, and keeping up with research. Use cutting-edge AI technologies to enhance teaching and learning.

- Knowing the right time to shift focus: AI is constantly evolving, which means that educational leaders need to be adaptable and able to change their approach when necessary. Being a life-long learner means being open to new ideas and being willing to learn from mistakes.

- Fostering a culture of learning: Having the power to influence the culture of learning is vital. By being lifelong learners themselves, they can model the importance of continuous learning and inspire others to do the same. This can lead to a more innovative and forward-thinking school culture, which will benefit both teachers and students.

- Asking for advice from their network: Being a lifelong learner also means connecting with other educational leaders in the field. This can help them stay up to date with the latest trends, exchange ideas, and collaborate on projects. By building a strong network, they can create a community of support.

We can all become leaders who develop these virtues who can develop these virtues so that true innovation can take place. I honestly believe we are at a crossroads right now. Ignoring AI now will exasperate the existing digital divide that many of our students suffer from.

AI STRATEGY

Introducing artificial intelligence into education requires a well-thought-out strategy to ensure that it's integrated correctly and effectively.

We can wait for governments or educational boards to write this, or we can get it done ourselves. This technology is already being used by your students and your staff, so I recommend you do the latter to stay up to date. This doesn't have to be a long-term or even a medium-term strategy. In fact, I'd argue that these would be near impossible due to the speed at which AI is developing. However, you can set the approach and attitude that your organization will take when discovering new developments in this field.

Let us look at the questions you will need to ask yourself and your organization to draw up this strategy. Then we'll take a look at an example.

WHY?

As Simon Sinek (2009) explains, start with why. It's a fundamental question that every educational institution needs to start with. The answer can be simple because without a strategy, introducing AI into education would be like navigating without a compass. It's a surefire way to get lost in the 'shiny new toy' wilderness.

The main question you need to answer is, "What is the goal of using AI in our organization?"

This answer needs to be formulated by you, as a leader, and your organization.

Some potential answers might be:

- To benefit from the efficiencies that artificial intelligence delivers so that our staff has a better work-life balance.
- To develop learners' skills so that they are prepared for success in their lives.
- To make smarter decisions using AI, so that we can develop as an organization with agility and speed.

Potential sub-questions to ask yourself as you explore this are:

- Why do our students need this?
- Why do our teachers need this?
- Why do our leaders need this?
- Why do our wider staff need this?
- Why are the benefits greater than the risks?
- Why are we choosing specific AI tools?

Once you pin down your 'why' of using AI, everything else will flow from that.

WHAT?

At its core, the 'what' is about setting clear and specific goals. It's about defining what we want to achieve. What do you want to deliver, and when do you want it delivered?

Here are some examples of goals you might want to achieve:

- AI tutoring systems to personalize some learning opportunities.
- Grading systems based on AI that can provide instant feedback to students.
- A school, college, or university chatbot that can answer frequently asked questions from students and parents.

- Speech recognition tools that can help English-language learners improve their pronunciation and fluency.
- AI-powered analytics that can identify struggling students early on and provide targeted interventions to help them catch up.
- An AI-powered accessibility suite that can help students with certain needs access resources.

HOW?

The 'how' is the most important question of this whole strategy-building process, because it ensures that the plan is executed successfully and meets the intended objectives. Without a clear route for implementation, the strategy can become fragmented, uncoordinated, and ultimately fail to achieve the desired outcomes.

The 'hows' should instill confidence in your community that success is not only possible but within reach. Whenever I think of the how question, I like to approach it from three different angles:

1. How will we continue to shape the vision?
2. How will we influence people?
3. How will we align people?

It will also be important to keep the leadership virtues in mind when developing the 'hows'. How will the strategy be a collaborative effort, how will it be inclusive of all, how will it be adaptable in the medium and long term, how will it be ethical and how will it help develop continued research and learning opportunities?

PRODUCING YOUR FIRST GUIDANCE DOCUMENT

Many governments and educational boards have yet to draw up guidance and short-term plans around the use of artificial intelligence in education. Some just do not even want to approach it and have actively banned AI. A short-sighted move that will inevitably widen the digital divide between their students and the students of more innovative schools.

One particular example of a fantastic guidance document is from the Department for Schools and Education of the State of North Rhine-Westphalia, Germany. They authored a document entitled *Handling Text-Generating AI Systems: A Guide for Action* (February 23, 2023) for all educational institutions in their state.

I want to take you through how this document presents information to their leaders and teachers and how I think they have succeeded in their approach. This will hopefully act as a guide for you to implement similar short-term guidance to your teams. I have included a translation of the full document from German into English as an appendix (Translated by Heinrich Niemann, March 2023).

1 START BY CULTIVATING CONFIDENCE

Crucially, they make their organizations aware that they know about this technology, giving confidence to their readers that they have done their research and due diligence. It will be important as a leader to get this message to your teams immediately if you haven't done it yet. I was recently asked by the UK Department of Education what my first steps would be if I were them and this is exactly what I told them to do as a first step.

ADDRESS THE LIMITATIONS

It is a smart move to address these concerns early on. Many teachers and parents will have worries about the use of artificial intelligence, from stories in the news. Showing that you understand these will also help to instill confidence and give the message that you have considered them and are mitigating against them. It's important to mention that AI text generators can produce incorrect information and biased answers.

MAKE IT CLEAR THAT AI CAN BE USED IN EDUCATION

Avoid confusing statements, and be very clear that open and constructive engagement with artificial intelligence is needed in the classroom. This document explains that educational organizations have an educational and pedagogical mandate to teach students about AI responsibly and safely. The classroom should be a safe environment where students can experience AI-based text generators and understand their potential and risks.

The document goes so far as to suggest practices for teaching with AI. The strategy involves formulating prompts to get desired responses from AI, checking the chatbot's outputs for errors, uncertainties, and gaps, and discussing functionality and effective use (our development of the PREP and EDIT method mentioned in Chapter 6 will give you a headstart).

IMPACT ON LEARNING AND SKILLS DEVELOPMENT

There are a lot of comments, mainly on social media, suggesting that AI will have a negative impact on literacy levels. As I have explained previously, the document from the Department for Schools and Education of the State of North Rhine-Westphalia argues that it is too simplistic to assume negative consequences without further reflection. The document lists some of the benefits of using AI to assist with individual support for students, particularly around individual inquiries, scaffolding, and different levels of text difficulty.

5 EXPECTATIONS FOR STUDENTS USING AI

Similarly to how the International Baccalaureate has allowed students to use AI (The Guardian, February 27, 2023), this document also takes the common sense approach of allowing students to use AI text generators, such as ChatGPT, so long as they must indicate them as a source. It also warns teachers not to create tasks that the AI can complete on its own. Instead, it encourages them to motivate learners to work independently through challenging and interesting tasks and to show why their own independent writing experiences are valuable.

It also lists some suggestions for how students can work in a way where their own skills and knowledge can be assessed, which include:

- Allowing them to work on topics from a self-chosen perspective.
- Varying the medium in which the tasks are completed.
- Promoting discussion-based skills so that learners orally justify their decisions.
- A conversational form of feedback that is not suited to the insertion of longer text passages from AI.

6   BENEFITS FOR TEACHERS

A lot of guidance on artificial intelligence tools for education starts with guidance for teachers, and many stop there. This document puts the learning and the students first, but it does go into the benefits for teachers. These are practical ways teachers can start using it now and start seeing benefits, such as a reduced workload.

7   LINKING THE APPROACH TO EXISTING STRATEGIES

The document does a good job of suggesting how learning about AI can be easily inserted into the curriculum and existing strategies for media literacy. This will be an important section for any guidance you give, but it will also take some planning to ensure existing strategies and curriculums have scope to include AI education. This will also help show stakeholders that AI is a development of the digital skills students are already learning and not something new to fear.

8   LEGAL AND PRIVACY GUIDANCE

Legal and privacy issues with text-generating tools like ChatGPT vary by country and organization. Work with data protection leads and professionals to use AI in practical and safe ways for students and staff. Avoid a blanket ban and find ways to work around limitations for maximum benefit.

The Children's Online Privacy Protection Act of 1998, commonly known as COPPA, is a federal law in the United States that places specific obligations on website operators and other digital and online service providers to safeguard the privacy of children under the age of 13. Under COPPA, websites and mobile apps must obtain verifiable parental consent prior to collecting or using any personal information of users under 13 years of age. Additionally, COPPA outlines the procedures and requirements for obtaining parental consent, the need for a privacy policy, and the legal responsibilities of the operator, including prohibitions on certain types and methods of marketing when targeting children under 13.

The General Data Protection Regulation (GDPR) of the European Union (EU) was enacted in 2018 to uphold people's rights regarding their data and is one of the world's most rigorous privacy and security laws. Although drafted and passed by the EU, GDPR imposes obligations on organizations globally, provided that they collect data from or target EU citizens and residents inside the EU. Article 8 of GDPR, also known as GDPR-K is the EU's equivalent of COPPA and pertains to conditions relevant to the child's consent concerning information society services. GDPR-K mandates that apps or websites targeted at children under the age of 16 (or younger, depending on the EU country) must obtain verifiable parental consent before collecting any personal information about the child. Moreover, it requires the controller to take reasonable steps to ensure, in such cases, that the consent is given or authorized by the holder of parental responsibility over the child, taking into account available technology.

9 LOOKING FORWARD

Lastly, this document ends on a positive note. It explains that this is short-term guidance that will have to be renewed periodically and that support will be available. Providing ongoing support for teachers through professional development and sharing of good practices will be important.

TRANSFORMING YOUR ORGANIZATION WITH AI

So far, we've explored how to be a leader in this new era and how to plan for short-term development with artificial intelligence. If we put this in the context of Vijay Govindarajan's Three-Box Solution, from Chapter 4, then we are merely optimizing the current system. This is not a bad thing, but we are still in Box One.

It will be crucial to start dedicating resources to Box Three and to listen out for the 'weak signals' of how this technology is advancing and the areas of society and education it is disrupting.

The Substitution, Augmentation, Modification, and Redefinition Model (SAMR) is a framework for evaluating technology integration in education. It was developed by Dr. Ruben Puentedura (2010), and although it is over thirteen years old, it can still offer educators an understanding of the different ways technology can be used to transform teaching and learning.

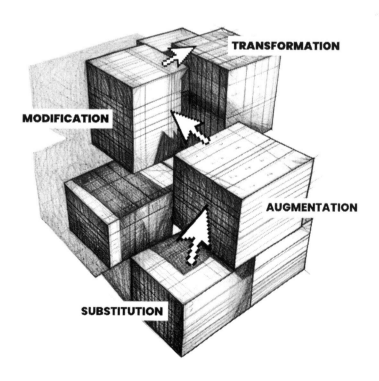

1 SUBSTITUTION

The first level of the SAMR model is substitution, which involves using technology to replace a traditional teaching method with a digital one. Here are some examples of how students, teachers, and leaders can substitute their traditional methods of practice with artificial intelligence:

This can benefit students by giving them the freedom to ask an AI chatbot any question they want and receive an answer in a similar way to asking a teacher. It can benefit teachers by creating lesson plans for them based on a precise set of requests.

Leaders can benefit from generating a policy document.

2 AUGMENTATION

The second level of the SAMR model is augmentation, which involves using technology to enhance a traditional teaching method. Here are some examples of how students, teachers, and leaders can augment their traditional methods of practice with artificial intelligence:

Students can use an AI text generator to craft a resume by using language and a professional structure. Teachers could benefit by using AI tools to find trends or common misconceptions in the work of a group of students, allowing them to address these at a group level.

One benefit to leaders could be using AI to edit a presentation so that it is more impactful in its language and imagery.

3 MODIFICATION

The third level of the SAMR model is modification, which involves using technology to significantly redesign a traditional teaching method. Here are some examples of how students, teachers, and leaders can modify their traditional methods of practice with artificial intelligence:

A student's experience of education could be modified by using a tool like ChatGPT to act as a learning mentor. Allowing the students to have an ongoing conversation where they receive support, guidance, tips, and feedback. Teachers can modify their lessons using a range of AI tools to generate animated movies of historical figures that teach part of the lesson. This allows more mundane lessons to become more engaging and offer a new dynamic to learning for their students.

Similar to students, leaders can modify their practice by using AI as a personal leadership coach.

4 REDEFINITION

The fourth and final level of the SAMR model is redefinition, which involves using technology to create previously inconceivable learning opportunities. We can not truly know how this technology will transform education mid- and long-term. However, even in these early days of the AI revolution, there are some ways that students, teachers, and leaders can redefine their traditional methods of practice with artificial intelligence:

Students can learn anywhere and at any time through personalized content generated specifically for them. Teachers can spend meaningful time guiding students and helping them form emotional intelligence, knowing that their AI ecosystem is helping students progress their learning and analyze data.

Leaders can have deep-level insights into the progress of all of their students, allowing them to intervene at the right moments and lead their staff with confidence.

It is important to note that the SAMR model does not necessarily represent a scale of the successful integration of technology. There will be some tasks where substitution and augmentation are entirely appropriate. However, as leaders, we must also strive for transformation so that our students and our staff receive the experiences needed for their long-term success.

A Template Artificial Intelligence Policy for Your Organization

I'm pleased to share with you this policy template that outlines how your school, college, or university can integrate artificial intelligence responsibly and safely.

As you know, artificial intelligence is rapidly evolving and has become an integral part of our daily lives. However, with this evolution comes the need for proper policies and regulations that ensure the safe and ethical use of technology, particularly when it comes to AI.

This template is not meant to be an exhaustive policy but rather a supplement to your existing digital, online, or technology policies. It is a guide to help you embed AI ethics and safety within your curriculum and staff structures while also highlighting the importance of having dedicated AI Ethics and Safety Officers.

As this technology changes and progresses at a fast rate, there will be a need to revisit your policy regularly and update it where appropriate.

In adopting this template, you'll need to work closely with your data protection officer and legal department to ensure compliance with data protection, laws, and regulations.

I encourage you to download this template and use it as a foundation for your school's policy. As you adapt and edit it, keep in mind the unique needs and circumstances of your institution.

By taking a proactive approach to AI policy, you'll not only be promoting responsible AI use but also preparing your students for a future where AI will continue to play an increasingly important role.

The Policy Template

1. INTRODUCTION

This Artificial Intelligence [AI] Policy supports the aims of the [School / College / University] in educating the [School / College / University] community to explore horizons in line with the digital world safely and responsibly. It aims to establish a framework for the ethical and safe use of AI technologies within the educational setting.

This policy applies to all members of the [School / College / University] community, including staff, students, and visitors. All staff (including volunteers) and any other users of AI technologies are expected to adhere to this policy.

The policy will be reviewed and updated as needed to ensure ongoing compliance with relevant laws and best practices. The date for the next review is _____.

2. RATIONALE

AI technologies have the potential to greatly enhance the educational experience, providing personalized learning opportunities, automating administrative tasks, and offering new ways for teachers to engage with their students. However, it is important to recognize the ethical and safety concerns surrounding the use of AI in the classroom.

[School / College / University] understands the responsibility to educate our faculty, students, and guests about the importance of AI ethics and safety issues. This policy is designed to help raise awareness and develop the appropriate behaviors and critical thinking skills that enable people to remain both safe and within the law when using AI technologies in and beyond the context of the classroom.

3. ROLES AND RESPONSIBILITIES

The _____ have ultimate responsibility for AI policy and delegate to _____ to confirm and report back that the policy and practices are embedded and monitored. The named AI Ethics and Safety Officers are the _____. All members of the [School / College / University] community are made aware of who holds these posts. It is the role of the AI Ethics and Safety Officers to keep abreast of current issues and guidance through organizations such as _____.

4. MONITORING

The [School / College / University] has appropriate filters and monitoring in place to facilitate the safe use of AI technologies. The AI Ethics and Safety Officers, together with relevant staff, are responsible for ensuring that AI technologies used within the [School / College / University] are compliant with data protection laws and uphold privacy rights.

5. STUDENTS

5.1 Inclusion

The School strives to establish a consistent message with parents regarding the responsible use of AI for all students, which in turn should contribute to the establishment and future development of the School's AI ethics and safety guidelines.

However, the staff is aware that some students may require additional support, including reminders, prompts, and further explanations to reinforce their existing knowledge and understanding of AI ethics and safety issues. For students with limited social understanding, careful consideration is given to group interactions when raising awareness of AI ethics and safety.

AI-related activities are thoughtfully planned and well-managed for these children and young people, ensuring they have the necessary guidance and support to use AI technology responsibly and safely.

5.2 Education

AI technologies are increasingly used across all areas of the curriculum. We believe it is essential for AI ethics and safety guidance to be given to students on a regular and meaningful basis. AI ethics and safety are embedded within our curriculum, with lessons addressing key areas of digital citizenship and AI-related safety.

6. STAFF

6.1 Data Security

Staff members have a responsibility to ensure the security of any personal, sensitive, confidential, and classified information when using AI technologies. Staff should not input the names of students, staff, members of the school community, or any other sensitive information about students and staff into an AI tool unless it has been declared officially safe to do so and approved in writing by the AI Ethics and Safety Officers.

6.2 Response to a Data Breach

In the event of a data breach, it must be reported immediately to _____. The [School / College / University] will follow the procedures outlined in the Data Protection Policy in reporting breaches to _____ and notifying exposed individuals.

7. INAPPROPRIATE MATERIAL OR UNETHICAL USE OF AI

Accidental exposure to inappropriate material or unethical use of AI must be immediately reported to _____. Deliberate exposure to inappropriate material or unethical use of AI must be reported to _____ and will be logged. Depending on the seriousness of the offense, there may be an investigation by _____.

Thoughts on AI From Educators

"...lean in. Be proactive. Act now in controlled prototypes to see the efficacy and impact."

Scott Hayden , Head of Digital Learning

"...get on board and understand this. It isn't going away."

Jon Tait, Deputy CEO

"...support teachers prepared to experiment with AI."

Jamie Smith, Executive Chairman

"...create an ethical guideline on the use of AI, equip teachers with the knowledge of AI through training on how to adopt and adapt to the transition."

Esther Albert, Psychology teacher & Human Intelligence Coordinator

"...staff in schools are used to having to evolve and adapt their pedagogy to reflect current thinking and provide the best environment for their learners."

Emma Darcy, Director of Technology for Learning

"...use it to make their life easier."

Lee Parkinson, ICT Mr P, Primary School Teacher and Teacher Trainer

Educational leaders need to...

"...invest in their strategy and... employ digital fit teachers. Besides that, they have to see that learning, school and teaching don't need to be in one place."

Dieter Möckelmann, EdTechWatcher

"...embrace technology and AI, so that they can teach their communities about effective governance and to impress the importance of skills and digital literacy for all stakeholders in their community."

Olly Lewis, Head of Digital Transformation

"...develop a whole school approach."

Martin Jones, Director

"...advocate for a national initiative that will stimulate further investment in the design, development, use and management of these services. Ethical frameworks need to be developed further to reflect advances in AI development."

Aftab Hussain, ILT and LRC Manager

"...embrace the power of technology and use it to enhance their teaching, not replace it. My advice: Get ahead of the curve before the curve knocks you down."

Mark Nichols, Future Leader

Share your advice on social media! What do educational leaders need to do regarding AI?

Use the hashtag #AICLASSROOM

CHAPTER 11

Embracing the Future:
Rethinking Education for a New World

"It's quite fashionable to say that the educational system is broken. It's not broken. It's wonderfully constructed. It's just that we don't need it anymore."

–Sugata Mitra,
Computer Scientist and Educational Theorist

There is no getting away from the fact that the main priority in education must be: "student achievement and preparation for global competitiveness by fostering educational excellence and ensuring equal access" (U.S. Department of Education, 2021). Education should equip students with the essential skills and knowledge to become accomplished individuals and valuable contributors to society. As a former philosophy teacher, I understand the concept that education can be an end in itself; however, the most important goal of education is to be successful in society. A large part of this success for our students will take place in their professions and the work that they perform as adults.

The world of work is undergoing rapid transformation due to technological advancements, which bring both opportunities and challenges. One of the biggest challenges is the need for new and more advanced skills, including social and emotional skills, higher cognitive skills, technological skills, and basic digital competencies.

The COVID-19 pandemic has accelerated the rate of technological adoption and changed workforce habits and expectations, leading to a rethinking of the role of work in people's lives. While many jobs may be lost as a result of technological adoption, many others will be created, and almost all jobs will change in some way. Schools, colleges, and universities will need to incorporate these skills in their curricula so that students thrive in this rapidly changing work environment.

The founder of deeplearning.ai, Andrew Ng, stated back in 2016 that "the biggest harm that AI is likely to do to individuals in the short term is job displacement, as the amount of work we can automate with AI is vastly larger than before" (Harvard Review, 2016). In the midst of this disruption, it is the responsibility of educators and educational leaders globally to ensure their students are given the skills to thrive in this new paradigm.

There will be a significant shift in the skills needed by workers, with demand for technological skills, social and emotional skills, and higher-level cognitive skills expected to increase. Additionally, educational systems need to focus on building competencies, such as cognitive, health, and social and emotional foundations, which are the prerequisites for further learning and acquisition of future skills. Ultimately, having this strong foundation is essential for workers to adapt to new ways of working and new occupations in an increasingly digitized world.

The World Government Summit 2023 (2023) has identified 56 foundational skills, split into the categories of Cognitive, Interpersonal, Self-Leadership, and Digital, that will help students thrive in the future of work.

This list will fluctuate and change as AI technology advances and the skills needed by humans develop. If I had to identify the most important skill in this list, I would choose self-development. Teaching students to learn is far more important than teaching them what to learn. As John Gatto Taylor (1991) stated:

> *As society rapidly changes, individuals will have to be able to function comfortably in a world that is always in flux. Knowledge will continue to increase at a dizzying rate. This means that a content-based curriculum, with a set body of information to be imparted to students, is entirely inappropriate as a means of preparing children for their adult roles.*

Artificial intelligence is increasingly replacing human labor. We have a duty to educate our students in the skills and work that have a low risk of being automated in the future and are projected to grow over the next decade.

One may wonder, what jobs are most insulated from the impact of artificial intelligence in the future?

The U.S. Career Institute (2023) curated a list of the 65 jobs with the lowest risk of automation. The jobs that are least at risk are often found in fields that value uniquely human qualities like empathy, creativity, and adaptability. In particular, the medical field stands out as a bastion of job security, thanks to the complex and ever-changing nature of medical work. Other professions that are least at risk include jobs in education, the creative sector, and personal services, such as hairdressing and massage therapy. The U.S. Career Institution stated that the jobs with the highest projected growth by 2031 are:

1. Nurse Practitioners: 45.7%
2. Choreographers: 29.7%
3. Physician Assistants: 27.6%
4. Mental Health Counselors: 22.1%

5. Nursing Instructors and Teachers, Post-Secondary: 21.5%
6. Coaches and Scouts: 20%
7. Athletic Trainers: 17.5%
8. Physical Therapists: 16.9%
9. Orthotists and Prosthetists: 16.8%
10. Occupational Therapists: 13.9%

These sectors will not be unaffected by artificial intelligence but will survive because human skills will be valued alongside AI capabilities. Therefore, it will be vital that our students learn how to work WITH artificial intelligence and distinguish their value separate from it. Are our schools, colleges, and universities ready to take on this challenge? They will be because educators and leaders like you are already taking the first steps in learning how to become essential teachers in the AI revolution.

Here are some ways education will benefit from artificial intelligence in the next ten years:

Personalized and Adaptive Learning

We can leverage the power of artificial intelligence by creating tailor-made educational experiences that cater to the unique needs, abilities, and interests of each individual student.

AI tools will continue to measure student progress and be able to design a personalized learning path for them. The AI system will adapt the content, pace, and difficulty of the curriculum to ensure that each student is challenged enough to learn but not so much as to get frustrated. Furthermore, artificial intelligence provides timely feedback and recommendations to students to help improve their learning outcomes.

AI Tutors

AI Tutors have the potential to transform the way our students learn. They provide students with guidance and support throughout their academic journey. By using natural language processing, they are able to answer students' questions and offer advice on how to improve their academic performance.

Unlike a human tutor, an AI tutor is available 24/7, providing students with support in and out of the classroom. This can be particularly beneficial for students who are struggling with certain topics or who need additional support to succeed in their studies.

Automated Grading and Feedback

We have benefited from automated grading and feedback for a number of years now with tools like Google Forms, but this will quickly advance with the new AI tools being developed. The ability to automate the grading of complex written work will become the norm. This will have a transformative impact on education at every level.

Artificial intelligence will be able to analyze a student's work quickly and accurately, providing instant formative feedback on their performance. This will save educators time and enable them to focus on providing more targeted support to struggling students.

Although artificial intelligence struggles with bias, the development of AI in education has the potential to reduce bias in grading. Traditional grading methods can be influenced by factors such as the teacher's mood, personal biases, or past experiences with a student. AI-powered grading systems will be able to provide consistent and objective feedback, eliminating these factors.

Virtual Learning Environments

Artificial intelligence will begin to enhance immersive learning experiences that bring realism and interactivity to virtual learning environments. These new experiences help students learn and develop skills in realistic scenarios that otherwise might be difficult to access, for example, participating in a surgery theater.

Furthermore, AI will assist educators with the creation and management of virtual reality content more efficiently. Existing AI tools can generate 3D models, textures, and animations, reducing the time and cost of content creation. AI can also analyze learner behavior in VR and improve the experience over time.

Predictive Analytics

Predictive analytics powered by AI has the potential to revolutionize the way education is delivered and received. Educators will have insights into student behavior, performance, and learning patterns. We will be able to predict what a student is likely to struggle with and create customized learning experiences that cater to their individual needs.

AI will identify students who are at risk of dropping out and provide early interventions to support their academic growth. This ensures that students receive the help they need, while also allowing educators to allocate resources more effectively.

Artificial intelligence will also help educators identify trends and patterns in student performance, which can be used to inform curriculum development and teaching strategies. With this information, educators will create more engaging and effective learning experiences that are tailored to individual students, resulting in better outcomes.

Language Translation

With AI-powered language translation, students easily access educational content in languages other than their native tongue. This enables them to learn from a wider range of sources and expands their knowledge beyond what is available in their primary language. It also facilitates instant user-friendly communication and collaboration between students from different countries.

Global Access

Students in remote or underserved regions of the world sometimes do not have access to quality education or skilled teachers. AI-based educational tools, such as chatbots and AI tutors, will provide immediate support to these students who may have questions or need additional assistance.

The use of AI in education democratizes access to quality education and provides learning opportunities for students around the world. Artificial intelligence helps us create a more inclusive and equitable education system that meets the needs of all learners, regardless of their geographic location or socioeconomic status.

Better Resource Allocation

AI helps identify areas where resources are underutilized. By analyzing data on student performance, educators can identify which resources are most effective and allocate them accordingly, by analyzing AI-powered data on student performance. Therefore, resources can be directed to areas where they will have the greatest impact, allowing for more efficiency.

Many organizations suffer from understaffing. By analyzing data and predicting future needs, educators can ensure that they have the right number of teachers and support staff in place to meet student and faculty needs. Resources can then be allocated more effectively, ensuring that students receive the support they need to succeed.

Life-Long Learning

As we integrate this technology deeper into our practice as educators, our students will develop the skills to be able to learn effectively with artificial intelligence tools. This moves us away from any notion that the teacher is the fount of all knowledge, which, of course, they aren't. As Paulo Freire (1970) explains, "The teacher is no longer merely the one who teaches, but one who is himself taught in dialogue with the students, who in turn, while being taught, also teach. They become jointly responsible for a process in which all grow." Our use and promotion of AI, alongside our teaching of key skills, will equip students to be able to learn from anywhere but also at any time, even after they leave us and become productive adults positively contributing to society.

It is necessary for us to assist our students in the development of their AI learning skills so that they continue to learn and unlearn in the ever-changing world in which we all live. The ability to be agile will be supported by technology that guides them and teaches them when they need it.

CHAPTER 12

Empathy and Algorithms: The Convergence of EI and AI

Technology continues to shape how we interact with and perceive our world, presenting us with an almost unbounded range of opportunities. Fundamental human traits will be just as important, if not more critical, amid this digital revolution; they will continue to form the foundations upon which a prosperous future rests. The Harvard Business Review (2019) defines emotional intelligence as "an individual's ability to accurately recognize, understand and manage their own emotions as well as that of others." People with high emotional intelligence understand others' feelings and select responses that will be met positively. The convergence of artificial intelligence and emotional intelligence (EI) is crucial for maintaining human relationships and interactions in the rapidly evolving technological landscape, emphasizing the importance of cultivating EI to work in harmony with AI.

According to Daniel Goleman (2005), there are four emotional intelligence domains: self-awareness, self-management, social awareness, and relationship management. Emotional intelligence is a critical factor in attaining successful outcomes. The importance of emotional intelligence in achieving success is well-established, as evidenced by a study by Bradberry (2009) that found that emotional intelligence is responsible for 58% of success in any role or career. It is no longer enough just to be competent; humans also need the intangibles of emotional intelligence.

In our rapidly advancing world, more than technical ability and knowledge are needed to keep up in the workplace, school, and everyday life. The benchmark for the success of humanity is changing; now more than ever, we need a robust variety of emotional intelligence skills if we hope to thrive in this new era. Understanding the four domains of emotional intelligence is essential in developing the skills necessary for effective interactions when using artificial intelligence in our daily lives.

Self-Awareness

Self-awareness is a metacognitive process that involves monitoring and regulating one's cognitive and affective states. Chinese philosopher Lao Tzu spoke about the importance of self-awareness when he said, "Knowing others is intelligence; knowing yourself is true wisdom. Mastering others is strength; mastering yourself is true power." Examining our thoughts, emotions, behaviors, and how they affect us and those around us allows us to gain insight into our lives—with a broader scope that leads to essential growth opportunities.

As artificial intelligence becomes more integrated into our society, we must consider the ethical implications of the systems that are being developed. Self-awareness helps us recognize the broader social and ethical implications of the systems we create and make decisions that align with our values and ethical standards. As artificial systems become more advanced, they are increasingly used to augment human decision-making. Self-awareness assists in understanding our decision-making processes and identifies areas where artificial intelligence can be most helpful in supporting or augmenting our decision-making while still being aware that we should also use human judgment.

Self-awareness is critical for ongoing learning and improvement. By being self-aware of our strengths and weaknesses, we can identify areas where we need to improve our skills and knowledge and where AI can be most helpful in augmenting or automating specific tasks. This leads us to the next domain, Self-Management.

Self-Management

Part of being able to manage ourselves is being able to manage our own emotions to respond effectively to different situations. The ability to regulate and control one's emotional reactions can be particularly pertinent in cases that may be challenging or stressful. We need to identify our emotions through self-awareness and use self-management to navigate those emotions appropriately.

Adopting a positive outlook and embracing the AI revolution can aid in overcoming challenges and uncertainties while opening up new opportunities for growth and innovation. However, it is critical to manage oneself effectively, particularly when encountering failure and frustration while learning and adapting to technology. Working through failure is a crucial aspect of self-management, and it's imperative not to let our emotions cloud our judgment.

In the book *Mindset: The New Psychology of Success*, Stanford University Professor Carol Dweck (2007) wrote about the power of mindset. She stated, "In a growth mindset, people believe that their most basic abilities can be developed through dedication and hard work—brains and talent are just the starting point. Cultivating a growth mindset is essential so that failure is not regarded as an end but as another stepping stone on the journey to mastery. Working through failure creates more resilient learners.

People with a growth mindset are more inclined to take on new challenges, work through failures, and continue working on their weaknesses. This certainly applies to learning and maximizing new technology like those that use artificial intelligence, including adaptive learning tools.

Adaptive learning tools align with the principles of a growth mindset by encouraging students to embrace challenges, learn from mistakes, and continuously improve. Adaptive learning tools use artificial intelligence to create personalized learning experiences that cater to individual student's needs, abilities, and performance. Here are some ways in which adaptive learning tools support a growth mindset:

- **Personalized learning**: AI-powered educational platforms are tailored to each individual's needs and abilities, helping learners work on their weaknesses at their own pace and instilling a sense of progress.
- **Real-time feedback**: AI can offer immediate feedback on performance, allowing learners to understand their mistakes, identify areas for improvement, and adjust their strategies accordingly.
- **Goal setting and tracking**: AI can assist learners in setting realistic goals, monitoring their progress, and providing insights on adjusting their efforts to achieve mastery.
- **Gamification**: AI can incorporate gamification elements into learning experiences, making the process of acquiring new skills more engaging and enjoyable. This approach can help learners view challenges as opportunities for growth rather than barriers to success.

There are numerous adaptive learning tools available, and through our research, DreamBox Learning and ALEKS are two of the best. DreamBox and ALEKS are adaptive learning platforms designed to enhance students' mathematical skills aligned with common education standards like the Common Core. DreamBox focuses on students from K-8, while ALEKS focuses on 3-12. While both employ adaptive learning algorithms for personalization, DreamBox focuses on game-based, interactive learning with real-time assessments, whereas ALEKS uses a structured approach with an initial "Knowledge Check" assessment. DreamBox also has a reading solution called Dreambox Reading, and ALEKS has chemistry, statistics, and more.

By leveraging AI's capabilities, learners will be better equipped to adopt a growth mindset, embrace challenges, learn from failures, and ultimately maximize their potential in a rapidly evolving technological landscape. One area in which a growth mindset is essential is in successfully utilizing the EDIT process of the PREP-EDIT framework.

The EDIT portion of the PREP-EDIT framework cycle plays a crucial role in individual's self-management when using artificial intelligence tools, as it involves adjusting and refining outputs based on feedback. This process requires emotional regulation and a growth mindset. It takes prompt engineering skills to give the proper inputs into AI tools to obtain relevant outputs. Being able to emotionally handle when we are not obtaining the desired outputs and being willing to continually adjust our approach until we are thriving instead of quickly giving up when we do not immediately find success is key to harnessing the power of a growth mindset in partnership with artificial intelligence. Students with a fixed mindset might think, "We get what we get from the outputs," while a growth mindset might think, "I don't have what I need yet, but I'll keep trying." Working through frustration and failure and maintaining a positive attitude that one will eventually get it right is essential to strengthening a growth mindset.

Having a growth mindset is essential for personal growth and self-improvement. By embracing the idea that our abilities and intelligence can be developed through hard work and dedication, individuals can take advantage of the benefits provided by artificial intelligence to make informed decisions that align with their intentions and values. Artificial intelligence is meant to collaborate with individuals and inform them. Still, individuals must also possess the skills and abilities to use this information to come to conclusions and courses of action based on human critical thinking that support developing more robust emotional intelligence. This is where the need for social awareness becomes evident.

Social Awareness

Social awareness refers to the ability to understand and navigate social situations and dynamics and to perceive and empathize with the feelings and perspectives of others. With an increased understanding of others, we act in ways that foster meaningful connections with those around us regardless of the particular context or situation. From deciphering body language cues to comprehending different societal norms, social awareness is essential to building relationships and successfully maneuvering through day-to-day interactions.

The emergence of AI-driven chatbots, such as ChatGPT, allows us to produce electronic communications instantly. This saves us precious time to allocate to what is most important: spending time with our families and building relationships with our students. However, the ease with which we can generate these communications creates a disconnect between the sender's and receiver's emotions. We can quickly generate a letter to parents, comments for a report card, or even an email to another person. Still, it is necessary to add a human element to ensure that all messages are appropriate before they reach their intended recipients. Doing so adds a personal touch, ensuring that context and tone accurately reflect what the sender wants their recipients to understand.

Understanding how to empathize with each other is essential for building a positive classroom culture. Showing compassion and consideration towards one another gives everyone in the class a chance to share their feelings and perspectives without judgment - this helps students learn from each other. Empathy helps students connect with others, build relationships, and respond compassionately to others' needs and concerns. It is fundamental for effective communication, conflict resolution, and social interaction. It can also help to reduce prejudice and discrimination by fostering greater understanding and acceptance of diverse perspectives and experiences.

AI can enhance empathy in the classroom by providing tools and resources that facilitate understanding, communication, and compassion among students. Please note that the use of these AI tools should always be in accordance with the school district or company policies and regulations. New features, tools, and possibilities are being created at a rapid pace, and here are some existing ways AI can contribute to building empathy:

- **Emotion recognition:** AI can analyze facial expressions, vocal patterns, and body language to detect emotions and provide insights into students' emotional states. This information can help teachers better understand their students' feelings and encourage empathetic interactions. A few AI tools that can be used are:
  - Affectiva: A software that uses facial expression analysis to detect emotions in real time.
  - Beyond Verbal: This platform analyzes vocal patterns and tones to detect emotions and moods.

- **Chatbots and virtual agents:** These tools can simulate realistic conversations with people from different cultural backgrounds, helping students develop empathy and understanding through engaging interactions. Examples include:
  - Replika: A chatbot that can simulate conversations, allowing users to practice empathy and understanding by engaging with artificial intelligence that adapts its responses to different contexts and emotions.
  - ChatGPT: Have students type in a paragraph or passage into the chatbot and prompt ChatGPT to respond or analyze the content from a particular perspective or run a sentiment analysis as mentioned in the EDIT framework. Chatbots might reflect bias, which is an excellent opportunity for students to analyze responses for this case! ChatGPT can also generate content in different languages and break down communication barriers.

- **AI-driven language learning tools**: Language learning is critical to understanding different cultures and fostering empathy. AI-powered language learning tools can provide personalized learning experiences and immersive practice environments, enabling students to connect with diverse backgrounds. Examples of these tools are:
    - **Duolingo:** Duolingo is a popular language learning platform that uses AI algorithms to personalize the learning experience and adapt to the individual learner's needs.
    - **Rosetta Stone:** Rosetta Stone's language learning platform combines AI-driven speech recognition and adaptive learning technologies to create a highly interactive and immersive learning experience.

- **AI-enabled social robotics**: AI-powered social robots can create realistic, human-like interactions, allowing students to practice empathy and understanding through engaging and dynamic scenarios. Examples include:
    - **Pepper Robot:** Pepper is a humanoid robot designed to interact with people using natural language processing, emotion recognition, and AI-driven behaviors. It can be used in educational settings to promote empathy and understanding.
    - **Tega:** Tega is a socially assistive robot designed for educational purposes, leveraging AI to create personalized interactions and experiences that promote empathy and understanding.

Artificial intelligence, while primarily focused on information, data, and facts, continues to evolve in its ability to approximate empathy and social awareness. As AI systems progress, they strive to understand better and adapt to human emotions, social cues, norms, and behaviors. This ongoing development brings optimism for the future of AI, as it aims to mimic social awareness more closely. Researchers and developers recognize the significance of ethical values and are taking measures to ensure that socially-aware AI systems are developed responsibly.

By leveraging data and advanced algorithms, artificial intelligence systems can make decisions independent of human input. AI offers valuable problem-solving insights, but it's crucial to assess its role as just one component within a larger decision-making process. Emotional intelligence helps individuals better understand and manage the ethical implications of artificial intelligence and ensure that AI-powered decisions align with human values. The insights gained from social awareness and understanding others can be actively applied to navigating relationships effectively.

Relationship Management

Relationship management is the ability to use the understanding of others' emotions and perspectives to manage, navigate, and foster relationships. AI-powered tools can assist in relationship management by building and maintaining rapport through analyzing communication patterns and providing suggestions for more empathetic and effective interactions. AI can support adaptability by monitoring changes in personal and professional environments. It offers data-driven insights that empower individuals to adjust their relationship management approach, an essential domain within emotional intelligence.

Relationships must be cultivated and nurtured. Learning the basics of healthy relationships through managing rapport, using effective communication techniques to ease difficult conversations, guiding conflict resolution for happier outcomes, embracing leadership qualities that foster team collaboration, and practicing adaptability- all form the foundation for successful interactions in our daily lives.

Effective communication involves expressing oneself clearly and listening actively to others to understand their perspectives. Conflict resolution is also an essential skill in relationship management. It consists of constructively identifying and addressing conflicts that satisfy the needs of all parties. Collaboration is also crucial as it requires working effectively with others towards a common goal, leveraging diverse perspectives and skills to achieve success. Lastly, adaptability is necessary to manage relationships effectively. It involves being flexible in one's approach to managing relationships and adapting to changing circumstances.

Collaboration is vital in a classroom setting for several reasons. It allows students to work together towards a common goal, leveraging each other's strengths and perspectives to achieve more than they could individually. This helps develop critical thinking skills and promotes problem-solving abilities. A necessary skill for working together on projects, such as project-based learning, problem-based learning, and genius hour, is developing and maintaining a schedule and goals to ensure accountability. AI assists students in navigating project management tasks together by recording notes, analyzing conversations, task reminders, and many other possibilities, allowing students to focus on working as a team toward their goals.

While most project management tools are designed primarily for businesses and teams, some can be adapted for use with students for group projects, task management, and collaboration. The following tools offer free plans or educational discounts, which make them more accessible for students:

- **ClickUp:** ClickUp offers a free plan that can be used by students for organizing tasks, managing projects, and collaborating with their peers. Its user-friendly interface and wide range of functionalities make it a good choice for students.
- **Asana:** Asana's free plan allows up to 15 team members, making it suitable for student group projects. Students can use Asana for task management, project tracking, and collaboration.
- **Monday.com:** Monday.com offers an educational discount, which can make their platform more affordable. With its customizable templates and features, students can use Monday.com to manage group projects and assignments and collaborate effectively.

Tom Moule, a senior AI specialist at Jisc, discussed in his podcast (Jisc, 2022) how artificial intelligence has the potential to enhance collaboration in several ways:

- **Intelligent grouping:** AI can help teachers form intelligent groups of students based on their skills, interests, and learning styles. This can help ensure that each group is balanced and that students work with others who complement their strengths and weaknesses.
- **Real-time monitoring:** AI can provide real-time monitoring of student interactions during collaborative learning activities, allowing teachers to identify potential issues and provide support as needed. This allows teachers to be more proactive when helping students.
- **Data analysis:** AI can analyze student data from collaborative learning activities to provide insights into group dynamics, such as how communication patterns influence learning outcomes. This can help teachers optimize joint learning activities and identify areas for improvement.

Collaboration fosters creativity and innovation. When students work together, they share ideas and develop new and exciting approaches to assignments or projects, including working with artificial intelligence. Tasks that can be accomplished with the collaboration of a student and artificial intelligence have the potential to be enhanced when multiple students work together to engage the artificial intelligence. For example, getting unique and diverse perspectives helps generate better inputs and outputs through collaborative discourse, strategizing, and problem-solving. Strong EI will allow students to navigate differences while building upon each other's strengths.

As research by Bradberry (2009) highlights, those with strong emotional intelligence are equipped to survive and thrive in the ever-shifting professional world. This is evident in that 90% of top performers in the workplace exhibit high levels of emotional intelligence. Although achieving success without emotional intelligence is possible, the odds are generally against it. As AI continues to disrupt traditional workplace structures, individuals with high emotional intelligence will be better able to navigate this new landscape's emotional and social challenges. They will be better equipped to understand the emotions and motivations of others around them.

Artificial intelligence will continue to advance and expand and become better at mimicking human behaviors. We must stay ahead of the curve and be lifelong learners to stay relevant and keep up with technological advancements. Not only will we need solid emotional intelligence to navigate society's continuous changes and evolution, but we must persistently learn how to apply what makes us human as an asset to technology. Balancing AI with EI will distinguish successful individuals in the AI revolution from those avoiding technology or becoming overly dependent on it for decision-making. The symbiotic relationship between algorithms and empathy will drive the future, allowing society to advance like never before.

EPILOGUE E

As we come to the end of the beginning of this journey into the world of artificial intelligence in education, it's simply astonishing to see the incredible pace at which AI is advancing. Since the beginning of this book, OpenAI has introduced the revolutionary GPT-4, taking a giant leap forward from its predecessor, GPT-3.5. As AI continues to evolve, so too will the opportunities to weave these extraordinary tools into our educational experiences.

GPT-4 is a multimodal model that establishes a new benchmark for foundational models in AI. It merges visual and textual data to significantly enhance comprehension, paving the way for AI-driven learning tools to broaden their horizons. The fact that GPT-4 outperforms GPT-3.5 in basic reasoning and human assessments is a thrilling prospect for the future of AI in education—a future where AI models can provide even more nuanced and sophisticated support for both students and educators.

The progress OpenAI made with GPT-4 by expanding its parameter base and refining the model through reinforcement learning via human input highlights the power of collaboration and iterative improvement. As we push the boundaries of AI in education, it's essential that developers, educators, and students alike come together to ensure these technologies cater to the diverse needs of learners across the globe.

In the last few days, Google has recently unveiled its innovative chatbot, Bard, in response to OpenAI's ChatGPT, prompting users to explore the similarities and differences between the two AI-driven platforms. As a groundbreaking Google chatbot, Bard is fueled by the LaMDA large language model, which enables it to accomplish a range of text-based tasks.

The genesis of Bard can be traced back to the meteoric rise of OpenAI's ChatGPT, which seemed to signal that Google was lagging behind in the tech arena. ChatGPT's potential to reshape the search industry and challenge Google's dominance in search advertising prompted a swift reaction from the tech giant. In fact, on December 21, 2022, just three weeks after ChatGPT's debut, the New York Times reported that Google had initiated a "code red" strategy to address this looming threat. A mere 47 days later, on February 6, 2023, Google announced the arrival of Bard.

At its core, Bard is driven by a "streamlined" version of LaMDA, a large language model trained on publicly available dialogues and web data.

The competition among tech giants like OpenAI, Google, Microsoft, and Amazon serves as a driving force for innovation. By nurturing a competitive environment, we're setting the stage for exponential growth in AI applications in education. Collaborations like those between OpenAI and organizations such as Microsoft, Khan Academy, Duolingo, and the Icelandic government reveal the incredible impact partnerships like these could have on educational outcomes.

As we witness the swift transition from lab to consumer-facing products, it's important to remain mindful of the challenges that lie ahead. As large language models like GPT-4 continue to grapple with issues of bias, falsehoods, and manipulation, the AI community must stay committed to tackling these obstacles, ensuring we create equitable and reliable learning tools for all.

As we embark on this exciting new chapter of AI in education, I invite you to share your experiences of GPT-4 and other AI-driven tools in the classroom. Join the AI Classroom Facebook group, or share your insights using the hashtag #aiclassroom on social media. Together, we can shape a future where AI and education form a harmonious partnership, empowering learners and educators to reach new pinnacles of knowledge and achievement.

"THE FUTURE BELONGS TO THOSE WHO PREPARE FOR IT TODAY."

Malcolm X

Vicki, a seasoned classroom teacher and Instructional Technology Director in southwest Georgia, has 18 years of experience teaching K-12 and five years with adults. A Georgia Tech graduate and world-traveling speaker, she is known for her philosophy of "innovating like a turtle." Vicki's focus is on supporting students and teachers facing unique challenges. As the author of the Cool Cat Teacher blog for 15 years, she has attracted over 100,000 monthly visitors and earned recognition as a top 50 education blog and an Edublog award finalist.

In the long term, I believe AI will impact how I work and live by...

...becoming an assistant. Already I replaced a human editor with two AI apps that help me edit. What it cannot do is help with structural editing. This big-picture work will need to be done by a human indefinitely. It cannot handle the big-picture visionary work of how I want to impact a reader or how I want to create a "driveway moment" on my podcast where someone sits in their car to listen to the end of a podcast before going in their house. Humans are uniquely creative, big-picture thinkers. Just as lower-level call centers went overseas, lower-level tasks will go "into the sea" of computing instead of to other humans.

The thing that worries me most about AI in my life is...

...that people are attributing human-like intelligence to AI. AI seems intelligent because of the repository of human work it has studied, but it is still a computing tool, albeit one fed by big data. We need to redefine our standards of working with AI. We have inherited a fractured, uncooperative, and depressed society from the last fifteen years of social media algorithm experimentation. When new tools emerge, new conversations must happen about the ethics and wisdom of their proper use and impact on society and especially our children.

How do you see AI changing education?

I am using AI built into software that helps me teach Python coding. I am teaching far more than I ever could teach having to grade and provide feedback on each item. This AI-aided assistant helps me focus on teaching the big-picture concepts of Python rather than being a human feedback machine tethered to my computer 24/7. This is great. The impact of AI on education will be immeasurable if we use it strategically. Students will need to be big-picture thinkers and problem solvers. They will need to know how to ask good strategic questions and good questions and prompts will become more important than ever.

AI will benefit education by...

...handling lower-level tasks. Teachers at this point in history have used up their personal reserves for handling crises and will perhaps only welcome true time savers instead of the technology du jour of the moment. We need tools that help us see the data and help it become actionable for parents, teachers, and students.

What should teachers who want to benefit from AI do?

I teach my students that there are two types of people with change: victims and victors. Throughout history, change happens and there are those who ride the wave and those who get buried by the wave. I'm not an advocate of new technology for new technology's sake. I am an advocate of using things that work. For example, when I needed a rotation schedule for students to take duty in my classroom, I recently asked ChatGPT to create a rotation in tabular form for six weeks. I had given it my students' names, and within moments, I had a table printed and on my board. This would have taken me an hour to create manually.

AI and pedagogy can work together because...

...if humans are intentional about the pedagogical practices and also seek to understand the AI tools available, then master teachers can take their students to new levels of critical thinking ability.

Educational leaders need to...

...be asking questions about data set integrity, bias, and AI accountability.

What are the consequences if schools, colleges, and universities ban new AI tools?

I'm not sure they can ban them. Just look at Netflix and streaming services that attempt to show one show in Europe and another in the US. People the world over are using VPNs to bypass IP filtering and watch what they want. Likewise, the problem is that AI detectors are not foolproof. I had a student paste a paper into a ChatGPT detector that he wrote two years ago in 2021. He asked if it was written by AI and it says it was. I know this student created this paper himself. So, if he'd been in a college environment with an AI detector, he would have been accused falsely.

What skills will students need to survive in the new AI world?

Students need to be creative, big-picture thinkers who can read and comprehend the text and creative works they consume. They will continue to need to read, better than ever likely. They will need to learn to be skeptical of what AI produces and to fact-check everything. They must understand that AI is not only fallible, that it can be biased. The idea of a "perfect robot" is flawed because the humans who program them are flawed, and the data sets studied by AI are flawed as well.

AFTERWORD BY PRIYA LAKHANI OBE

Priya Lakhani OBE is the Founder CEO of CENTURY Tech, an artificial intelligence education technology company that develops AI-powered learning tools for schools, colleges, universities and employers across the world. Priya was awarded Business Entrepreneur of the Year by the UK Chancellor in 2009 and Officer of the Order of the British Empire in 2014. She was appointed to the UK government's AI Council in 2019.

The AI revolution is growing louder. Though many of us are already using AI every day, these encounters are likely to take the form of asking your voice-activated digital assistant to make a call or play your favorite song. Without you even having to instruct it, AI technology might block a fraudulent transaction for you, make a personalized learning recommendation to your child, or calculate the optimal route to your destination. But these are relatively inconspicuous.

In recent months, spurred on by the launch of ChatGPT, AI has become far more visible and consequential. AI will only continue to manifest and will become increasingly inescapable. Soon, it will be radically improving healthcare with machines identifying ailments alongside humans. Transport and infrastructure will be overhauled, while AI will help to prevent cybercrime and terrorism. Many unpleasant and risky jobs like mining will be taken care of. The fourth industrial revolution is upon us.

Today, most of us are either living with, working with, or building AI. In less than a decade, every single one of us will be. AI has disrupted every sector in the world. Even areas that seem less reliant on technology right now do not exist in a vacuum, cut off from the supercharging power of AI. As a society, we are quite unprepared for the radically different way of life that has gone from looming on the horizon to infiltrating every use of technology in our daily lives. This lack of preparedness includes our approach to research and development, business policy, public services, and education despite the obvious useful potential of AI.

Despite society's general heel-dragging toward technological revolution, pioneers and experts are spurring us forward. In many sectors, AI has already been proven to be transformatively effective. AI has huge implications and applications to improve experiences and outcomes, especially in sectors where large amounts of data are generated. Despite the habit of Hollywood films and TV boxsets focusing on the dystopian power of technology, AI has the power to do a huge amount of good on this planet. Many areas such as medicine, urban planning, infrastructure, climate change, and conservation, in addition to equality, equity, and accessibility, have already seen the benefits of AI.

Medicine has proved particularly fertile ground for the application of AI. Algorithms can be used to help doctors make certain diagnoses easier to determine, supporting medical professionals and improving patient care. In Seoul in 2018, medical researchers developed an AI algorithm to analyze chest x-rays in order to detect abnormal cell growth, a potential indicator of cancer. When compared to practicing diagnosticians, the algorithm outperformed 17 out of 18 doctors. A similar application, also in 2018, was developed by researchers at Google AI Healthcare to identify breast cancer tumors from lymph node biopsies. When tested on two separate datasets, the algorithm was able to correctly identify the cancerous tumors with 99 percent accuracy.

In public infrastructure, there are a wealth of applications of AI, especially those that could enhance our public transit systems and streamline our commutes. Some of these will already be familiar, such as live chatbots and route planners that warn us of delays in real time and suggest ways to augment our journeys. Other applications may not be so familiar to the average commuter, such as machine learning algorithms that predict bus and train congestion, allowing operators to make informed decisions to keep networks flowing. Algorithms can also be used for predictive maintenance works, reducing costs and the likelihood of accidents. Large datasets compiled by urban developers and city government departments can be used to support planning of new transport links and renovations also. Some of these are achieving results already. City Brain, Ali Baba's urban AI project, which was already in 22 cities by 2019, has reduced traffic jams in Hangzhou by 15 percent.

The biggest issue on the global horizon is climate change, and AI will have a role to play here, too. AI algorithms can be used to analyze datasets of weather and temperature patterns to help us make informed decisions that will have a real impact to help the planet. Companies can use AI technology to accelerate the pace at which they reduce emissions and decarbonize. One company in California is looking at the damage risk to buildings and infrastructure from natural disasters with AI, and another based in New York is tracking and analyzing real-time data from floods to reduce risk and save lives. The Ocean Cleanup research team is using AI "object detection algorithms" to analyze GoPro footage across global waters with a target to have cleaned up the world's oceans by 2040. AI also has a role in wildlife conservation with a project in Hawaii that has used AI for a decade to help reduce instances of birds flying into electricity cables.

While there will certainly be challenges for governments to improve access to new AI technologies, the technologies themselves can have applications in reducing inequalities (as long as they are trained on non-biased datasets). AI technologies are already being used to improve accessibility for people with disabilities. Some of these technologies will be well known. Voice recognition software can help those with disabilities in the home, for example, to control appliances, set the temperature, or send text messages hands-free. Text-to-speech software on smartphones can read aloud important written documents for people with a visual impairment, who can also benefit from the support offered by image recognition technology. Instantly generated AI closed captions can also be used to support those with hearing difficulties. These and other assistive technologies are also being used to improve experiences for students with disabilities, for example, by supporting accessibility course content and for testing and qualifications.

AI is already being used in education across the globe by personalizing how we learn. In 2022, the UNESCO Mahatma Gandhi Institute of Education for Peace and Sustainable Development declared that personalized learning should be a right for every student. Advanced AI recommender engines personalize learning by analyzing learning data to choose the right next step for each individual student to fill a knowledge gap, address a misconception, or stretch and challenge. Automatic marking and data analysis by education platforms are helping us leverage new insights to target interventions and support for learners in real-time before it is 'too late' (i.e., after they have received their exam results). New applications of language learning models are just now entering the classroom now that ChatGPT has captured people's imaginations.

The rapid development of generative AI, such as Open-AI's GPT-4, Stability AI's Stable Diffusion, or Google Bard, and platforms leveraging deep learning models to personalize education and provide deep insights is an opportunity. The transformative power of AI can transform our education systems for the better. Personalized learning will support students to scale new heights of potential. Digital automation and machine learning will free teacher time and energy from bureaucracy, data collation, and resource creation, allowing them to have more agency across their practice.

Freeing up teacher time is essential. Education is different from other sectors — children are not workers or mechanical devices and should be treated accordingly. Our work at CENTURY Tech shows that technology and AI can hugely benefit the learning process. But students' developing minds can only be nurtured by loving humans. Sadly, our education system is so badly run that educators are leaving the profession in droves, their natural passion for teaching stretched to the limit by a system that is not fit for purpose. In 2015, the UNESCO Institute for Statistics stated that

> by 2030, an additional 68.8 million teachers will need to be recruited just for primary and secondary: 20 million are required to expand access to primary and secondary school and 49 million are needed to replace those who leave the workforce...Research shows that the quality of teachers is a major determinant of children's learning and well-being.

Global education systems are not fully prepared for this revolution. We have not yet equipped our millions of teachers and tutors (there are close to 85 million teachers worldwide) with the infrastructure, training, or skills to leverage these tools for the benefit of learners who will enter this radically different AI-powered world. Our schools still look largely the same as they did one hundred years ago. Digitally, we've gone from a blackboard to an interactive whiteboard - and that's about it.

An AI-ready education must go far beyond the brick-and-mortar of traditional schooling, with lifelong learning becoming the expected norm. Here, we are particularly failing — the number of British adults participating in learning, for example, is at its lowest on record, dropping by four million in the last decade. The age of automation requires wholesale changes to education that have, so far, not materialized. If we are to thrive in the burgeoning AI age, everyone needs robust data literacy. Everyone should be learning how to thrive in a data and technology-driven environment from an early age. Even if automation does create more jobs than it destroys (800 million by 2030, according to McKinsey), many of these will be unrecognizable to those of today. The skills that will be required to thrive, such as 'soft skills' like teamwork, the ability to adapt to unusual environments, and learning how to learn, are lacking in education. If ChatGPT and LLM technologies have demonstrated anything over the last few months, it is that the human skills that differentiate us from a machine need to be nurtured and developed, and we need to work together to develop our education and assessment systems to reflect this.

It is essential that educators are aware of how to use this technology to augment teaching and learning for the better. AI can help our education system become more nimble so it can react to a rapidly-changing environment. AI technology can be leveraged by teachers across the globe, helping to reduce their workload and support them deliver their best lessons. It can also be used by learners to improve their performance and progress to better outcomes. But these technologies must be well understood.

This is why *The AI Classroom* is a vital and timely resource that addresses the need for integrating artificial intelligence in education. Dan, Amanda, and Brad have provided this comprehensive guide that offers invaluable insights and practical advice for educators and educational leaders who are looking to embrace the AI revolution in their teaching practices and curriculum development.

Handling Text-Generating AI Systems: A Guide for Action

Department for Schools and Education of the State of North Rhine-Westphalia, Germany

Ministerium für Schule und Bildung
des Landes Nordrhein-Westfalen
Völklinger Straße 49
40221 Düsseldorf
Telefon 0211 5867 - 40
poststelle@msb.nrw.de
www.schulministerium.nrw
© MSB 02/2023

Translated by Heinrich Niemann, from the original German text:
https://www.schulministerium.nrw/system/files/media/document/file/handlungsleitfaden_ki_msb_nrw_230223.pdf

Introduction

Text generators based on artificial intelligence (AI) are capable of producing texts of such quality that it is often difficult to tell whether they were produced by a human or not. Since the end of November 2022, when the text generation AI ChatGPT was released and made freely accessible, many questions have arisen for everyday school life. What exactly are text-generating AI applications? How can the new possibilities offered by AI applications be handled? Can AI applications be used in the classroom? What legal framework applies? Do I, as a teacher, have a direct benefit for my own activities? Can AI be used in the classroom in the future, and how will it change teaching? Although the questions cannot be comprehensively answered at this time, we would like to provide you, as educators, school management, teacher training institutions, and members of school supervisory bodies with initial information and guidance on AI applications with this action guide. Due to the dynamic developments in the field of AI, it will be necessary to update the action guide for dealing with text-generating AI systems regularly.

The commercial products mentioned in the document (e.g. ChatGPT, DeepL, you.com, BARD) are mentioned in this text as examples of the underlying technology, but this is not associated with an implicit or explicit advertisement or evaluation of these products.

What are text-generating AI (such as ChatGPT) and what can they achieve?

Even though ChatGPT currently dominates the discussion and is therefore mentioned as an example in this text, there are numerous other AI applications in the fields of art and video production, research, translation, or as planning and structuring aids that are changing our work and learning processes and are therefore also important for teaching and learning in schools. It is expected that further text-generating AI applications will quickly come onto the market; in the past few weeks, for example, the AI-powered search engine you.com or BARD have already attracted attention.

ChatGPT is a chatbot that can answer questions, summarize or evaluate texts, write poems or computer programs, translate texts, create multiple-choice tests, and much more in various languages. It is noteworthy that ChatGPT is capable of taking into account the context between consecutive text inputs, creating the impression of a conversation.

The chatbot generates extensive responses to the user's text inputs based on the language model GPT (generative pre-trained transformer). The responses vary with each input, as the text is generated anew each time. Simply put, the algorithm has learned which character strings frequently follow each other in a text.

Text creation: With clear instructions and questions, texts can be created in a predetermined text form or style.

Text editing: The AI text generator can also be used to edit existing texts. The chatbot can offer a possible structure for a text, help with formulations, or suggest corrections.

Text evaluation: Likewise, the AI text generator can evaluate created texts according to predetermined criteria (AES - Automated Essay Scoring). This makes it possible to receive quick and direct feedback and to improve one's own skills as well as to steer writing processes through direct feedback.

The term "text" is to be understood broadly here: ChatGPT can also offer mathematical equations or generate and analyze computer programming.

Why can text-generating AI applications lead to misinformation?

Texts can be created much faster, easier, and on a larger scale than before through the use of text-generating AI. Even if an AI-generated text contains mostly reliable facts, it may also contain false statements that appear to be based on facts. However, as these tools become better, they will be more difficult to detect.

Therefore, it is particularly important to focus on the topic of "misinformation" in education. Students should be made aware that the generated responses may be flawed or incomplete. For example, ChatGPT's training was completed in the summer of 2021, so the world after that time is still unknown. Text-generating AI such as ChatGPT also fills "knowledge gaps" with new combinations of text fragments or embellishments. The underlying language model is trained to create texts that read as if they were written by a human. Since the AI application learns by machine, it is also difficult for developers to predict which response will be generated in response to which input. If training were optimized to only output reliable facts, it could often lead to no response being given, which is not the intended purpose of the language model. The system thus focuses more on eloquence than on truth. In addition, there is also a risk of making incorrect or incomplete statements through text generation itself, as the creation of the text is based on probabilities. The produced content must, therefore, not be accepted uncritically but must be controlled by learners. This is only possible if learners have acquired sufficient knowledge about the subject beforehand.

This makes media literacy even more important. The ability to distinguish fake news from facts based on one's own secure knowledge will become increasingly important.

Does AI provide neutral and unbiased answers?

The training data for ChatGPT is based to a large extent on English-language texts. It can, therefore, be assumed that this alone creates a predominantly Western view of the world as the basis for the texts generated by the AI. However, precise statements on this cannot be made, as the model is not transparent to the scientific community. Nevertheless, there are already approaches to training AI with data sets in different languages and from many different countries to create a more diverse language model. However, the problem remains that very large data sets are needed for training, which can only be found on the internet. As a result, it often happens that widespread prejudices and ethically morally questionable texts are included in the data used to train the AI. Filtering out unwanted training data is not possible, as many suitable texts would also be filtered out. Alternatively, the outputs of the chatbot could be checked and filtered so that offensive content is no longer displayed or replaced by predetermined answers. However, targeted user inputs can still generate insulting text snippets.

The "human" filter remains crucial here. A certain amount of problematic content can be prevented through subsequent training. However, it is more important to be aware when using the chatbot that articulate texts are not necessarily true and, above all, are not an indication of the intelligence or even consciousness of the AI.

How should this new capability be approached in education?

The accessibility of AI text generators is currently difficult to assess in terms of their impact. Experts from science and research unanimously emphasize that the effects of such AI on the education system and the world of work will be immense. In light of the educational and pedagogical mandate of schools, the education system must therefore address these new developments and their effects. Depending on the perspective, AI can offer opportunities and open up new perspectives or pose new challenges or even dangers. Both perspectives must be taken into account. We, therefore, ask you to engage openly and constructively with the new possibilities and to address them in the classroom.

Can a text-generating AI be used in the classroom?

The use of AI applications will increasingly gain importance in many areas of life and work. In the interest of the educational and pedagogical mandate of schools, which also includes responsible and safe handling of media in the digital world (§ 2, 6 no. 9 Education Law of North-Rhine-Westphalia SchulGesetz), it is also the task of schools to familiarize students with AI within the framework of teaching and to experience together in a protected environment how AI-based text generators work, what potentials, but also what risks are associated with them. A ban on addressing and using AI as a teaching tool in the classroom cannot be a viable response in the context of an extremely dynamically developing world in which students live. It is therefore important for teaching and schools to open up further and to reflect on the developments together with the students. It is evident that AI is of great interest to students and can thus be strongly linked to their lives.

In what context should engagement with AI applications take place?

The Media Competence Framework for North-Rhine-Westphalia or the digital key skills that are used in vocational education provides the framework in which engagement with AI-based text generators is meaningful: students should know their functional scope and learn to use them creatively, reflectively, and purposefully (1.2 MCF NRW), evaluate the produced information (2.3 MCF NRW), as well as understand and consciously use the basic functionality (6.1 MCF NRW).

When engaging with text-generating AI applications, three essential aspects should be taken into consideration:

- **The technological perspective:** How does an AI text generator work?
- **The sociocultural perspective:** What are the societal impacts of using AI?
- **The application-related perspective:** What can the AI application be used for, and what should be considered?

Implementation suggestion

To address the application-oriented perspective in teaching, it can be tried out together how to cleverly formulate prompts (= requests or instructions directed to the AI) to obtain the desired response. There are numerous instructions available online for this purpose. In addition, the outputs of the chatbot can be checked for errors, uncertainties, and gaps. Particularly in the natural sciences and mathematics, misinformation or incorrect results can often be found, which can be used as a starting point for a discussion about the functionality and effective use of the chatbot. (Example experiment: Solving a simple quadratic equation: The formula used by ChatGPT is uncommon in schools, and the chatbot makes an error in the last step. All learners can understand this mistake, and as a differentiation strategy, students can verify that the given formula is valid.)

What legal and practical conditions must be observed when using AI in an educational context?

In the context of the use of AI applications in education, various legal aspects must be considered, particularly concerning the processing, evaluation, and possible transfer of personal data, which cannot yet be conclusively assessed. This is also because the respective application possibilities and usage conditions of AI applications may vary.

Regardless, the use of AI applications in education - like the use of an online platform or app - must only occur while adhering to the applicable and known data protection requirements. The responsibility for compliance with school data protection lies with the head of the respective school. It must be carefully assessed to what extent the personal data of users are collected, and if necessary, technical or organizational measures must be taken to protect such data.

Information on what data the provider of an AI application processes can be found, in particular, in the privacy policy and terms and conditions. These may include data that is fundamentally necessary for use, such as when creating an account (age limits may need to be considered), as well as data that arises during use (automatically). A provider must be transparent about its data processing and, in particular, about the right to deletion.

Regarding the various usage scenarios in schools and the existing knowledge about the usage conditions of an AI application, such as ChatGPT, the following assessments and recommendations can be made:

The use of ChatGPT in education with students' own devices or via their accounts/email addresses cannot be recommended given the current factual and legal situation (especially concerning data protection requirements).

If teachers have voluntary access to ChatGPT or other AI applications, they can use them to work with the application in class. As with all other applications, it must be ensured that no personal data of students is transmitted. This would be the case, for example, if prompts establish a connection to the class or individual students.

It is recommended to inform parents about the type of use of an AI application in class and the framework of legally permissible options in the context of educational partnerships. Providing information on AI applications in participation committees can also help to alleviate any existing uncertainty.

How the use by students with their accounts may be possible in the future depends on the design of the terms and conditions and data protection policies of the application(s) in each individual case.

For practical school purposes, initial assessments from the perspective of school data protection officers can be helpful, which can be found, for example, at https://unterrichten.digital/2023/01/23/chatgpt-datenschutz-unterricht-schule.

What impact can the text-generating AI application have on students' writing skills?

What consequences can the text-generating AI application have on the development of students' writing skills? So far, there is no scientific evidence about the effects of incorporating text-generating AI applications on the development of basic writing competencies. Although it is certainly true that writing skills are mainly developed through one's own efforts, a direct deduction of negative consequences is too simplistic. Especially concerning students who may require more individual support, the possibilities of using a text-generating AI application must be further reflected upon (e.g., individual inquiries regarding text comprehension, scaffolding, and different levels of text difficulty in class).

Can AI be used to support the learning process?

A learning-friendly use of AI can contribute to expanding language, writing, and evaluation skills. It is necessary to design the use of AI didactically in terms of subject-specific and cross-disciplinary competencies (e.g., media competencies or digital key competencies of vocational colleges). For example, the texts generated by the AI can be examined for correctness, consistency, style, etc. Furthermore, working on factual accuracy or arguments is possible.

Scaffolding: In addition to supporting the processing of texts, AI can also provide individual assistance in other areas during the learning process. For example, it is possible to simplify or translate texts during internet research. In addition, learners can have concepts explained to them again and answer follow-up questions, and have appropriate examples or analogies searched for them.

Creation of exercise material: A text-generating AI can create self-tests to check whether students can correctly reproduce the content of a text. These gap-fill exercises, multiple-choice tests, or questions with answer choices can later be used for repetition and practice. The testing formats could also be integrated into learning management systems, such as Learning Management System for all public schools and recognized alternative schools in North Rhine-Westphalia, and made available as a practice opportunity for the class or course.

The defined evaluation criteria for a learning product can be used with the help of AI for any time available, timely formative feedback. It should be clear to students that this is feedback to adjust the learning process and not a performance evaluation because the teacher is not directly involved in the feedback. The criteria must be not only transparent but also understandable for students to be able to work with the result meaningfully.

AI-generated texts can be used in the classroom in multiple ways as a basis for discussion or as a topic of discussion. On the one hand, they can serve as brainstorming, for initial orientation and structuring or for collecting arguments, but on the other hand, the creation of content must always be discussed. Since the texts are created based on an AI-based language model, correctness is not necessarily given. Learners must be guided to increasingly check the content against their prior knowledge independently. In addition, the texts created by AI must also be considered from a values perspective, as values, norms, and ethical aspects do not play a role in the creation of the text by AI.

How can teachers establish rules with students about how the use of AI in texts can be referenced?

If the students voluntarily use text-generating AI tools, they must, of course, indicate them as a source because only then can the teacher determine what performance the learner has achieved and evaluate it. Currently, citation rules that indicate AI as a source are being worked on in the scientific field. Based on this, a regulation for indicating the use in a school context could look like this:

"In producing this text [or image or programming code, etc.], X [=name of the AI-assisted tool] was used. I controlled the AI with the following prompts [=instructions or questions for the AI]: 1._____, 2._____ "

The advantage of this type of indication is that the teacher can evaluate how extensive the use of AI was. It can also be assessed how competent the student controlled the use of the AI. The text generated by the AI should be included for evaluation.

How do I handle it if students use AI but do not disclose it?

The general principles for "scientific" work and performance evaluation still apply: If external aids are used, they must be fully disclosed. This also applies to the use of an AI application. Texts created using a text-generating AI are less easily identifiable as plagiarism than those copied and pasted from websites or texts because the AI-generated texts are not always identical. Strictly speaking, this is not plagiarism, but rather the use of an application to create a text. It is currently unclear whether it will be possible to develop reliable software that can detect AI-generated texts. Experts believe that such software would rather be used as a training opportunity for an AI system to improve.

Even if it is not plagiarism in the strict sense, not indicating that the text or parts of it were generated using AI is a deception about authorship. If the use of AI has been explicitly excluded in the assignment, it is also the use of an impermissible aid and an attempt to deceive. For tasks that are not carried out on-site in the school under supervision, teachers, as always, have the opportunity to check the degree of independent work of students: in this context, teachers have a high level of professional experience and can, among other things, recognize in classroom discussions whether students have completed products that they have created at home for the performance assessment independently or with impermissible assistance. Just as tasks in the home environment were not allowed to be created with the help of third parties, they must not be provided with a technical aid that is not adequately indicated. This also involves teaching students that it is in their own interest to independently complete learning tasks assigned to them (including homework, which might not be graded) and to correctly indicate any aids and sources used.

If there are acts of deception or other irregularities, the procedure is based on the principles of performance evaluation (§ 48 SchulG) and the relevant regulations of the examination regulations (in particular § 6 paragraph 7 APO-SI, § 13 paragraph 6 APO-GOSt, § 20 APO-BK).

To avoid situations that are stressful for both students and teachers, the tasks should be designed preventively so that they cannot be completed exclusively with the help of AI.

How can I create tasks that are less susceptible to being exclusively completed by AI?

With sufficiently complex questions, it is apparent that texts created in the first step by a text-generating AI application do not necessarily meet the requirements. Often, multiple, very specific questions and corresponding subject matter knowledge are necessary to create appropriate texts for the assigned task. Training and mastering this type of control is a perspective that is important to convey to students. It is possible to motivate learners to work independently through challenging, interesting tasks and to show why their own, independent writing experiences are important to be able to reflectively evaluate the quality of both their own and others' texts. Addressing this perspective can be successful, especially in the cooperation between teachers and learners.

All of the mentioned aspects will contribute to the need to further develop learning and performance tasks. It is already advisable to combine existing formats for checking learning performance in such a way that they consider the work processes of the students and are less susceptible to being exclusively processed through the targeted use of AI.

For projects or term papers, for example, this could mean including their own, individual research task of an empirical nature or series of experiments that are tailored to the specific teaching situation. The guidance of the work process also becomes significantly more important. In conversation with the learner, it becomes clear to what extent he or she has dealt with the content. In addition, a final presentation with a discussion about the work can illustrate that the student independently completed the work or that passages of text generated with AI were not used without reflection.

In the classroom, it is necessary to motivate and guide learners to shape their learning process through creative, challenging, and real-world related tasks, opening up learning arrangements, and implementing peer approaches. Essential impulses for a learning-promoting education in the digital world can be found in impulse paper II.

Tools for the further development of tasks

If individual references are included in the learning and performance tasks, the AI cannot easily take them into account, so the individual contribution on the part of the learner is necessary. For example, if a survey in the class, an experiment, mapping, data collection, personal hobby, a self-selected focus about the place of residence or a comparison with the presentation of a classmate is included, AI text generators cannot fully take over the task. Additionally, working on a topic from an individual, self-chosen perspective can contribute to the motivation of learners.

A change in format or media in the task means that learners must independently implement their findings. While AI can provide ideas for creating a poster, an explanatory video, a podcast, a song, or a still image, suitable implementation and, thus, engagement with the content must be carried out by the learners. Additionally, this approach can promote argumentative competencies in learners, as they are increasingly asked to justify their own decisions, analyses, or formats.

Formative assessment - i.e., observation, feedback, or feedback accompanying the development process - can also contribute to ensuring the independence of the work submitted. It also promotes the motivation and acceptance of learners to write their own texts, as they can be further improved based on repeated personalized and timely feedback. Instead of writing several ever-new texts for the class, fewer but better, repeatedly revised texts are produced. Additionally, the continuous feedback contact between teacher and student makes it less likely to insert longer text passages that come from an AI.

What benefits could it have for me as a teacher?

In the discussion of the possible applications of text-generating AI, diverse opportunities also arise for teachers: Teachers can benefit from the use of AI text generators in preparing for class by generating differentiation options, diagnostic tests, ideas for implementing the class or initial corrections of products created by the learners. Thus, texts can be simplified and offered at different levels, analogies and examples can be found, or assessment formats can be created. Texts could be pre-corrected regarding grammar, spelling, and sentence structure. A media-competent use also means that data protection regulations must be followed, so no student data may be entered.

Outlook

Not only the school sector but also universities are currently intensively dealing with the consequences of text-generating AI applications. All discussions and publications by scientists are currently focussing on the 3 statements below:

1. A ban on the use of AI is unrealistic and unsustainable.
2. Instead, it is necessary to establish the potential and risks for teaching and learning.
3. Dealing with AI must be negotiated between teachers and learners and must be transparent and legally secured.

There is a high level of agreement that a competent handling of AI applications is essential for successfully dealing with future demands in education, study, work, and everyday life; for this reason, schools cannot turn a blind eye.

It requires a joint effort of schools, education authorities at all levels, and teacher training and development to further develop the 3 aforementioned areas. Therefore, the Ministry of Education will continue to deal with these developments and provide information on the topic to all relevant bodies.

ACKNOWLEDGMENTS

This book is dynamic in its approach to exploring the thoughts and wisdom of educators from all over the world. It is important to us that you understand how artificial intelligence is already changing education and how it might continue to develop in the years to come, from the keyboards of those who are doing it. Our contributors are mainly educators like you, using AI to streamline their workload, transform learning and prepare their students for the exciting world they live in.

Thank you to all who contributed.

Aaron Maurer, STEM Lead
Aftab Hussain, ILT and LRC Manager
Aileen Wallace, Teacher of Modern Studies
Aimee Coelho, Teacher in charge of Media and English teacher
Alaina Clark-Weinstein, COO TeacherGoals Publishing
Andy Kent, CEO of Angel Solutions
Anne Kasa, Instructional Technology Coach
Ben Whitaker, Educational Consultant
Bob Harrison, Visiting Professor University of Wolverhampton
Bruno Avelar Rosa, Professor
Bryan Zevotek , STEM Educator and Author
Carla Bell, Digital Lead and Home Economics Teacher
Caroline Law, English Language Arts teacher
Charlotte Beeney, Director of Digital Literacy
Clara Hawking , Head of Wellbeing
Conall MacLoingsigh, Assistant Head - Digital Learning & Data
Conrad Taylor, Business Learning & Technologies Manager
Dan Jones, Middle School Teacher
Daren White, Academic Technologies Lead, Academies Enterprise Trust
David Price OBE, Author and Consultant
Dieter Möckelmann, EdTechWatcher
Dr. Chris Lensing, Superintendent
Dr. Rhonda Moffit, EdD and Gifted Specialist

Eirik Hernes Berre, Co-Founder Curipod
Elissa Malespina, School Librarian and School Board Member
Emma Darcy, Director of Technology for Learning
Esther Albert Psychology teacher & human intelligence coordinator
Garrett Smiley, CEO of Sora Schools
Guang Wu, Middle Years Mathematics Learning Leader
Heather Brown, K-5 math interventionist and STEAM teacher
Heinrich Niemann, Head of Languages at Box Hill School (Ret.)
Jamie Smith, Executive Chairman C Learning
Jens Aarre Seip, CEO, Curipod
Jennifer E. Womble, Conference Chair, FETC
Jon Neale, Edtech Consultant
Jon Tait, Deputy CEO
Katie Storey, Head of Digital Learning - Prep Schools Trust
Kerry Murby, Teaching, Learning and Assessment Quality Improvement Leader
Lee Parkinson, ICT Mr P, Primary School Teacher and Teacher Trainer
Marcin Sztomberski, MYP Coordinator
Mark Nichols, Future Leader
Martin Jones, Director Value Added Education
Mats Larsnäs, Teacher and edtech consultant
Matt Jessop, Head Teacher
Melissa McBride, Founder of the Metaverse Education Council and CEO at Sophia Technologies.
Mick McMurray, Educator, San Diego, CA
Nathan Michael Wilfong, Special Education Teacher & Behavioral Trainer
Nicky Blackford, Assistant Headteacher Teaching and Learning
Nicolas Cole, Author, Co-Founder Ship 30 for 30 & Premium Ghostwriting Academy (PGA)
Olly Lewis, Head of Digital Transformation
Priya Lakhani OBE, Founder and CEO of Century Tech
Richard Grainger, COO/Director at Everybody Counts
Ross McGill, Teacher Toolkit
Scott Hayden, Head of Digital Learning and Teacher
Shane McComb, Digital Learning Leader
Sharifa Khatun, Coordinator of Computer Science & Digital Innovator
SJ White, Teaching and Learning Specialist
Steve Dembo, Director of Technology and Middle School CSAI Teacher
Tammi Scheiring, Teacher of Computer Science, Cybersecurity and AI
Tom Tuthill, Director of Collaboration and Innovation, Malvern College
Vicki Davis, Cool Cat Teacher Blog, IT Director
Wassim Jouini (boredgeeksociety), Head of AI at a LegalTech

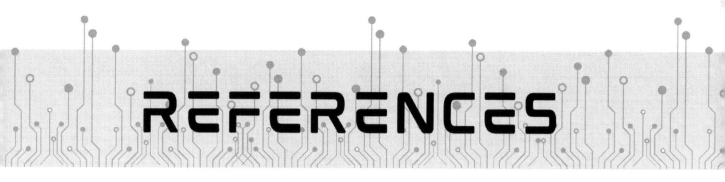

REFERENCES

Chapter 1

Yalalov, D. (2022, December 8). ChatGPT passes the Turing test. Metaverse Post. https://mpost.io/chatgpt-passes-the-turing-test/

Kurzweil, R. (2005). The singularity is near: When Humans Transcend Biology. Palgrave Macmillan UK.

Chapter 2

Jack Clarke [@jackclarkSF]. (2023, February 12). A mental model I have of AI is it was roughly-linear progress from 1960s-2010, then exponential 2010-2020s, [Tweet]. Twitter. https://twitter.com/jackclarkSF/status/1624564977117057024?s=20

Chapter 4

Govindarajan, V. (2016). The Three-Box Solution: A Strategy for Leading Innovation. Harvard Business Review. https://store.hbr.org/product/the-three-box-solution-a-strategy-for-leading-innovation/15029

Walker, M., Worth, J., and Brande, J.V. (2019). Teacher Workload Survey 2019: Research Report. UK Government, Department for Education. publishing.service.gov.uk

Texthelp. (n.d.). Inclusion: The Key to the Future of Education. https://www.texthelp.com/resources/inclusion-the-key-to-the-future-of-education/

Chapter 5

VOGELS, E.A. (2021, June 22). Digital divide persists even as Americans with lower incomes make gains in tech adoption. Pew Research Center. https://www.pewresearch.org/fact-tank/2021/06/22/digital-divide-persists-even-as-americans-with-lower-incomes-make-gains-in-tech-adoption/

Christodoulou, D. (2023, January 20). ChatGPT: Exams should be protected and the tech regulated. Schools Week. https://schoolsweek.co.uk/chatgpt-why-ai-should-be-banned-from-assessment-and-regulated/

National Literacy Trust. (2023, March 9). What is literacy? https://literacytrust.org.uk/information/what-is-literacy/

Chapter 6

Marr, B. (2019, January 29). Artificial Intelligence Has A Problem With Bias, Here's How To Tackle It. Forbes. https://www.forbes.com/sites/bernardmarr/2019/01/29/3-steps-to-tackle-the-problem-of-bias-in-artificial-intelligence/

Jenkins, H., Clinton, K., Purushotma, R., Robison, A. J., & Weigel, M. (2006). Confronting the Challenges of Participatory Culture: Media Education for the 21st Century. MacArthur Foundation.

National Association for Media Literacy Education. (n.d.). Core Principles of Media Literacy Education. https://namle.net/resources/core-principles/. Stanford History Education Group. (n.d.). Evaluating Information: The Cornerstone of Civic Online Reasoning. https://sheg.stanford.edu/civic-online-reasoning.

UNESCO. (n.d.). Media and Information Literacy: Curriculum for Teachers. https://en.unesco.org/themes/media-and-information-literacy/curriculum-teachers.

Chapter 7

Unleash Learning. (n.d.). Unleash the Science of Learning – Retrieval Practice. https://www.retrievalpractice.org

Bloom, B. S. Engelhart, M. D. Furst, E. J. Hill, W. H. & Krathwohl, D. R. (1956). Taxonomy of educational objectives: The classification of educational goals. Vol. Handbook I: Cognitive domain. David McKay Company.

Chapter 8

CAST. (2018). Universal Design for Learning Guidelines version 2.2. https://udlguidelines.cast.org/

Chapter 10

Harrison, B. (2023, March). In the Ultimate Guide to Artificial Intelligence in Education book, we are equipping teachers, students and leaders. [Post]. LinkedIn. https://www.linkedin.com/feed/update/urn:li:activity:7037357439033188353 commentUrc=urn%3Ali%3Acomment%3A%28activity%3A7037357439033188353%2C7037365147037365148%29&dashCommentUrn=urn%3Ali%3Afsd_comment%3A%287037365148287037365%2Curn%3Ali%3Aactivity%3A7037357439033188353%29

Bible Gateway. (n.d.). Proverbs 29 - King James Version. https://www.biblegateway.com/passage/?search=Proverbs%2029&version=KJV

Sinek, S. (2011). Start with Why: How Great Leaders Inspire Everyone to Take Action. Getinvestable.

Department for Schools and Education of the State of North Rhine-Westphalia. (2023). Handling Text-Generating AI Systems: A Guide for Action.

The Guardian. (n.d.). ChatGPT allowed in International Baccalaureate essays. https://www.theguardian.com/technology/2023/feb/27/chatgpt-allowed-international-baccalaureate-essays-chatbot

Power School. (2021, April 13). SAMR Model: A practical guide for K-12 Classroom Technology Integration. https://www.powerschool.com/blog/samr-model-a-practical-guide-for-k-12-classroom-technology-integration/#:~:text=The%20SAMR%20Model%20is%20a,Augmentation%2C%20Modification%2C%20and%20Redefinition.

Gates, B. (2023, March 21). The Age of AI has begun. Gates Notes. https://www.gatesnotes.com/The-Age-of-AI-Has-Begun

Chapter 11

World Government Summit 2023. (2023). The Skills Revolution and the Future of Learning and Earning.

https://www.mckinsey.com/~/media/mckinsey/industries/education/our%20insights/the%20skills%20revolution%20and%20the%20future%20of%20learning%20and%20earning/the-skills-revolution-and-the-future-of-learning-and-earning-report-f.pdf

U.S. Department of education (n.d.). Federal Role in Education. https://www2.ed.gov/about/overview/fed/role.html

Gatto, J. T. (2002). Dumbing us down: The hidden curriculum of compulsory schooling. New Society Publishers.

Andrew, Ng. (2016, November 9). What Artificial Intelligence Can and Can't Do Right Now. Harvard Business review. https://hbr.org/2016/11/what-artificial-intelligence-can-and-cant-do-right-now

Freire, P., & Ramos, M. B. (1970). Pedagogy of the oppressed. Seabury Press.

Chapter 12

Bradberry, T., & Greaves, J. (2009). Emotional intelligence 2.0. TalentSmart.

Dweck, C. S. (2007). Mindset: The new psychology of success. Ballantine Books.

Goleman, D. (2005). Emotional intelligence: Why it can matter more than IQ. Bantam Books.

THE SCIENCE OF READING IN ACTION
BY MALIA HOLLOWELL

This is not just a book, it's a teaching movement. With 67% of U.S. kids not proficient in reading, according to 2022 data, the status quo isn't working.

This book tackles the main obstacles: training, tools, and support offering:
- Evidence-based insights on teaching reading, dispelling social media myths
- Solutions for common challenges facing struggling readers
- Ready-to-use activities and strategies that simplify brain-friendly reading instruction
- A method to help students memorize words 10X faster than with flashcards
- Techniques to ensure no student falls behind

Written by Malia Hollowell, a certified educator and Stanford alum, this book is your all-in-one guide for making reading instruction effective and engaging.

TEACHING IN SYNC
BY ERICA TERRY AND LYNÉA LAWS, PH.D.

Teaching In Sync is a comprehensive guide to co-teaching success, covering everything from building a strong relationship with your co-teacher to utilizing AI for co-planning and incorporating technology for progress monitoring. With research-backed advice and a touch of NSYNC inspiration, this book will help you hit all the right notes in co-teaching.

Unlock the power of co-teaching with:
- 20+ downloadable resources
- Time-saving strategies to efficiently co-plan & progress monitor
- 50+ assistive and instructional technology resources
- 15+ AI prompts designed for co-teachers
- In Sync co-teaching framework

HEARTLEADER
BY MATTHEW BOWERMAN

When you become part of a school community, it's all about authentic relationships. It's all about authentic love.

From the classrooms to the neighborhoods, in every role, when you lead from the heart, what kind of impact will you create with those you serve?

Heartleader begins with an origin story, becoming a trauma-responsive, K-12 field guide for every member of a school community. It gets to the heart of the matter, asking us to consider who we are, the why of our service, and how we will let love shape every move we make.

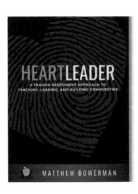

CHILDREN'S BOOKS

www.teachergoals.com/books

PETER O'METER
BY TRICIA FUGLESTAD

Join *PETER O'Meter* in the world of #RobotProblems, where you help him manage his emotions in a retro-futuristic world.

This book combines interactivity and augmented reality for an immersive experience.
- Emotional Robot: Help PETER O'Meter with his feelings.
- Interactive Story: Engage in a retro-futuristic world.
- Augmented Reality: Use the Quiver app to bring the story to life.
- Reader's Influence: Your decisions guide PETER's journey.

Experience a unique narrative adventure that's both emotionally engaging and technologically innovative.

MONSTERS HAVE MANNERS
BY JEFF KUBIAK

Dive into the enchanting world of *Monsters Have Manners* by Jeff Kubiak a charming children's book that teaches kids about the importance of kindness and manners through the adventures of River and his monster friends.

This beautifully illustrated book features augmented reality coloring pages that come to life, making it a truly interactive and immersive reading experience. Ideal for children ages 3 to 8, *Monsters Have Manners* is a delightful read-aloud that belongs on every child's bookshelf.

River loves monsters. He loves drawing monsters, dressing up as a monster, and even pretending to be a monster. But no one loves his monster manners. Not even the monsters. One night, the monsters visit River, and it changes everything!

MARKERTOWN
BY AMANDA FOX

A heartwarming story about kindness, inclusion, and finding your place in the world. Gift a copy to someone you love today.

After a long day of coloring, the markers head home to their boxes—but Glitter can't find her cap! As Glitter journey's through Markertown, she meets a group of repurposed markers that help her envision a different future. But can they save her ink in time?

Markertown is a story that commends kindness and friendship. It embraces upcycling not only markers, but parts of ourselves along our journey. Readers should walk away understanding that true sparkle and shine come from within.

So let the mark you leave on the world be one of kindness!

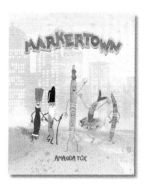

NEW AND UPCOMING TITLES

**BLUEPRINT FOR INCLUSION
BY REBEKAH POE**

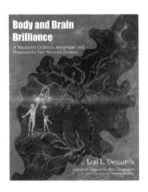

**BODY AND BRAIN BRILLANCE
BY DR. LORI DESAUTELS**

**MODERN PBL
BY DAN JONES**

BULK ORDERS

www.teachergoals.com/books/bulk-orders

GET MORE FOR LESS WITH TEACHERGOALS PUBLISHING!

Need copies for your coworkers or staff? Bulk order your favorite titles and enjoy exclusive discounts. Ask about signed copies and book studies to enhance your reading experience.

Big savings and great learning opportunities await with every bulk purchase!

Made in United States
Orlando, FL
11 September 2024

51412577R00211